A Guidebook for Teaching
READING

Pauline L. Witte

Allyn and Bacon, Inc.   **Boston • London • Sydney • Toronto**

This book is part of A GUIDEBOOK FOR TEACHING Series

 217234

Library of Congress Cataloging in Publication Data

Witte, Pauline L.
  A guidebook for teaching reading.

  (A Guidebook for teaching series)
  1. Reading (Secondary education)   2. Developmental
reading. I. Title. II. Series.
LB1632.W57   1985   428.4'07'12   84–11153
ISBN 0–205–08202–5

Printed in the United States of America

10 9 8 7 6 5 4 3 2 1   89 88 87 86 85 84

Dedication

To my students at
Middleton High School
Middleton, Wisconsin

About the Author

Pauline L. Witte is a reading specialist in Middleton, Wisconsin where she teaches developmental reading to students in grades 10–12, works with poor readers at the elementary level, and serves as a reading consultant to classroom teachers. She also has served as a staff associate at the Wisconsin Research and Development Center. Dr. Witte earned her M.S. and Ph.D. in reading at the University of Wisconsin.

Gene Stanford, *Consulting Editor for the Guidebook for Teaching Series,* received his Ph.D. and his M.A. from the University of Colorado. Dr. Stanford has served as Associate Professor of Education and Director of Teacher Education Programs at Utica College of Syracuse University and is a member of the National Council of Teachers of English and the International Council on Education for Teaching. Dr. Stanford is the author and co-author of several books, among them, *A Guidebook for Teaching Composition, A Guidebook for Teaching Creative Writing, A Guidebook for Teaching about the English Language,* and *Human Interaction in Education,* all published by Allyn and Bacon, Inc.

Contents

PREFACE   xi

Chapter 1   **ORGANIZING THE COURSE**   1
The Place of the High School Reading Class in
   the Total School Reading Program   1
Organizing for Instruction: Students and
   Objectives   3
Organizing for Instruction: Materials   4
Selected Learning Experiences   5
Resources for Teaching   9

Chapter 2   **IDENTIFYING READING NEEDS**   11
Performance Objectives   11
Content Overview   12
Learning Experiences   16
   Topic 1:   Using Standardized Tests and Other
                Published Diagnostic Instruments   16
   Topic 2:   Evaluating Vocabulary Learning Skills   18
   Topic 3:   Identifying Comprehension Needs   20
   Topic 4:   Evaluating Study Skills   24
   Topic 5:   Assessing Rate of Comprehension   25
Assessing Learning Experiences   26
Resources for Teaching   27

Chapter 3   **REINFORCING WORD IDENTIFICATION SKILLS**   29
Performance Objectives   29
Learning Experiences   30
   Topic 1:   Building Word Awareness   30
   Topic 2:   Learning to Read: A Review of the
                Process of Phonic Analysis   32

            Topic 3:   Using Word Identification Strategies
                       at the High School Level   35
            Assessing Learning Experiences   37
            Resources for Teaching   38

Chapter 4   **IMPROVING READING COMPREHENSION SKILLS**   39
            Performance Objectives   40
            Learning Experiences   40
                Topic 1:   Using Background Information   40
                Topic 2:   Reading Is Reasoning   44
                Topic 3:   Applying Comprehension Skills   49
            Assessing Learning Experiences   54
            Resources for Teaching   54

Chapter 5   **DEVELOPING AND USING STUDY STRATEGIES**   57
            Performance Objectives   58
            Learning Experiences   58
                Topic 1:   The Study Skills Project   58
                Topic 2:   Prereading Strategies   61
                Topic 3:   Underlining   64
                Topic 4:   Writing Marginal Notes   66
                Topic 5:   Notetaking and Summarizing   68
                Topic 6:   Student Questioning   71
                Topic 7:   Outlining   72
                Topic 8:   Graphic Overview   74
                Topic 9:   Selecting and Using Study Techniques
                           to Prepare for Tests   76
            Assessing Learning Experiences   78
            Resources for Teaching   79

Chapter 6   **TEACHING RATE FLEXIBILITY**   81
            Performance Objectives   82
            Learning Experiences   82
                Topic 1:   Developing Reading Flexibility   82
                Topic 2:   Improving Rate of Comprehension   88
            Assessing Learning Experiences   91
            Resources for Teaching   91

Appendix A   **ADDRESSES OF PRODUCERS OF RESOURCES**   93
Appendix B   **REPRODUCTION PAGES**   95
Appendix C   **FEEDBACK FORM**   249

Preface

A Guidebook for Teaching Reading is designed to provide practical ideas and resources for teaching a reading course at the secondary level. The activities and presentations are designed for a developmental reading course or a study skills course offered to students who have generally good reading skills but who would like to learn to read and study more efficiently. Some suggestions for adapting these activities for poor readers are also included.

The topics covered in *A Guidebook for Teaching Reading* are setting up a reading course, reading diagnosis, vocabulary development, comprehension, study skills, and rate of comprehension. The materials and activities included can provide the content for a one semester course; the real intent, though, is that teachers use these activities to supplement their own instructional ideas.

The theme of developing awareness of one's own thinking-reading processes is carried throughout the book, as is the related idea that students must be actively involved in the process if they are to really learn. These themes reflect the influence of recent research on how human beings read, learn from reading, and remember what has been read. The reader who can reflect on his or her own thought process can make better reading and studying decisions. He or she can say such things as "I already know this information, so I will read it quickly," or "This information is all new to me; I must take more time to read, reread, or take notes."

The readings in *A Guidebook for Teaching Reading* are selected from content area texts, newsmagazines, and newspapers. They were chosen because they contain meaningful information for secondary students and provide a reading-studying challenge. One article, for example, is excerpted from a secondary school level psychology text and, in very readable language, explains how human beings receive and process information. Although the article is not especially difficult to read, the concepts are complex. This article then is used in several activities to demonstrate how to use study strategies taught in this text, such as writing marginal notes and constructing graphic overviews. Another article from a newsmagazine focuses on the issue of the American Indians' right to preserve the sacred burial grounds of their ancestors versus the right of archaeologists who want to dig up Indian graves in order to study the past. This article is used as the basis for an activity designed to help students develop the comprehension skill of critical evaluation.

A key activity included in *A Guidebook for Teaching Reading* is the "Study Skills Project." This project or activity can span a six to eight week period and is the vehicle used to help students apply to content area courses the skills and strategies learned in the reading course. After a particular strategy is introduced, students are given reading class time to apply that skill directly to reading assignments current in other courses. Specific procedures for organizing this project are presented in detail, and handouts that can be used to help structure the project are included.

The secondary reading course is an important one because it provides an opportunity for students to learn about process—the processes of reading, learning, and thinking. Through a reading course, a student can gain perspective and self-understanding that can be used to improve learning in all areas. This book is one approach to organizing and teaching a secondary reading course. Hopefully, it will serve as a useful resource to others who are teaching students how to read and study.

A Guidebook for Teaching READING

1

Organizing the Course

THE PLACE OF THE HIGH SCHOOL READING CLASS
IN THE TOTAL SCHOOL READING PROGRAM

For at least three decades, organizations such as the International Reading Association, the national Right to Read effort, and a wide variety of individual reading educators have been insisting that reading instruction at the postelementary level ought to occur primarily in content area courses.[1] Since most students have acquired essential reading skills by the time they reach fifth or sixth grade, the focus for reading instruction in the later school years changes to that of using reading as a way of learning. Many reading educators believe that postelementary content area teachers can most effectively provide this instruction because they can teach reading skills and study strategies in context. If a particular text or portion of a text is troublesome to students, teachers in subject areas such as science, social studies, or literature are in the position to teach the necessary reading skills and simultaneously provide students with the opportunity to apply those skills.

Because of this emphasis on reading in the content areas, less attention has been paid to the postelementary reading class. Perhaps some reading authorities feel that the high school or junior high reading course reaches too few students or jeopardizes the content area program becuase it directs the reading staff's energy toward teaching instead of consulting. Some educators have even directly criticized the postelementary reading course, suggesting that the skills taught are not readily applicable to the reading tasks students face in their regular classes.[2]

In spite of this criticism and lack of attention, the reading course is still prevalent in grades six through twelve in the United States today. Greenlaw and Moore[3] surveyed a sample of junior and senior high schools throughout the country, asking

1. P. L. Witte and W. Otto, "Reading Instruction at the Postelementary Level: Review and Comment," *Journal of Educational Research* 74 (1981): pp. 148–158.
2. D. Kirby, "Professional Publications: Reading and the English Teacher," *The English Journal* 67 (1978): pp. 84–85.
3. M. Greenlaw and D. Moore, "What Kinds of Reading Courses Are Taught in Junior and Senior High School?" *The Journal of Reading* 25 (1982): pp. 534–536.

teachers to respond to the question, "In your school, is reading taught as a separate course?" The majority of the respondents (77 percent) indicated yes. Many of the courses described by the teachers who responded were remedial but a substantial number (44 percent) said that developmental courses were offered in their school and 36 percent reported that an accelerated reading course was part of their school's curriculum. Earlier surveys of postelementary reading instruction show that the existence of separately taught reading courses is not a recent innovation.

Hill[4] reviewed twenty five surveys of secondary reading activity published between 1942 and 1970. His summary table shows that planned reading instruction at the postelementary level most often took place in a developmental, corrective, or remedial class, or was considered part of an English class. Freed[5] surveyed 242 postelementary schools and found that 55 percent of junior high schools and 22 percent of senior high schools included a required reading course in their instructional program. After an informal review, Early (1973)[6] concluded that the reading class is one of the major vehicles for teaching reading at the postelementary level. These surveys clearly indicate that somehow the secondary reading class must be a realistic response to a felt need on the part of public school teachers, students, and administrators. Schools continue to offer reading courses—sometimes as a requirement but often as an elective—and students continue to enroll.

The purpose of this guidebook is to provide practical ideas and resources for teaching a secondary reading course. It is written with the hope that a strong reading course will enhance the total school reading program. In an effective reading course, students can be taught techniques and strategies that will positively influence their performance in content area courses. Then content area teachers observing students' improvements can perhaps begin to understand the value of the process skills taught in a reading course and appreciate the expertise of the reading specialist.

The study skills project described in Chapter 5, "Developing and Using Study Strategies," is designed to demonstrate to students how the skills taught in a reading course can be applied to other classes. Through a combination of serendipity and deliberate planning, the project can help teachers become more aware of effective reading and studying strategies.

When students in the reading course construct a careful outline or draw a graphic overview from one of their content area texts, they sometimes show this work to their subject area teacher. Also, sometimes teachers themselves notice a positive change in a student's performance and observe the study techniques this student is using.

The study skills project can also help reading staff members become familiar with the content area subjects taught in the school as students bring texts and assignments from other classes into the reading course. This familiarity can enable reading specialists to begin conversations with teachers about interesting aspects of their courses, to compliment teachers on effective techniques they are already using and, as relationships develop, to offer suggestions for improvement. In this direct way the reading course can assist reading specialists to develop their roles as consultants. Creditibility is also established when content area teachers see that reading specialists spend at least some time effectively teaching the same very real students that they are teaching.

4. W. R. Hill, "Characteristics of Secondary Reading: 1940-1970," in *Reading: The Right to Participate*, P. B. Greene (ed.). Twentieth Yearbook of the National Reading Conference (Milwaukee, Wis.: National Reading Conference, 1971), pp. 20–29.
5. B. F. Freed, "Teaching Reading in the Secondary Schools: Survey of State Department of Education and Selected School Districts," (Philadelphia: Research for Better Schools, 1972), pp. 1–34.
6. M. J. Early, "Taking Stock: Secondary School Reading in the 70's," *Journal of Reading* 16 (1973): pp. 364–373.

ORGANIZING FOR INSTRUCTION: STUDENTS AND OBJECTIVES

Sometimes students are assigned to a reading course on the basis of specific needs. College-bound students might be scheduled into an accelerated or critical reading course or students with poor academic skills might be placed in a reading-study skills course or a reading lab. Although some schools attempt to organize reading courses to meet specific student needs, it seems safe and realistic to say that, more often than not, students in any one high school reading course differ greatly from one another in terms of reading ability, motivation to achieve, and post-high school goals.

The activities in this guidebook are designed to be used with a wide variety of students. Good readers will be able to read many of the materials presented independently, only needing your direction to help them organize what they have learned through reading and to apply this learning to other situations. Some students will need more of your assistance when they are involved in the act of reading. The activities in this guidebook that show how the essential ideas in a passage can be found and evaluated ought to be particularly useful for these students. An important aspect of all of the activities is the active involvement of all students in the process of learning about their own minds and reading-thinking-studying behaviors. It is hoped this approach will capture and sustain the interest of even discouraged and poorly motivated readers.

Specific performance objectives are stated for the topics of each chapter in this guidebook. The overall objectives for the reading course have a broader focus, reflecting the belief that the skills and behaviors taught can benefit students as they become lifelong readers and learners.

PERFORMANCE OBJECTIVES

As a result of the learning experiences in this course, students will be able to:

1. Become confident, independent readers and learners.

2. Discover their reading/thinking strengths and weaknesses and appreciate errors as opportunities to learn.

3. Increase their knowledge and use of new words in as many subject areas as possible.

4. Learn to reflect on and evaluate whatever they read.

5. Increase the level and accuracy of their reading comprehension.

6. Develop effective study skills for content area courses.

7. Increase their rate of comprehension.

8. Develop the ability to alter reading pace according to their purpose for reading.

9. Experience personal and social growth through broad reading experiences.

ORGANIZING FOR INSTRUCTION: MATERIALS

To improve their reading, students must read. The desire to read can be stimulated in the reading course by using interesting, meaningful materials to provide the basis for teacher-directed instruction and by having books and reading suggestions available for student recreational reading.

Instructional Reading Materials

Though the material in this guidebook can be used as it is presented to form the curriculum for a secondary reading course, it is not intended for that purpose. The book is designed so you as the teacher can select units and activities that best suit your conception of the reading class, style of teaching, and the type of students you teach.

Many of the activities in this guidebook are based on materials from magazines, newspapers, poetry and short story anthologies, and content area textbooks. Materials are selected from a wide range of sources in order to include a collection that provides meaningful, practical reading experiences for secondary students. You may want to use many of the activities just as they are presented on the Reproduction Pages. You might also want to use some of the activities as models to create materials of your own. Perhaps a current national or world issue captures your interest or your students express a deep concern about a crucial social or political issue; a relevant article from a newspaper or magazine on such a topic, developed into a learning experience, can help students realize that the skills taught in the reading course do apply to real life. Students can be encouraged to compare what they read with what they see and hear on television and then ponder the question of which of the two media prompts them to think more freely and critically. Most magazine articles can be reproduced in small numbers for classroom use. If you are uneasy about infringing on copyright restrictions, a telephone call to the publishers of even national magazines is not very costly and is usually reassuring. Editors of local newspapers are usually very cooperative, doing all they can to encourage teachers to use the newspaper. They understand that students who learn how to read newspapers in school have a better chance of becoming regular newspaper purchasers and readers later on.

In addition to the materials provided in this guidebook and activities that you develop, there are a number of published materials that can contribute to effective instruction in a reading course. Many of these materials are described in subsequent chapters, and a list of publishers' addresses is included in Appendix A.

Recreational Reading Materials

An important component of a reading course is a "free reading time," when students are given an opportunity to read for enjoyment. Procedures for this free reading time are included in number 7 of the Learning Experiences described below. In order to make free reading workable, the reading room must be supplied with materials students will enjoy. Some ideas for obtaining materials and providing reading suggestions for students follow:

1. To supply your classroom with books, try to arrange discount plans with a book outlet or book–store; if it helps, join the English Department in ordering. Order from discount paperback sources when students place orders. If finances are especially slim or nonexistent, ask students to bring and share books they already have. Maybe fellow faculty members will also make a contribution.

2. Try to get free magazines from a book outlet. Often if the outlet returns only the covers of the magazines, it is reimbursed and the magazines may be given away free of charge. Book stores will sometimes also do this.

3. Ask the school librarian to keep a special rack in the library for bestsellers and books of current movies or television specials.

4. Set aside a portion of a bulletin board for students to tack up note cards listing titles of books they want to recommend to other students. The cards can include a brief description of the book and ought to be signed by the person making the recommendation.

5. Pass around a ditto master headed "Preferred Reading List" and have each student suggest one favorite book. Ask them to include brief testimonials. Run off the ditto and distribute three copies to each student.

6. Obtain lists of suggested books for college-bound students from your state English teachers association or from the American Library Association. Make multiple copies and make these copies available to your students.

SELECTED LEARNING EXPERIENCES

The following activities are designed to introduce the reading course to students so that they can understand the purpose of the class and begin thinking about reading and setting goals for their own improvement. You may want to use these activities as they are presented during the first week of school, or modify the approach to suit your own purpose and style. The Reproduction Pages mentioned in the text can be found at the end of the book. Use these to make duplicating masters or overhead transparencies.

1. Many secondary students feel disorganized. Constantly moving from class to class with only a narrow locker as a home base is often unsettling particularly for those students who have just come from an elementary school where they had one room, one teacher, and one desk. Although many of your students may have been coping with moving from room to room for several years, some may still have problems being in the right place at the right time with the right materials. One of the essential characteristics of good students is a sense of organization. A reading course can help students to develop this sense.

    Below are steps listing a procedure for setting up a central file box in which each student keeps a file folder containing the handouts, book lists, charts and other materials needed for class.[7] Students pick up their folders at

---

7. I would like to acknowledge Bernice Bragstad, reading specialist at LaFollette Senior High School, Madison, Wisconsin, for her contributions to *A Guidebook for Teaching Reading*. I am indebted to her for helping me understand the overall conception of the reading course and for the idea of using the file folder system described here.

the beginning of each class session and return them to the file box at the end of each class. Though this system may seem like a small thing—perhaps just a gimmick—it really does help to establish a sense of organization and of belonging to a class.

A. Find a cardboard box that is slightly larger than a manila folder and cover it with adhesive shelf-liner. This is the central file box for holding student folders. Use cardboard dividers to separate classes from one another.

B. Distribute a folder to each student. Instruct them to write their name and the number of their class hour on the top tab.

C. Stress that they are *not* to take the folders with them when they leave the class. The folders are to remain in the file box.

2. Reproduce "Content of the Reading Course" (Reproduction Page 1) as a transparency, or draw a copy of the chart on the chalkboard. Instruct students to draw this same chart on the front of their folders. Tell them that this course will be different from other courses they have experienced. They will not be focusing on one subject, such as science or literature, but on processes for learning. The chart they have just drawn summarizes all the processes included in the reading course. After your students have drawn the chart, discuss it using the following comments as a guide:

• "Thinking and Becoming" are written in the center of the chart because reading is a thinking process. As we become better readers we also become better thinkers. As we think and read, our minds grow and we become more than we were.

• *Comprehension:* The emphasis in the first part of this unit is on helping you to learn more about what happens in your mind when you read. The second part of the unit includes activities designed to help develop comprehension skills such as determining the main idea of a passage and using the organizational structure provided by an author.

• *Vocabulary:* Often students simply skip words they do not know when they are reading and therefore miss the opportunity to expand their thinking by learning the new concept the word represents. The purpose of this unit is to help you become aware of unknown words as you read and to encourage you to use effective word-attack strategies to determine their meaning.

• *Extensive reading:* One of the goals of this course is to improve your reading by encouraging you to read more and to find enjoyment in reading. Class time will be set aside for recreational reading in order to help you accomplish this goal. As a class, we will share what we have read in order to help you expand your reading interests.

• *Rate flexibility:* Many students do not read efficiently: they read all materials at the same rate and do not concentrate completely on the material. Early in the course you will have an opportunity to find out how fast you read. As the course progresses you will do activities that ought to improve your concentration and help you select reading rates that suit your purpose for reading.

- *Study skills:* The study skills unit in this course is organized around a study skills project. After you have been taught a particular study skill, you will be instructed to apply that skill using material from another course. This application procedure is called the *study skills project*. The intent of this project is to show you how study skills can be applied and to help you improve your grade in another course.

3. Distribute copies of "Student Information Sheet" (Reproduction Page 2). Ask students to fill it out carefully. Explain that the purpose of this sheet is to help you learn about student reading and studying needs so you can plan the course accordingly, and that filling out the sheet ought to encourage students to begin thinking about their own reading and studying behaviors.

4. Reproduction Page 3, "Why Take A Reading Course?" consists of a newspaper article entitled, "Our Next Disgrace: Why Johnny Can't Log On." This article concerns the notion that students who graduate from our nation's high schools have inadequate reading skills. According to the author of the article, many graduates are ill-prepared to cope with the vast amounts of printed information that will come their way in our complex society.

   Distribute copies of this article to your students, explaining that this article gives some reasons why it is so important for them to improve their reading skills. Then follow the steps below to guide your students as they read and to discuss the content of the article.

   - Read the first three paragraphs aloud as your students follow along reading silently. Begin the discussion by asking questions such as:

     a. Are "long-suffering mascot of national illiteracy" and "standardbearer of our collective disgrace" two different ways of saying the same thing?

     b. What does the author mean by these two phrases?

     c. What do you suppose an "Information Revolution" is?

     d. What is a watershed? (You might have to ask a student to look this word up in a dictionary).

     e. What does the author mean when he calls the Information Revolution "a watershed in human development"?

   - Instruct students to read the fourth paragraph silently and to underline the key ideas. Then ask them if they underlined the sentence that explains that more than 50 percent of the work force is involved in processing and communicating information.

   - You read the next five short parapraphs aloud. Tell students to think about the sentence: "Self-styled experts will speculate endlessly why Johnny can't log on."

   - Tell students to read paragraphs 11–13 silently and to prepare to answer the question: "What is the real crisis?"

   - Ask for a student volunteer to read paragraphs 14–17 aloud. Then ask: "Where does Rudolph Flesch place the blame?" If you wish, explain to your students the difference between "Look-and-Say" and phonics approaches to teaching beginning reading.

- After students have read paragraphs 18–20 silently, ask: "What does Roger Farr blame for the decline?" Once students have answered this question, continue with: "Whose reasoning is more believable, Flesch's or Farr's?"
- Explain that paragraphs 21, 22 and 23 present three more possible causes for the decline in national literacy. Tell students to read these three paragraphs, looking for these possible causes.
- Give students time to finish reading the article then ask:
  a. What are some of the important points being made in the last portion of the article?
  b. Are any solutions to the problem given?
  c. Do you personally agree that there is a problem?
  d. Do you think your own reading skills are good enough to help you achieve what you want to achieve?
  e. If you agree that there is a problem, how would you solve it?
  f. What does the author really mean by the term "log on?"

5. Because students are usually very interested in how fast they are able to read, a reading rate check is often a good activity for the first week of class. However, stress that speed is not of primary importance but understanding is essential. Also explain that the rate check as well as the other types of evaluation done in the course will help students understand their own strengths and weaknesses so they can work toward improvement.

   The procedure for determining reading rate is discussed under Topic 5, Chapter 2, "Identifying Reading Needs." A reading passage, comprehension questions, and the reading rate graph are included on Reproduction Pages 18–22. Follow the procedure as described under Topic 5 with one additional beginning step: ask students to staple the "Reading Rate Graph" (Reproduction Page 21) to the inside of the folder they keep in the central file box.

6. Distribute copies of "Personal Book List" (Reproduction Page 4) to students on the first or second day of class. Tell them that they are to fill in the list with the titles of at least ten books before the end of the week or before they are given free reading time. Explain that they will be expected to bring one of these books with them for the designated reading time. If necessary help students fill out their "Personal Reading List," pass a ditto-master around the class and have them make recommendations as suggested under the heading "Organizing for Instruction: Materials," above.

7. The practice of scheduling blocks of time for free reading during the school day or a class period has been credited to Lyman Hunt of the University of Vermont, who called the procedure Uninterrupted Sustained Silent Reading (USSR). This procedure is a good one to include in the reading course because it gives students an opportunity to practice their reading skills, and the com-

mitment of time to reading shows students that teachers and administrators sincerely value it.

The procedure for free reading is very simple. First, students must bring materials with them for the designated reading time or use materials they have previously chosen in the reading room. (To ensure an effective free reading time, require your students to preselect books or prepare a "Personal Book List" as described in Activity 6 above.) The second requirement for free reading is that students must read for the entire time allotted—that means no working on homework and no talking.

Some teachers prefer to set aside one day of the week, such as a Friday, for free reading. Others set aside ten or fifteen minutes at the beginning of each period. Both procedures work well. The ten- or fifteen-minute reading period at the beginning of each period helps students get settled and into a state of mind conducive to learning. On the other hand, having an entire class period to read allows students to become more involved.

RESOURCES FOR TEACHING

Below is a list of resources that provide useful background information for teaching the concepts and topics of this chapter. Addresses of publishers can be found in the alphabetical list in Appendix A.

Bean, Rita, and Wilson, Robert. *Effecting Change in School Reading Programs.* Newark, Del.: International Reading Association, 1981. Suggestions are offered for reading specialists who would like to function as resource persons within their schools. Topics such as communication, interpersonal and decision-making skills are discussed in this booklet. The authors have a realistic perspective on the role of the reading specialist and the difficulty of working as a consultant to teachers.

Kummer, Robert. "Reading as an Elective." *Journal of Reading,* 1976, *19,* (8), 640–643. The article describes a reading course offered to high school juniors and seniors and offers suggestions for organizing and grading students in a high school level reading class.

Newman, Susan, and Prowda, Peter. "Television Viewing and Reading Achievement." *Journal of Reading,* 1982, *22,* (7), 666–670. The authors have analyzed the reading and television viewing behavior of over 7,500 students. They report a negative relationship between reading achievement and television viewing at all grade levels. Their findings suggest that reading for pleasure should be emphasized and television viewing monitored.

O'Rourke, William. "Research on the Attitudes of Secondary Teachers toward Teaching Reading in Content Classrooms." *Journal of Reading,* 1980, *23,* (4), 337–339. The results of a questionnaire sent to 480 Nebraska teachers are reported. According to O'Rourke, the attitudes of these content area teachers toward teaching reading as part of their courses were positive. The article concludes with recommendations for more course work and staff development for content area teachers.

Smith, R. J., Otto, W., and Hansen, L. *The School Reading Program.* Boston: Houghton Mifflin Co., 1978. This is a source book for developing the school reading program from kindergarten to grade twelve. It includes discussions of basic skill instruction as well as in-service guidelines.

2

Identifying Reader Needs

Students who enroll in a high school reading course in most cases do so because they feel they have a reading problem or have an idea that they need to improve some of their academic skills before going on to college. Some have a general notion of what their weaknesses are. They say, "I read too slowly," "I have trouble remembering what I read," or "When I read I don't know when I should take notes." But they often do not understand their difficulties well enough to make an organized attempt to improve.

High school students have the capacity to think about their own thinking and by doing so they can become more effective learners. Therefore, the results of both formal and informal diagnostic approaches can be used not only by teachers to plan instruction but also by students to focus their own learning efforts. The activities included in this chapter are designed to involve teachers and students in the process of identifying reading needs in order to work toward improving reading and studying skills.

The content overview and the first topic in this chapter deal with formal standardized and general informal types of reading diagnosis. The rest of the topics include diagnostic activities corresponding to the four major units covered in the reading course: vocabulary, comprehension, study skills, and rate of comprehension. The standardized and general forms of diagnosis, as well as some activities from each of the four topics, can be used at the beginning of the course to gain a general perspective of student needs in all areas. Teachers may choose to use some of the diagnostic activities later as each unit is introduced.

PERFORMANCE OBJECTIVES

As a result of the learning experience in this chapter, students will be able to:

1. Gain insight into their own reading strengths and weaknesses in the areas of:

   a. general reading

---

   b. vocabulary

   c. comprehension

   d. study skills

   e. rate of comprehension

2. Decide which reading and study skill areas should be the focus for their efforts toward improvement.

3. Develop their understanding of the reading process by experiencing the many aspects of diagnosis.

CONTENT OVERVIEW

The term *formal* is often used to refer to standardized tests that have been normed. This means that the test has been administered to large groups of students selected to represent the range of abilities and backgrounds in the United States population. The raw scores resulting from these large-scale testings are converted to percentage and stanine scores. Students can then compare their own scores with these scores to gain a perspective on how their reading ability compares with other students at the same grade level across the nation. But standardized tests are only one form of diagnosis. There are many informal methods, such as study-skill inventories and comprehension measures based on actual classroom materials, that are more appropriate than standardized tests for many diagnostic purposes.

The purpose of this content overview is to describe how standardized tests can be used in a reading course, explain their limitations, and provide a background for interpreting standardized scores to students. It is hoped this overview will assist teachers to select and use standardized tests appropriately.

When to Use Standardized Tests

Standardized tests are an objective means of evaluating student abilities and comparing their achievement with other students. This objective comparison can help us decide if students are making good progress and therefore need to be encouraged and stimulated to continue developing their reading skills, or if they have reading problems and need special help to correct their deficiencies. This type of assessment is often called *survey-level diagnosis*[1] or *general diagnosis*.[2] It is usually done on a class or large-group basis. The terms survey level or general diagnosis correctly imply that the results are useful for preliminary screening, not for diagnosing specific reading weaknesses. Standardized test results can give an indication of which students are likely candidates for special corrective or remedial help. Additional diagnostic materials and procedures should be used to determine the specific kind of help that a particular reader needs. Methods for identifying individual reading strengths and weaknesses will be discussed later in this chapter.

---

1. W. Otto and R. Smith, *Corrective and Remedial Teaching*, 3rd ed. (Boston: Houghton Mifflin, 1980): p. 48.
2. G. Bond, M. Tinker, and B. Wasson, *Reading Difficulties: Their Diagnosis and Correction*, 4th ed. (Englewood Cliffs, New Jersey: Prentice-Hall, 1979): p. 168.

The results of standardized tests can also aid in planning instruction by giving an indication of the range of reading ability within a class. Such an indication can help teachers make decisions about how to present the content in a reading course. If the range of ability in a class is small, much of the course content can be taught on a large-group basis. If the range of ability is wide, more small-group or individualized instruction is necessary.

Guidelines for Selecting and Using Standardized Tests

Results of standardized tests can provide useful information for the purposes of making instructional decisions if tests are carefully selected and their limitations are known. The following section can be used as a guide for selecting standardized reading tests.

1. *Do the objectives of the standardized test reflect the objectives of the reading course?* Karlin[3] points out one of the major shortcomings of standardized reading tests when he indicates that they are "too narrow in scope" and "do not reflect all that we call reading." This problem is not easily remedied. Even though much intensive research and thought has been devoted to it, reading experts and learning psychologists are not able to identify and define "all that we call reading." The best reading teachers can do is decide, based on our own knowledge and experience, what it is we call "reading" and then choose the standardized tests that most accurately reflect our decision in light of the kinds of skills and behavior we want to stress in our courses.

   A well-constructed standardized test manual contains clearly stated test objectives. The test authors' definition of reading and philosophy of reading instruction should also be included so we can make comparisons easily and select a test that most nearly matches our own teaching objectives and philosophies.

2. *Can the test be administered easily?* Check several factors related to the administration of a standardized test before making a selection:

   A. Are the directions clear and easy to understand?

   B. How much time is required to administer the test?

   C. Can the test be easily and quickly scored?

   D. Are there several forms of the test so that one can be used at the end of the course to give an indication of improvement?

3. *Does the test measure what is says it does? Is the test a valid one?* Reading test publishers usually answer this question by establishing a case for two types of validity, content and concurrent. *Content validity* is established for a particular test either by asking reading experts to indicate whether or not the test does in fact measure reading ability, or by comparing the content of the test with the content of reading programs commonly used throughout the country. *Concurrent validity* is established by comparing the scores of one reading test with scores of another reading test. For example, a publisher producing a new reading test compares scores from the new test with scores from an established

3. R. Karlin, *Teaching Reading in the High School,* 3rd ed. (Indianapolis: Bobbs-Merrill, 1977): p. 82.

reading test. If the scores on the new test reflect the same patterns as the scores on the established test, then the new test is said to have concurrent validity.

We should view the test publishers' descriptions of their tests' validity with some skepticism. As Estes and Vaughan[4] point out, the claim for content validity "depends on acceptance of what amounts to a very narrow and probably unrealistic definition of reading" and the claim for concurrent validity is "circular reasoning." If Test 1 is like Test 2, then Test 2 is like Test 1. This does not mean that both tests are true measures of reading. As reading teachers, we are probably better served by selecting a test that reflects our course objectives as suggested in the first guideline discussed in this section than by accepting the test publishers' claims for validity at face value.

4. *Is the test reliable?* The reliability of a test reflects the precision of the instrument. High *split-half reliability* indicates that the two halves of the test, or the odd- and the even- numbered items, are consistent in what they are measuring. *Alternate-form reliability* indicates that the two forms of a test are consistent with each other. A well-constructed test should have split-half and alternate-form reliability of at least .90 or better. Remember that the reliability of a test tells nothing about *what* the test is measuring: it is only an indication of the consistency within the test.

5. *Do the test publishers provide adequate information for interpreting the scores?* Much of the controversy that has surrounded the use of tests in recent years has involved the interpretation of test results. Test scores can easily be misinterpreted, especially if the test publishers do not provide adequate information or do not stress the limitations of their tests. Reading teachers ought to consider the following factors as part of the test selection process:

   A. *Description of the norming sample.* Standardized tests enable us to compare our students with other students at the same grade level. Therefore it is important for the test publisher to provide a description of the types of students that were used to establish the norms for the test—the students against whom we make our comparisons. This norming group should be very similar to the type of student we have in our class so we can be sure we are comparing only reading abilities, not other factors such as race, sex, cultural environment, or geographic area.

   B. *Explanations of raw scores, percentile ranks, stanines, and grade level.* A good test manual should provide a description of each type of score, explaining what they mean in terms of that particular test. The following is a brief general description of how these scores can be used.

   Raw score: The raw score is simply the number of items that a student answers correctly on the text. This score does not enable us to make comparisons with other students in a formal way. However, we can use raw scores to make informal comparisons. For example, we might want to compare a student's raw score from the beginning of the course

4. T. H. Estes and J. L. Vaughan, *Reading and Learning in the Content Classroom* (Boston: Allyn and Bacon, 1978): p. 53.

with the same student's raw score at the end of the course as a rough measure of improvement.

Percentile ranks: Percentile ranks do provide a means for comparing students. The percentile rank indicates the percentage of the norm group that obtained a raw score equal to or less than a particular score. For example, if a student scored at the 75th percentile, this would mean that 75 percent of students in the norm group obtained the same or a lower raw score and 25 percent of the norm group obtained a higher score.

When using percentile ranks, keep in mind that they do not represent actual amounts of ability. A difference of 25 percentile points does not mean that one student has 25 percent more reading ability than another. Furthermore percentile ranks do not represent equal units. For example, the performance difference between ranks 20 and 25 may be greater than that represented by the difference between ranks 40 and 45. Since the percentile rank units are unequal and represent very small units, it would not be appropriate to use percentile ranks to measure growth.

Stanines: Stanines are scores that range from a low of 1 to a high of 9. Stanine 5 represents average performance. Like percentiles, stanines provide a means for comparing students. However, stanines do represent approximately equal units and provide a realistic unit for describing reading growth. For example, if a student's performance improves enough to move from one stanine to the next higher, this is an indication that reading growth has occurred.

Grade level: Grade level is more appropriately used for discussing reading scores at the elementary level than it is for discussing reading scores at the secondary level. At the elementary level, it is possible to describe how the reading performance of a typical first grader would differ from that of a typical second grader. The same is not true at the secondary level. It is difficult, if not impossible, to explain how the reading skills and behavior of a ninth grader would differ from those of a tenth grader.

6. *Is speed a factor in the test?* In order for the test norms to be used appropriately, the reading test must be administered as directed in the manual. This means that the time limits must be followed exactly. If the time limits are short, speed is more than likely a factor in the test. In this case, the test probably does not measure what it says it does but instead measures how quickly a student can react. In other words, the speed factor contaminates what we are trying to measure. For this reason, it is important to choose a test with adequate time limits so that most students are able to finish.

7. *Can the subtests be used for diagnostic purposes?* Though some standardized test publishers claim that their instruments can be used to diagnose reading strengths and weaknesses, reading experts such as Estes and Vaughan[5] and Farr[6] maintain that this claim is not supported by a sound knowledge of the reading

Estes and Vaughan, *Reading and Learning in the Content Classroom*, pp. 53–54.
R. Farr, *Reading: What Can Be Measured?* (Newark, Del.: International Reading Association, 1969): p. 61.

process. The practice of using subtest scores to plan a remedial program for students is based on the incorrect assumption that the reading subskills measured by a particular reading test do in fact measure all of the parts of the whole we call reading. As mentioned earlier, we are not able to define the reading process in exact terms. We have some ideas about the specific skills necessary in order to be an effective reader, and we know that instruction in these skills has helped many children learn how to read. However, we do not have a pat definition of the reading process and we cannot say that we know what all the subskills of reading are. The real danger of using the subtests of standardized reading tests diagnostically is that this procedure can lead us to a simplistic view of the reading process. Based on subtest scores we might be inclined to say, "Student A scored poorly on subtests one, two, and three. Therefore, I will provide remedial instruction in those subskills and solve this student's reading problem." Unfortunately, it is not that simple. Standardized tests and their subtests can give a general picture of our students' reading strengths and weaknesses; however, the careful reading teacher will recheck these impressions using more specific ways of identifying reading needs.

The "Resources for Teaching" section at the end of this chapter contains a selected list of current standardized reading tests and other more informal published diagnostic instruments. A brief description of what the test purports to measure, the date of publication, the time needed to administer, the grade levels, and the number of forms for each are included in the list. In addition to the guidelines given above for selecting and using tests, there are many other resources teachers can use to learn more about tests and testing procedures. A number of these sources are also listed in "Resources for Teaching."

LEARNING EXPERIENCES

Topic 1: Using Standardized Tests and Other Published Diagnostic Instruments

1. The procedures for using most standardized tests are similar. After you have selected an appropriate test, decide which subtests you wish to use and then review the directions for administering carefully.

   Introduce the test to students by explaining the purpose and limitations of standardized tests, using the information given in the content overview as a guide. You might also want to indicate that the grade (or whatever form of final evaluation) students receive in the reading course does not depend on their scores on standardized tests, but that the purpose of this testing is to help students understand their weaknesses so they know where to begin the process of working toward improvement. Finally, explain the purpose and type of skills assessed in each of the subtests students will be taking.

   Administer the test to students following the directions given in the manual and adhere strictly to the time limits. After the tests have been scored, either by you or by the students themselves, interpret the scores using the following procedure:

A. Make multiple copies of the tables in the test manual showing the stanines and percentile ranks. Distribute these to students.

B. Explain again that it is important for students to understand their own scores so that they can gain insight into their own reading strengths and weaknesses.

C. Show students how to find their stanine and percentile scores in this manual. Some students may be discouraged by their scores, so stress that it is not the score itself that is important but how much they are able to improve by gaining insight into their reading problems.

D. Have students record their scores. (A record sheet and a procedure for recording scores are described in the following activity.) Then ask students to reflect a moment on their lowest subtest scores. You might pose questions such as:

   a. Did you expect a low score in this area?

   b. Have you received low scores in this area on previous tests?

   c. Did you find the subtest where you scored lowest to be particularly difficult?

E. Explain that you will administer another form of the test at the end of the course. Students will then be able to compare their final scores with their scores from this first testing to gain an indication of the kind of improvements they have made.

2. The "Reading Improvement Plan" (Reproduction Page 5) consists of a sheet students can use to record their scores and results from both the initial testing done in the reading course and any tests or inventories they may respond to when a unit is introduced. This reproduction page is called a "Reading Improvement Plan" because students will use it to record the information they will need to set goals for reading and study improvement. It contains space for students to record scores from standardized tests taken at the beginning and at the end of the course and space for them to record scores from specialized tests given in the areas of vocabulary, comprehension, study skills, and rate of comprehension.

   Whenever students have completed a test, direct them to record their scores on this sheet. This procedure of recording scores from a variety of instruments on one sheet ought to help students analyze their reading behaviors and provide a basis for them to think about their own mental activities.

3. The term "Informal Reading Inventory" (IRI) was originally used to describe a diagnostic tool developed by classroom teachers and was based on classroom materials. The IRI was designed to assess the reading needs of individual students at the elementary level and disabled readers at the postelementary level. Most IRIs consist of a series of graded passages followed by comprehension questions. A teacher administers the IRI by asking a student to read a selected passage orally. Any oral errors such as omissions, substitutions, or miscalled words are recorded. Following this, the teacher asks the student a series of five to ten questions. The number of oral reading errors and the comprehension errors can be evaluated according to a set criteria to determine the grade level

at which reading instruction would be most beneficial. This procedure can be varied by having the student read the passage silently or by asking the student to recall the events in the passage without prompts or cues from the teacher.

This type of procedure gives teachers an opportunity to observe students as they read and struggle to gain meaning from print. Unlike the scores from standardized tests, results from IRIs can give specific information about the difficulty level of material a student can handle. The major drawback of IRIs is that they require individual testing sessions and thus are impractical to administer to every student in a reading course, even though this would probably be an ideal way to obtain information about student reading needs.

In most reading courses, there are a few students who seem to have exceptional needs. They score poorly on standardized tests and other group assessment measures and generally seem to have a great deal of difficulty dealing with printed materials. Administering an IRI to this type of student is worth the time and effort needed to gain information about the type and severity of problem the student has.

An IRI based on classroom materials is probably the most useful; but the development of such a diagnostic tool requires time, expertise, and experience. Fortunately, there are a number of published assessment instruments that follow the IRI format. Many of these are well constructed, containing all the needed testing materials as well as specific guidelines for administering, evaluating the results, and planning subsequent instruction. Any one of several of these instruments helps teachers to evaluate students with special needs. A list of recommended published diagnostic instruments that follow the IRI format is given in the "Resources for Teaching" section of this chapter under the subheading "Individual Tests."

Topic 2: Evaluating Vocabulary Learning Skills

1. Most standardized reading tests contain subtests designed to measure the extent of a student's general vocabulary. In many cases, this vocabulary knowledge is measured by asking students to choose a word from a list of four or more that best completes a sentence or to select a word that means the same or nearly the same as another. Most tests also include some items that require students to analyze the context to determine the meaning of a word, and a few contain subtests that measure student ability to find meaningful parts within words as well as their knowledge of prefixes and suffixes. Some standardized tests designed for secondary students even contain a phonics analysis subtest.

   After students have taken the vocabulary portion of a standardized test and have recorded their scores, take a few moments to discuss the vocabulary subtests. The following questions can be used to direct the discussion.

   A. Did the subtest measure general vocabulary or did it include terms from specific content areas?

   B. How was vocabulary knowledge measured? What type of format was used?

   C. Did the subtest measure the ability to structurally analyze words?

   D. Did the test measure the ability to use context to define words?

   E. Did the test measure phonic analysis skills?

Following this discussion, ask students to note on their Reading Improvement Plans (Reproduction Page 5) the type of vocabulary skills the subtests measured. Tell them to keep these scores in mind when they analyze the results from the diagnostic activities that follow. Explain that it is important to look for patterns in their scores. They may have scored poorly on one test simply because they did not understand the questions or were uncomfortable with the format. However, if they score poorly on two tests that measure similar skills but use different formats, this, perhaps, is an indication of a real weakness.

2. "Structural Analysis Assessment" (Reproduction Page 6) consists of three subtests:

A. Identifying Meaningful Word Parts

B. Using Meaningful Word Parts

C. Using Suffixes

The purpose of the first subtest is to provide information about students' ability to locate the meaningful parts within a word. The second subtest requires students to apply their knowledge of the meaning of common prefixes and root words, and the third subtest assesses the students' ability to use suffixes to alter a word's grammatical function in a sentence.

Distribute copies of Reproduction Page 6 to your students and read through the directions for each subtest with them. Allow them as much time as they need to complete the test. Then collect the tests and score them yourself or have students correct their own papers. The procedure of having students correct their own papers is recommended: not only does it save some of your time, but it helps students to understand their errors and perhaps even why they made them. Of course, if the test is being used to evaluate students for the purpose of determining a course grade, self-correction is not appropriate. If you are having students correct their own papers, you may first want to write answers to the items yourself and then read your own answers aloud or you may ask for student volunteers to read their responses. Student answers may vary and a variety of responses could be considered correct for many items. This assessment is not a difficult test and for many students it may simply serve as a review of word-attack strategies that they ought to be using as they read; but for poor readers at the high school level this assessment may help to identify areas of weakness.

After the subtests have been scored, ask students to record their results in the form of a percentage at the bottom of the "Structural Analysis Assessment" and/or have them record their scores on the "Reading Improvement Plan" (Reproduction Page 5). After recording the scores, review the word-attack strategies this assessment required students to use. They are listed below, and you might want to ask students to write this list beneath their subtest scores.

• Look for meaningful parts within words.

• Work at finding the meaning of words by using your knowledge of meaningful word parts.

• Realize that suffixes do not change the meaning of words but that they do alter words so they can be correctly used in sentences.

3. Textbooks in almost all content areas rely extensively on contextual definitions to explain the meaning of new words and terms. The ability to use these contextual definitions effectively is an essential one for high school students. Reproduction Page 7, "Using Context Clues," consists of brief excerpts from numerous content area texts. Each excerpt contains an underlined term or word that is also defined within the excerpt. The purpose of this assessment is to determine if students can use the context in a variety of situations to write a definition showing that they understand the meaning of a technical term.

Distribute copies of Reproduction Page 7. Read the directions to students and stress that they are to write a definition using their own words —they are not to simply rewrite the information given in the passage. Allow students ample time to complete this assessment. Then collect and evaluate their responses. If students have correctly defined a term, have used at least some words not used in the original text, or have varied the phrasing, score the item correct. Return Reproduction Page 7 to students and discuss any questions or comments they might have.

4. "Vocabulary Concepts Assessment" (Reproduction Page 8) is designed to evaluate student knowledge of the concepts and ideas presented in Chapter Three, "Reinforcing Word Identification Skills." This assessment can be used either as a pretest to determine how much students already know about the content of a unit, or as a posttest to evaluate student learning.

After you have distributed copies of Reproduction Page 8 to students, ask them to place a check on the appropriate blank, depending on whether they are taking the assessment as a pretest or as a posttest. Instruct them to read each item carefully. Allow time for every student to finish. Then either collect and grade their papers or have students correct their own work. An answer key is provided below.

ANSWER KEY—VOCABULARY CONCEPTS ASSESSMENT

| 1. b | 3. d | 5. d | 7. c | 9. d |
| 2. c | 4. f | 6. b | 8. b | 10. b |

Topic 3: Identifying Comprehension Needs

1. Interest in the reading comprehension process is a fairly recent phenomenon. Even though much research has now been done, the most that can be said safely is that we have sharpened our focus. We still do not have an adequate understanding of what happens when a reader understands the message that appears on a printed page.

Most standardized reading tests include one or more comprehension subtests. Some of these subtests attempt to diagnose a student's comprehension strengths and weaknesses by including items designed to measure literal and inferential comprehension or other skills such as the ability to determine the main idea of a passage or understand cause-and-effect relationships. However, researchers and reading educators cannot really be sure that comprehension does consist of these subskills even though they seem to be reasonable components. Most researchers will only go so far as to say that comprehension is based on a general language ability and an ability to reason while reading, and most reading experts and educators will say that standardized reading tests appear to be valid measures of this global ability.

Because the assessment of comprehension is not an exact science, it is important to involve students in the process so they do not just accept a score as an indication of their ability, but learn to evaluate the adequacy of their own thinking as they read.

Following the administration and scoring of a standardized reading comprehension subtest, ask students to record their scores on Reproduction Page 5 (Reading Improvement Plan) and then discuss the test. You may want to use the following questions to guide the discussion:

- Did you find the test difficult? What caused you difficulty?

- Could you remember the answers to questions or did you find that you had to go back to the passage to reread?

- Did you have enough time to complete the test?

- Do you think the passages in the test were similar to the types of material you read as part of your regular school work?

- As you read the passages in the test did you ask yourself questions like:

  a. Do I understand what I'm reading?

  b. Does what I think I understand make sense?

  c. What point is the author trying to make?

- Do you think your score reflects your true reading ability?

2. Paraphrasing what has been read, or rewriting the material using different words but keeping the author's message intact, seems to be an effective way of demonstrating that a reader has understood a written message. To write an acceptable paraphrase, a reader must be able to see or understand the meaning (deep structure) that underlies the words and the sentence construction used by the author (surface structure), and then from their own store of words and sentence construction knowledge reform the message so that the original meaning can be grasped by another reader or listener.

For these reasons, asking students to write paraphrases does give an indication of their ability to read and comprehend. Of course, paraphrases can not be scored as objectively as standardized tests. A fair amount of judgment is needed to evaluate student responses. Nevertheless, the paraphrasing process can help teachers develop an insight into students' reading strengths and weaknesses.

"Paraphrasing Assessment" (Reproduction Page 9) consists of ten familiar phrases and statements. Even though most people would say that they have a general idea of what these statements mean, many would find it a challenge to restate or paraphrase the ideas.

Distribute copies of Reproduction Page 9. Read the directions to your students and make sure that they understand that they are to change more than just one or two words. Collect the papers when students have finished. Use your own judgement to score the responses. You may find that many students had difficulty with some of the items. For example, a number of students who responded to a sample version of this activity were unable to accurately paraphrase "If wishes were horses then beggars would ride." They seemed unable to make the necessary inferences that would result in a paraphrase to the effect that if people could obtain everything they wished for, no one would lack for anything. These students were asked if changing the statement to: "If wishes were cars then beggars would ride" would have helped. They indicated that they did not think this change would have made any difference. Apparently the idea of wishes being equated with cars was as difficult to understand as the equating of wishes and horses. After you have returned your students' papers you may choose to discuss the paraphrases by:

- Asking students to verbally share particularly well-written paraphrases

- Explaining items that caused difficulty for many students

- Discussing the meaning of some of the items

3. The process of writing a summary requires skills similar to those used when writing paraphrases. The reader must understand the material and rethink the meaning of the information in order to rewrite the passage in a briefer form. To get an indication of how well students understand longer passages, select a brief front-page or human-interest article from your local newspaper. (See Chapter 1, Section, "Organizing for Instruction: Materials," for more information about selecting and using newspaper articles.) Reproduce the article and distribute copies to your students. Explain that they are to write a summary of seventy-five to one-hundred words that includes the important ideas conveyed in the article. Give students all the time they need to complete this activity.

   Return the summaries to your students after you have graded and scored them. Conclude the activity by pointing out the ideas you had expected students to include in their summaries. You might also write a summary of the article and distribute this to students and ask them to compare their responses with your own.

4. Many people report that they have mental images when they think and read. They say that these images take the forms of sights, sounds, smells, tastes, and even tactile or kinesthetic sensations. Some researchers who have studied the phenomenon of mental imagery (Shepard[7] and Pavio[8]) suggest that some people often use mental images when they think, while other people's thinking takes a verbal or concept-level form. No one really understands the imagery phenomenon very well because it is a difficult area to research. Scientists cannot get into someone's head and look at the pictures; they have to rely on what people report about their own thought processes, and self-reports can often be inaccurate. Several studies have shown though (Irwin and Witte[9] and Cramer[10])

7. R. N. Shepard, "The Mental Image," *American Psychologist*, February (1978): pp. 125–137.
8. A. Pavio, "Language and Knowledge of the World," *Educational Researcher* 3 (1974): pp. 5–12.
9. J. W. Irwin and P. L. Witte, "College Readers' Mental Imagery, Comprehension, and Attitude with Abstract and Concrete Expository Material," *Reading World* 20 (1980): pp. 35–43.
10. E. H. Cramer, "A Study of the Relationship Among Mental Imagery, Reading Comprehension, and Reading Attitude of Eleventh and Twelfth Grade Students," (Doctoral Thesis, University of Wisconsin, Madison, 1975).

that this ability to form mental images while reading is related to good comprehension, and that people who have mental images as they read like what they read better.

Reproduction Page 10, "An Imagery Inventory," consists of a series of sentences or statements taken from novels, magazines, newspapers, tax forms, and so forth. Some sentences were selected because they seemed to have the potential to evoke many images, while others were picked because they seemed to stimulate few if any images. There are no normative data for this inventory so it is not appropriate to use it as an instrument to evaluate an individual's tendency or ability to conceive images. However, it seems to be useful as a way of introducing the idea of imaging while reading and to help students become aware of mental imagery as they read.

Distribute copies of Reproduction Page 10 to students along with copies of Reproduction Page 11, "Imagery Response Form," which is designed to accompany the inventory. Read through the directions carefully with your students. After students have finished the inventory, ask them to share their responses to particular items. You might ask, for example, "How many people rated item number five high in imagery value?" Then ask for volunteers to explain the types of images they had. You may find that one person in a class marked an item as evoking vivid images while the next person marked the same item as evoking no images. The ensuing discussion of why one person had an image and another did not may show how background experiences play an important role in reading. Item number nine on the inventory, for example, describes a step in the process of preparing a recipe. A person who has never cooked may report no image while a person who cooks a great deal not only mentally visualizes but also smells and tastes what is being described.

5. Both common sense and research evidence[11] suggest that the ability to reason while reading is a key factor in effective comprehension. The *Watson-Glaser Critical Thinking Appraisal* is one of the few instruments that attempts to evaluate this ability through the use of a systematized format. When taking the test, students are asked to perform a variety of complex thinking operations. They are instructed to:

A. Evaluate the degree to which a particular inference follows from a given statement of facts.

B. Recognize if an assumption has been made.

C. Determine if a specific deduction can be made, given a particular statement.

D. Decide whether or not a proposed conclusion follows beyond a reasonable doubt from the information given in a paragraph.

The Watson-Glaser Critical Thinking Appraisal consists of fairly difficult reading and reasoning tasks and would be a challenge for average and above average readers. Poor students would no doubt become extremely frustrated while taking it. So the instrument is not recommended for remedial or corrective classes. Students in developmental or advanced reading courses might be

---

11.   J. A. Holmes, "Basic Assumptions Underlying the Substrata-Factor Theory," in *Theoretical Models and Processes of Reading*, 2d ed. H. Singer and R. Rudell (eds.) (Newark, Del.: International Reading Association, 1976), pp. 597–618.

stimulated by this test and gain some insight into their own thinking behavior. The address of the publisher of the *Watson-Glaser Critical Thinking Appraisal* can be found in the alphabetical list in Appendix A.

Topic 4: Evaluating Study Skills

1. The "Study Skills Self-Assessment" (Reproduction Page 12) is an informal instrument designed to assess general study habits. The items in the inventory are directly related to study and reading behaviors covered in this guidebook. A number of the items assess the students' awareness of the specific study approaches presented in Chapter 5 (Developing and Using Study Strategies). Reproduction Page 12 can be used as a pretest for this unit.

   Distribute copies of the "Study Skills Self-Assessment" to your students. Read through the directions with them, including the instructions for the "Response Evaluation" on Reproduction Pages 13 and 14. After students have completed the assessment and evaluated their responses, instruct them to record the name of the skill area in which they scored lowest on the "Reading Improvement Plan." Explain to students that they should place special emphasis on this area when it is taught as part of the reading course.

   Note: This instrument can be used as a posttest when the study skills unit or the entire course is completed.

2. The *Learning Styles Inventory* (1980) developed by Albert Canfield (the address of the publisher can be found in Appendix A) is designed to assess how students believe they react to:

   A. Learning conditions such as course work organization, peer and teacher relationships.

   B. Type of content, i.e., numeric, qualitative, inanimate, and people.

   C. Learning mode, i.e., talking, reading, ironic or direct experience.

   A fourth scale is designed to reflect students' expectations of how well they feel they will do in school.

   The directions for completing the inventory are complex and ought to be carefully explained to students. After students have completed and self-scored the instrument, the scores require thoughtful interpretation. This interpretive step is an important one and may be accomplished by using a class discussion format. The manual included with the "Learning Styles Inventory" provides a detailed, in-depth discussion of the characteristics the scales are designed to measure. By discussing what high and low scores in each area mean, students may learn more about their own patterns of goal setting, the influence their friends have on their class performance, and their own expectations for themselves. Used at the beginning of the course, this instrument seems to stimulate self-appraisal and to establish in the minds of students the idea that growth in reading and studying is based on self-understanding and an inner desire to improve.

3. Many high school students seem to have only vague conceptions of how they spend their time. To a certain extent, their poor class performance is not due to not knowing how to study but to the fact that they do not study or even set aside time to study. Reproduction Page 15, "Weekly Schedule," consists of a form students are to fill in by writing the activity they were involved in at a particular time. The purpose of this activity is simply to help students begin to think about how they spend their time.

When students were presented with just a blank sample version of this schedule, they seemed to have great difficulty figuring out how to fill it in. They did not seem to be able to devise methods for dividing up the time spaces to fit their own schedules or to show how a particular activity was repeated at the same time every day. Reproduction Page 16 "Sample Weekly Schedule," was developed to help solve this problem. This reproduction page simply shows how some typical student might fill in the schedule. Students appeared to find Reproduction Page 16 helpful. At least, they asked fewer questions and filled in their blank schedules more deliberately and effectively.

After students have filled in Reproduction Page 16, distribute copies of "Time Analysis of a Week" (Reproduction Page 17). Students may want to use some of the information from their weekly schedules to fill in this sheet. When students have completed this task, you may want to discuss how students use their time. The following questions might help to focus such a discussion:

- Does the amount of unaccounted for time you have surprise you?

- Are you generally satisfied with the way you spend your time?

- Do you feel you waste time?

- Do you want to change the way you use time?

- How could you change the way you use time?

- How do you imagine that you will spend your time when you are out of school?

Topic 5: Assessing Rate of Comprehension

Determining students' rate of comprehension is an interesting assessment procedure to use during the initial diagnostic activities in a reading course. Most students seem curious about how fast or how many words per minute they read. This activity is designed to give an initial indication of how fast students can read a simple piece of narrative prose. Detailed discussions of procedures for determining rate and improving rate of comprehension are included in Chapter 6 of this guidebook.

Distribute Copies of Reproduction Pages 18, 19, and 20. Explain that the following procedure will be used to determine students' rate of comprehension:

1. They will be instructed to begin reading the article "The Kalahari Desert" (Reproduction Page 18) at a specific time. All students will begin reading at the same exact time. No student will begin reading until a signal is given.

2. Starting with thirty seconds (:30), the time used will be recorded on the board every ten seconds, i.e. :30, :40, :50, 1:00, and so on.

3. As soon as students finish reading, they are to write the time that is currently on the board on their papers.

4. Next, students will answer the comprehension questions on Reproduction Page 19, "Comprehension Check—*The Kalahari Desert.*"

5. Following this, students will turn to Reproduction Page 20, "Reading Rates for *The Kalahari Desert,*" to locate their reading time in minutes and seconds. In the corresponding column, they are to circle the number of words they read in one minute.

When all students have finished answering the comprehension questions and have found their reading rate, briefly discuss the reading and ask students to score their own comprehension questions. The correct answers to the "Comprehension Check" are as follows: 1. c, 2. c, 3. a, 4. c, 5. e, 6. c, 7. d, 8. b, 9. d, 10. a.

Now distribute copies of Reproduction Page 21, "Reading Rate Graph." You may also want to make a transparency of Reproduction Page 22, "Reading Rate Graph: (Demonstration Sample)," to use as you explain the procedure for filling in the graph. Instruct students to:

1. write the current data in the box with the "1" in it on the graph.

2. write the number of items they had correct on the "Comprehension Check" over the total number of questions, i.e., 10/10, 9/10, and so on, in the bottom box labeled "Comp. Score."

3. count up five lines from the box with the "1" in it and mark an "X" in the sixth box, or the box above the fifth line.

4. write the number of words they read per minute in the margins next to the fifth line.

The reason for going up five lines to mark the first reading is that some students may read more slowly when they encounter more difficult future readings. Allowing five lines provides space for recording lower rates. After students have successfully recorded their comprehension scores and their rates on the graph, ask them to transfer these scores to the "Reading Improvement Plan."

ASSESSING LEARNING EXPERIENCES

To determine if students have gained some insight into their own reading and studying strengths and weaknesses, request them to take out and study carefully the "Reading Improvement Plan," which ought to include the scores or results from the various tests and inventories they have taken as part of this unit. You might then ask them some or all of the following questions:

1. Which are your strongest skill areas?

2. Which are your weakest skill areas?

3. In which areas do you most want to improve? Draw a star in the margin next to this area.

To further assess what students have learned, ask them to write a brief paper describing what they have learned either about their own reading, thinking, and studying behaviors in general or what they have learned about themselves in one specific area such as their ability to schedule time, to use mental images while reading, or to think critically.

RESOURCES FOR TEACHING

Below is a selected list of resources useful for teaching the concepts and topics of this chapter. It is divided into two categories: "Books, Pamphlets and Articles" and "Formal and Informal Tests and Inventories." Addresses of publishers can be found in the alphabetical list in Appendix A.

Books, Pamphlets, Articles

Blanton, W.; Farr, R.; and Tuinman, J. (Eds.). *Reading Tests for the Secondary Grades.* Newark, Del.: International Reading Association, 1972. This includes a discussion of criteria teachers may use to review tests. Commonly used standardized tests available at the secondary level are reviewed.

Daffelmeyer, Frederick A. "A Comparison of Reading Test Results in Grades Nine and Twelve." *Journal of Reading,* 1980, 23, (7), 606–608. Many standardized reading tests yield both vocabulary and comprehension scores. Though some authorities suggest that students can be classified according to the balance between their reading comprehension scores and their vocabulary scores, Daffelmeyer suggests that this type of classification may be misleading. He cites evidence indicating that differences in the scores may be due to the fact that a particular vocabulary subtest may be more difficult than a particular comprehension subtest or vice versa. The author maintains that test results must be examined carefully and used cautiously.

Drahozal, Edward C., and Hanna, G. S. "Reading Comprehension Subscores: Pretty Bottles for Ordinary Wine." *Journal of Reading,* 1978, 21, (5), 481–487. This article discusses the problem of using the subtest scores of standardized reading comprehension tests for diagnostic purposes. The authors cite numerous other authorities and include evidence from some of their own research to demonstrate that the subtests of standardized tests that obstensibly measure different skills such as inferring or recognizing the main idea may be measuring virtually the same skill. Thus the results from these subtests would have little or no real diagnostic value.

Farr, Roger. *Reading: What Can Be Measured?* Newark, Del.: International Reading Association, 1969. This includes research information on measurement and evaluation and provides a thorough discussion of such topics as the problem of measuring reading subskills, variables related to reading performance, and guides to and indexes of reading tests and reading test reviews.

Johns, Jerry L. "Do Comprehension Items Really Test Reading? Sometimes!" *Journal of Reading,* 1978, 21, (7) 615–619. The author cautions test users to study the items in standardized reading comprehension tests carefully. He cites examples of specific items from published tests that can be correctly answered by students who have not even read the passage.

Lehr, Fran. "Testing Reading Comprehension at the Secondary Level: Informal Measures." *Journal of Reading,* 1979, 23, (3), 270–273. A source of ideas for using informal measures to assess secondary students' reading abilities. Included are descriptions of how to adapt informal reading inventories to the secondary level, a model for developing a reading and study-skills inventory, and descriptions of materials that can be obtained through the Educational Resources Information Center Clearinghouse on Reading and Communications Skills (ERIC/RCS).

Mehrens, William A., and Lehmann, Irvin J. *Measurement and Evaluation in Education and Psychology.* New York: Holt, Rinehart, and Winston, Inc., 1973. A standard textbook on testing and evaluation providing background information on such topics as the development of evaluation techniques in education, basic principles of measurement, and the development and use of teacher-made and standardized tests.

Schell, Leo M. (Ed.). *Diagnostic and Criterion-Referenced Reading Tests: Review and Evaluation.* Newark, Del.: International Reading Association, 1981. This source reviews and evaluates frequently used individual and group-administered reading tests. The reviews include an overview of the test, discussions of the norming sample, the test's reliability and validity, and conclusions drawn by the author of the review.

Schreiner, Robert. *Reading Tests and Teachers: A Practical Guide.* Newark, Del.: International Reading Association. 1979. This guide discusses how to select tests, how to develop valid and reliable tests, and how to use tests for planning instruction.

Formal and Informal Tests and Inventories

GROUP TESTS

California Achievement Test: Reading. Test Bureau/McGraw-Hill, 1978. Grade level: 6–12: Time to administer: 50–75 minutes; Measures: vocabulary, story skills, comprehension in different types of material; Forms: 2.

Gates-MacGintie Reading Tests. Houghton Mifflin, 1978. Grade level: 7–9 (Survey F); Time to administer: 44 minutes; Measures: speed and accuracy, vocabulary, comprehension; Forms: 3.

Iowa Silent Reading Test. Harcourt Brace Jovanovich, 1973. Grade level: 6–12; Time to administer: 60 minutes; Measures: vocabulary, comprehension, reading efficiency; Forms: 1.

Metropolitan Achievement Tests: Reading, Advanced. Harcourt Brace Jovanovich, 1978. Grade Level: 7–9; Time to administer: 46 minutes; Measures: vocabulary and comprehension; Forms: 2.

Nelson-Denny Reading Test. Houghton Mifflin, 1973. Grade Level: 9–16; Time to administer: 40 minutes; Measures: vocabulary, comprehension, and rate; Forms: 2.

Sequential Tests of Educational Progress, (STEP) Reading. Educational Testing Service, 1978. Grade level: 4–14; Time to administer: 45 minutes; Measures: comprehension; Forms: 2.

Stanford Diagnostic Reading Test: Blue Level. Harcourt, Brace, Jovanovich, 1978. Grade level: 9–12; Time to administer: 90 minutes; Measures: comprehension, vocabulary, decoding, and rate; Forms: 2.

INDIVIDUAL TESTS

Classroom Reading Inventory. William C. Brown, 1973. Grade level: 2–8; Time to administer: varies; measures: word recognition, oral and silent reading comprehension, spelling; Forms: 3.

Diagnostic Reading Scales. CTB/McGraw-Hill, 1972. Grade level: 1–8; Time to administer: varies; Measures: word recognition, oral and silent reading comprehension, listening comprehension, word attack and auditory discrimination; Forms: 1 (includes supplementary passages).

Sucher-Allred Reading Placement Inventory. Economy Company, 1973. Grade level: 1–9; Time to administer: 20 minutes; Measures: word recognition and oral reading comprehension; Forms: 1.

Woodcock Reading Mastery Tests. American Guidance Service, 1973. Grade level: K–12; Time to administer: 50 minutes; Measures: letter identification, word identification, word attack, word comprehension, and passage comprehension; Forms: 2.

3

Reinforcing Word Identification Skills

Students at the postelementary level who read are able to do so because they know how to identify words. They have learned that certain sounds are associated with certain letters and they can make these associations so quickly that in most cases they are unaware of the process. Most students also have some skill in analyzing unknown words by dividing them into meaningful parts, and in finding the meaning of words by analyzing the context in which they appear.

In other words, most secondary students have acquired basic word identification skills. The purpose for including a unit on vocabulary development or word identification in a reading course is primarily to reinforce skills students already have. The first topic in this chapter deals with building word awareness and encouraging students to actively apply the word identification skills they already have when they encounter unfamiliar terms in print. Included under the other topics are activities designed to help students review and further develop these skills.

PERFORMANCE OBJECTIVES

As a result of the learning activities in this chapter, students will be able to:

1. Realize that vocabulary improvement is an attitude toward learning.

2. Increase their understanding of words.

3. Develop their appreciation of words.

4. Use word-attack strategies appropriately.

5. Use dictionaries and thesauruses as aids for increasing their word knowledge.

LEARNING EXPERIENCES

Topic 1: Building Word Awareness

1. Articles, books, selected passages—in fact all the printed materials used in a reading course—are sources for words and provide opportunities for vocabulary growth. Students need to be encouraged, coaxed, and directed to notice new words, think about their meanings in context, and look them up. For this reason, it is important to point out consistently words in the printed materials used in a reading course that might be new or only somewhat familiar to students. The following activity may be used as a model for using materials available to classroom teachers to develop word awareness.

   Distribute copies of "Mrs. Joe Gargery" (Reproduction Page 23), a selection from Charles Dickens's *Great Expectations*, and instruct students to read the article. In addition to noting the vocabulary used, ask your students to pay attention to the way Dickens so quickly and seemingly easily develops a very remarkable character. When your students have finished reading, have them turn the page over and ask them to write any words they found that were unfamiliar to them. After students have suggested some words, involve the class in trying to use context to define them. If students are unable to locate any unfamiliar words, tell them to turn back to the article. Point out words like "impregnable" or "trenchant" or ask them what it means to spread in an "apothecary" kind of way. Chances are good that no one will be able to define these terms, at least not quickly. After some suggestions of contextual definitions have been given, ask someone to look each term up in the dictionary. Ask students to explain how the dictionary definition helps to clarify the meaning of the word as it is used by Dickens. Explain to students that this procedure of identifying and then using context or a dictionary to define an unfamiliar word is one that ought to help them expand their vocabularies.

2. The approach described in Activity 1 above can be systematized by providing students with a means of recording and organizing the words introduced in class readings or discussions. "Recording New Vocabulary Words" (Reproduction Page 24) can be filled out by students when they encounter new words. Writing the word, its context meaning, and dictionary definition, and then using the word in a sentence, gives students some of the practice needed to assimilate a new word into their vocabularies. Students may keep these slips in their reading folders and review them periodically or else the procedure can be formalized by following the steps below:

   • Point out a word like "trenchant" when it occurs in a reading. Pass out copies of Reproduction Page 24 to students and guide them through the process of filling out a slip for "trenchant."

   • Stress that it is important for students to write a sentence with the word in it.

   • Each time a new word occurs in a subsequent reading or class discussion, ask students to fill out a slip. This may seem time consuming and tangential to the topic at hand, but the process helps students better understand what they are reading and at the same time helps them expand their vocabularies.

- Periodically collect and evaluate these slips.

3. Estimates of the number of words in our modern English language indicate that we have a total vocabulary of well over one million words. Three-quarters of these words, however, belong to specialized fields such as medicine, computer technology, carpentry, and many other fields. Most of us use and recognize only about 30,000 to 60,000 words. The majority of the words in our language are unknown to most of us and are highly specialized. Even the most literate people are not likely to have vocabularies of much more than 100,000 words.[1] The number of words is simply too immense; no one could learn, remember, and use all of them. The sheer number of words also means that a random approach to vocabulary development is not effective. Learning isolated lists of vocabulary words or using self-help word books for vocabulary development can easily result in studying words that students might never need to know or have the occasion to use. Instead, it is more effective for students to focus their vocabulary-building efforts on four areas:

    A. *The word knowledge needed to function as world citizens and people in a democratic society who make political decisions.*

    B. *The words and terms associated with an individual's chosen profession or vocation.*

    C. *The word knowledge needed to be an intelligent consumer.* (Today, people need to understand terms associated with foods and food processing in order to make intelligent nutritional choices. Understanding specialized vocabularies is also important when making decisions about clothing, housing materials, or automobiles.)

    D. *The word knowledge associated with recreational activities.* (Sports, arts and crafts, music, and games all have specialized vocabularies that we need to know in order to appreciate fully and discuss our interests with others.)

    Introduce this activity by explaining to students that the English language has more words than any one person could possibly learn. Use the information given above regarding the number of words in our language to emphasize to students the importance of carefully selecting the words they will think about and learn.

    On the chalkboard, write the four areas for focused vocabulary development given above. Briefly discuss each area and ask students to give examples of words that could be included in each area. Request that students take notes on this discussion. Suggest that they include the four areas for focused vocabulary instruction and the examples given by class members in their notes.

    To provide additional opportunities for students to develop their understanding of focused vocabulary development, the two activities directly following this one are based on printed materials containing words associated with consumerism and recreational activities.

4. "Word Knowledge Associated With Recreational Activities" (Reproduction Page 25) is a newspaper article dealing with sports. Ask students to read this account of a golf tournament. Tell them that the purpose of the exercise is to help them

---

1. Mario Pei, *The Story of Language*, (New York: J.B. Lippincott, 1966), p. 85.

become aware of the number of technical terms used in the everyday world. Instruct them to draw a line under terms whose meanings are unknown to them. Discuss the words that students have underlined and have students familiar with terms used in professional golf provide definitions for the rest of the class.

5. This activity is similar to Activity 4 except that it is based on an excerpt from a magazine dealing with the domestic arts. The article is about preparing food and includes terms associated with cooking and with various cuts of meat. Distribute copies of Reproduction Page 26, "Word Knowledge Needed to Be an Intelligent Consumer." Ask students to read the article and to underline unfamiliar terms. Again discuss the underlined words and have students who are knowledgeable about cooking define these words for the rest of the class.

Topic 2. Learning to Read: A Review of the Process of Phonic Analysis

1. As mentioned in the introduction to this chapter, most students at the high school level have learned letter-sound correspondences to the degree that they can associate letters with sounds in an almost automatic, unconscious fashion. When readers are able to make letter-sound correspondences rapidly, they can be said to have mastered decoding skills. Most students reach this point at about the fourth grade. After this mastery is attained, readers have more mental energy available to focus on comprehending the printed page. The purpose of the following activity is to help students appreciate the extent to which they have mastered phonics, or the process of associating letters with sounds.

The English language is notorious for inconsistencies in letter-sound correspondence; we have silent e's, p's, and b's, and *ph*, *f*, or *ugh* can represent the same sound, to list a few of the more obvious ones. Reproduction Page 27, "Rephonixed Reading Test," consists of a short passage describing a commercial product followed by a comprehension quiz. Some of the words, however, have been respelled using alternative letters to represent a particular sound. Ask students to read the passage and answer the comprehension questions. Some students will be able to decode this passage quickly and most students will be able to complete the task successfully if given some time. Ask for a volunteer to read the passage aloud and then correct the comprehension questions. The correct answers are as follows: 1. d, 2. c, 3. c, 4. b, 5. b. Conclude the exercise by explaining to students that they were able to decode the passage because they had learned that letters representing certain sounds form words and that words can be put together to form sentences that convey meaningful messages. Even though words were spelled in an unfamiliar manner in the passage, students understood the process of decoding and reading so well they were able to overcome the inconsistencies. The passage for the "Rephonixed Reading Test" appears below, reprinted with regular spelling patterns.

Rephonixed Reading Test

Reverse Announces Two New High Performance Tennis Shoes
With Something in Them No One Else Has

Now there are two Reverse Tennis Shoes designed around the way the world's top tennis players play the game.

Both have the unique Reverse bioflex outersole that maximizes the flexibility and control in your forefoot area—the portion of your foot on which you play the most crucial part of your game. So both shoes give you extra traction.

Plus, both give you the kind of comfortable fit only a Reverse can because they're made on the advanced Reverse last. So when you wear them, you get the same kind of increased endurance they give the champions.

Feature for feature they beat every shoe in their class. Try on a pair and see how it feels to be one of the world's top tennis players today.

2. Because high school students learned to read so long ago, many have probably forgotten how or what exactly they did learn. In some respect, the process of learning to read may be a mystery to them. The purpose of this activity is to give just a brief review of a few basic concepts that are part of beginning reading instruction. Students may be interested in getting a perspective on how much progress as readers and as students they have made. Reproduction Page 28, "Basic Concepts Involved in Learning to Read: Letters, Words, and Sentences," consists of the sentence "The sun is a star." This sentence is part of an achievement test given at the end of kindergarten and demonstrates three important concepts kindergartners are expected to have learned: First the child is asked to put an "X" on a letter. Next the child is instructed to draw a circle around a word. Finally he or she is asked to draw a line under a sentence. Some kindergartners do well on this test. But others may not know what a word is. They draw a circle around a letter or several letters instead. Also, many kindergartners do not know what a sentence is. At the high school level, we take for granted knowing what a word is and what a sentence is, but they are concepts that none of us knew at one point in our lives and that all of us had to learn.

Make transparencies of Reproduction Pages 28 and 29. Place the transparency of Reproduction Page 28 on an overhead and then, using the information given above, explain to students what kindergartners are asked to do with the sentence "The sun is a star."

Then place the transparency of Reproduction Page 29, "Basic Concepts Involved in Learning to Read: Letter-Sound Correspondence," on the overhead. The following comments may help you guide the discussion:

A. Point to the box on the top left hand portion of the page. Explain that many common approaches to teaching beginning reading involve the child in a process like the following:

    a. The child carefully inspects a letter such as an "N."

    b. The child prints the letter.

    c. The child draws a circle around the picture whose name begins with the same sound as the letter's name.

B. Beginning readers do one or several pages of such activities, working with only one letter. Then they perform the same procedures again until they learn all the beginning consonant sounds. Following this, they are instructed to listen for ending sounds, vowels, and sounds in the middle of words. They are taught to associate these sounds with appropriate letters by following the procedure of inspecting and printing the letters and selecting pictures whose names contain the sounds.

C. After beginning readers have had practice associating letters with pictures, they may be given a more complex activity requiring them to reverse the process. The second row of pictures on Reproduction Page 29 contains pictures of a box and a walrus. Below each picture are four letters. Children are asked to choose the one letter out of the four that represents the sound at the end of the word "box" or the word "walrus."

D. Once children understand the concept that letters represent sounds, one of the next important steps to becoming a reader is learning how sounds are blended when they form words. To help children learn how to blend, teachers instruct beginning readers to inspect words carefully, begining at the left and moving to the right. As teachers slide their hand under a word, they slowly say the word demonstrating how the sounds are blended.

E. While children are being taught letter-sound correspondences and sound blending, they are also experiencing reading as a process of communication. Through stories that are read to them, stories they compose and dictate for their teacher to write, and numerous other methods such as labeling objects in the classroom, children are taught that reading is an important way in which human beings communicate ideas.

F. When children have learned the basic concept that letters correspond to sounds and that sounds form words that convey ideas, the most important thing they need to do to become readers is to practice what they have learned until they become highly skilled. Certainly there are other skills, such as learning to identify main ideas and supporting details, that children need to know. But it is very important that children at the elementary level have many opportunities to practice phonic skills by reading simple meaningful materials.

3. There are few reading/learning situations in which high school students are required to employ phonic analysis. Once students have learned to associate letters and sounds and have had the opportunity to practice these associations until they can make them almost automatically, there is little need to sound out words. Long, difficult words are sometimes an exception, however, especially if students need to pronounce such words when participating in class discussions or if they want the words to become part of their speaking vocabularies.

If students are not able to ask someone for the correct pronunciation of a word, their main recourse is the dictionary. To increase awareness of this source of assistance, distribute copies of any standard dictionary to individual students or small groups of students. Point out that there is a guide to pronunciation at the front of many unabridged dictionaries and that most dictionaries have pronunciation guides at the bottom of each page. Review these guides with students, asking for volunteers to say the words and sounds presented in the guides. Then ask a student to describe how these guides can be used to learn the correct pronunciation of main entry words. Student responses ought to include the idea that a key to pronunciation is often given in the main entry portion of the dictionary and the guide at the bottom of the page is to be used if students have difficulty interpreting the specialized letter forms and signs that make up this key.

Topic 3. Using Word Identification Strategies at the High School Level

1. Structural analysis—the process of identifying words by dividing them into known meaningful parts—and contextual analysis —defining words by analyzing the context in which they appear—are common terms used to describe word identification strategies readers use after they have mastered phonics or decoding skills.

   To introduce this topic to students, point out that these strategies, structural and contextual analysis, involve thinking processes that are very different from those used by readers to make letter-sound associations. Phonic analysis is based on the assumption that once readers can sound out a word, they will immediately know what the word means because that word is already part of their listening and speaking vocabularies. On the other hand, structural and contextual analysis are used by readers to identify the meaning of words that are unknown to them or not part of their listening and speaking vocabularies. Readers employ a reasoning process whereby they use the known meaning of parts of words and their knowledge of the context in which a word appears to define a term that is unfamiliar.

   Explain to students that doing exercises that deal with isolated words or sentences may not help them learn how to apply structural and contextual analysis as much as learning to use these strategies when they are reading complete passages. For this reason, the purpose of the following activities is to review several ideas concerning the application of structural and contextual analysis and to provide an in-depth opportunity to develop contextual analysis skills.

   To conclude this introductory discussion you may want to stress the following:

   - Phonic analysis is used by beginning readers to sound out a word they will then recognize because it is part of their listening and speaking vocabularies.

   - Structural and contextual analysis are strategies used to determine the meaning of unknown words or words that are not part of readers' listening and speaking vocabularies.

   - Students can most effectively learn to use structural and contextual analysis by applying these strategies when they are reading complete passages.

2. When students encounter an unknown word while reading, they ought to be able to quickly decide which word-identification strategy would be most appropriate. If meaningful parts can be identified, then stopping to analyze the prefixes, roots, or suffixes that make up the word would probably be an effective strategy. Sometimes words can be quickly defined by studying the context. At other times both structural and contextual analysis are necessary in order to comprehend difficult terms. But some words defy any type or combination of word analysis and readers are required to consult an outside source such as a teacher, another student, or a dictionary. The point here is that students need to have flexibility when they come upon unknown words in print.

   The purpose of the following activity is to provide practice in selecting appropriate word-identification strategies and to impress upon the students the idea that it is important to take a flexible approach when seaching for the meaning of unknown words. Distribute copies of Reproduction Page 30, "Choosing

Word Identification Strategies." Explain that students are to write "SA" on the blank in front of those words they think they can identify through structural analysis. Indicate that they may write SA for a word even if they can only identify the meaning of part of the word. When students have finished writing, discuss their responses. You may want to make comments similar to the following as you direct the discussion:

- There are no correct or incorrect responses. Knowledge of word parts will vary from individual to individual.

- If students can only identify the meaning of a portion of a word, ask them to explain the meaning of that portion and ask if other students can provide assistance in defining the complete word.

- Ask students if they experienced frustration as they tried to identify those words presented out of context.

- Ask if students think they often rely on context to help them learn the meaning of words when they are reading on their own.

- Explain that the purpose of this activity is to help students:

  a. develop the habit of looking for meaningful parts in words.

  b. realize that it is often necessary to use several strategies in order to identify unknown words.

3. Reproduction Page 31 contains lists of some common prefixes, roots, and suffixes. These lists can be used in several ways to help students develop the awareness that they can sometimes determine the meaning of unknown words by looking for the meaningful parts. First, review the three lists with your students. Beginning with the list of prefixes, request that students read through the prefixes and their meanings silently. Then ask for volunteers to give additional examples of the prefixes being used with different root words and suffixes. Use this same procedure to review the lists of common roots and suffixes.

   A second activity involving the three lists is to have students form small groups or "word committees." The purpose of the activity is to provide an opportunity for students to play with words and to get some experience manipulating roots and affixes. Assign each group five prefixes, five root words, and two or three suffixes from the lists. The number of affixes and roots assigned is arbitrary, depending on the amount of class time available and the interest and ability of the students. Tell students that, as a group, they are to write lists of five to ten words (again the number is arbitrary) that contain each prefix, root, and suffix you assigned. Stress that the activity is not one that will be graded, but that students are to think of as many words as quickly as they can. Hopefully, students will stimulate each other and become adept at and comfortable with the process of forming words, and as a result of this activity they will be encouraged to use structural analysis when they encounter unknown words in subsequent readings. After the groups of students have finished writing their lists, ask someone from each group to tell the class how many words his or her group thought of and to give a few examples of some of the more interesting words.

4. "Types of Context Clues" (Reproduction Page 32) consists of a list of types of context clues or typical ways in which context is used to define terms. The examples that follow each of the context clue types are based on the definitions of the same two terms, "peripheral nerves" and "nervous system." The term and the context used to define the term are underlined. These same examples are used over and over in order to emphasize the differences among types of context clues.

   Discuss these context clue types with students and point out that there are several other ways of using context to define or identify unfamiliar terms that are not as straightforward as the context clue types listed. These include:

   - *Tone:* The way an author uses words to describe a person, setting, or event can develop a feeling or mood that aids a reader in defining an obscure term.

   - *Pictorial:* Many content area texts include drawings or pictures that define terms or clarify terms that are already defined in text.

   - *Experience of the reader:* Sometimes a term is described or an idea is developed by referring to experiences that are common to most people. Reflecting on these experiences can help readers define unfamiliar terms.

   Conclude this discussion by asking students if they can think of any other ways in which words are defined in context. Emphasize that "Types of Context Clues" (Reproduction Page 32) is not meant to be a definitive list. The purpose of Reproduction Page 32 is simply to cause students to think about the different methods writers use to clarify or explain the words and terms they use.

5. Reproduction Page 7, "Using Context Clues" was presented in Chapter 2, "Identifying Reading Needs," as a measure of students' ability to use context clues. It can be used to provide practice in identifying types of context clues.

   Ask students to write definitions for the terms given on Reproduction Page 7 if you have not already asked them to do so as part of earlier diagnostic activities. Then working either individually or as a class discussion activity ask students to determine the type of context clue that is used in each of the fifteen items on Reproduction Page 7. There may be some differences of opinion because there are similarities among the types of context clues. The goal of this exercise is to help students develop an awareness of the general use of context, not to teach them that there are absolute types of context clues.

ASSESSING LEARNING EXPERIENCES

The extent to which students have mastered the concepts and skills presented in the chapter can be measured by having students submit for evaluation the final products of almost any of the activities suggested earlier.

1. Divide the class into small groups of about five students. Ask each group to develop lists of words that would come under each of the four areas for focused vocabulary development listed below:

   A. The word knowledge needed to function as world citizens and as people who make political decisions in a democratic society.

B. Words and terms associated with an individual's chosen profession or vocation.

C. The word knowledge needed to cope with living in a modern society.

D. The word knowledge associated with recreational activities.

2. Have students write one paragraph explaining when and how they would use phonic analysis, structural analysis, and contextual analysis.

RESOURCES FOR TEACHING

Below is a selected list of resources that can provide further background information for teaching the concepts and topics of this chapter. Addresses of publishers can be found in the alphabetical list in Appendix A.

Burmeister, Lou "Vocabulary Development in Content Areas Through the Use of Morphemes." *Journal of Reading,* 1976, *19,* 481–487. In this article Burmeister suggests that content teachers can aid student vocabulary development by teaching the morphemes (the smallest unit of meaning in language) that are common to their particular subject area. For example, students in social studies can be taught that words such as *autocracy, autobiography,* and *automat* have the same base, the morpheme "auto."

Cunningham, Patricia. "Decoding Polysyllabic Words: An Alternative Strategy." *Journal of Reading,* 1978, *21,* 608–614. This article describes a compare and contrast strategy for identifying unfamiliar words. The author includes lessons and examples that show how students can match eight words they already know to parts of unknown words.

Ehri, Linnea; Barron, Roderick; and Feldman, Jeffrey. *The Recognition of Words.* Newark, Del.: International Reading Association, 1978. The three articles in this pamphlet contain a discussion of a model of how children learn to recognize words and how they learn to associate printed words with speech sounds. These articles provide some insight into the process of learning to read.

Estes, Thomas, and Vaughan, Joseph. *Reading and Learning in the Content Classroom.* Boston: Allyn and Bacon, 1978. Chapter 7 of Unit 2 in this text includes suggestions for evaluating vocabulary knowledge and skill.

Suggestions for helping students develop meaningful vocabularies are provided in Chapter 13 of Unit 3.

Hill, Walter. *Secondary School Reading: Process, Program, Procedure.* Boston: Allyn and Bacon, 1979. Several chapters in this text contain detailed descriptions of effective word-attack behaviors and suggestions for diagnosing vocabulary strengths and weaknesses. Ideas for developing instructional activities are also included.

Johnson, Dale, and Pearson, P. David. *Teaching Reading Vocabulary.* New York: Holt, Rinehart, and Winston, 1978. The purpose of this text is to help clarify some of the terminology associated with vocabulary development and to provide suggestions for diagnosis and teaching. This book is a particularly appropriate resource for teachers working with poor readers at the secondary level.

Lee, Joyce. "Increasing Comprehension through Use of Context Clue Categories." *Journal of Reading,* 1978, *22,* 259–262. Included in this article are descriptions of a variety of methods teachers can use to provide needed instruction in the use of context clues. The author discusses the value of using classification systems for teaching context clues and offers suggestions for modifying the cloze procedure to help students take advantage of context clues.

Kaplan, Elaine, and Tuchman, Anita. "Vocabulary Strategies Belong in the Hands of Learners." *Journal of Reading,* 1980, *24,* 32–34. Five strategies for actively involving students in the process of learning vocabulary in a meaningful context are described in this article. All these strategies require a high level of student and teacher participation.

4

Improving Reading Comprehension Skills

The purpose of reading, of course, is to comprehend an author's message and to learn from that message. Yet, if asked to define comprehension, most of us would have difficulty. We might respond with something like: "Comprehension is understanding what you read." But that kind of statement neither defines the process nor explains what happens inside people's heads when they read. Definitions of reading that are credible tend to be so general and circular that they say nothing. Attempts to define comprehension in specific terms most often seem incomplete or even erroneous. Recently, reading educators and researchers have devoted much time and effort to studying comprehension, but they are still reluctant and essentially unable to arrive at a pat definition. Most seem to agree, though, that the background experiences of the reader, the ability to quickly and accurately recognize words, and the ability to reason while reading are key factors in comprehension.

The existence of a fourth factor—specific comprehension skills—is a matter of controversy. Some reading educators maintain that comprehension is a unitary process closely related to if not synonomous with thinking and reasoning. They recommend holistic approaches to instruction, such as encouraging students to form mental images, read widely, or study how concepts are organized and developed. Other reading experts maintain that comprehension is developed through learning and applying specific skills, such as determining the main idea of a selection or locating supporting details.

This lack of agreement is really more stimulating than discouraging. Different points of view encourage creative thought on the part of all who are involved in teaching reading. Despite the lack of consensus, recent emphasis on reading research has resulted in some intriguing insights and new approaches to helping students understand and learn from print.

Activities that reflect some of these recent developments in reading comprehension research have been included in this chapter. Topic I consists of activities designed to encourage students to use the information they already know—the background experiences that are stored in their memories. Activities that focus on the development of reading and reasoning skills are presented under Topic II. Topic III includes a variety of activities centering on specific skills related to the comprehension tasks of high school students.

PERFORMANCE OBJECTIVES

As a result of the learning activities in this chapter, students will be able to:

1. Reflect on their own reading/thinking process.

2. Realize they ought to review what they already know about a topic before they begin an assigned reading.

3. Develop strategies for using the information they already know as they read.

4. Improve their ability to reason while reading.

5. Increase their comprehension by learning to recognize more effectively important ideas and use the organizational structure provided by the author.

6. Develop skill in paraphrasing in order to demonstrate that they have understood what they have read.

LEARNING EXPERIENCES

Topic 1. Using Background Information

1. A number of researchers[1] studying human memory and learning have developed a theory or way of conceptualizing how we remember and how we use memories to learn new information. According to this theory, information gained through experience is put into an organizational framework called a *schema* (*schemata* in the plural) and thus is stored in our memories. These schemata or memory units are not passive storage containers for ideas; they are actively involved in the process of comprehending information. This theory of memory seems to be a reasonable one and perhaps can provide students with some insights into their own mental processes.

   This activity and the one that follows are designed to be used as part of the same lesson. Together, the two activities ought to help students understand how information is organized and stored in the form of schema and how this stored background information can be used to learn new information. First, duplicate Reproduction Pages 33–35, "Schemata for Water," in the form of

---

1. R. C. Anderson, "Schema-Directed Process in Language Comprehension," in *Cognitive Psychology and Instruction,* A. Lesgold, S. Pellegrino, S. Fakkima, and R. Gaser (eds.), (New York: Plemen Press, 1978), pp. 82–110. D. Rumelhart and D. A. Norman, "Accretion, Tuning and Restructuring: Three Modes of Learning," in *Semantic Factors in Cognition,* J. W. Cotton and R. L. Klatzky (eds.), (Hillsdale, New York: Erlbaum Associates, 1978), pp. 37–61.

transparencies to serve as illustrations. Then explain as follows: A particular student might have the idea or schema for water that includes the information that water is something we drink, wash in, and cook with (see Reproduction Page 33). Another student who is an avid swimmer also conceptualizes water as something we drink, wash in, and cook with, but has stored additional information about the buoyancy of water. Each person's schema for a particular concept is almost certain to be different from another's because we have all had different experiences.

Now suppose the student who has the schema for water containing the information that water is something we drink, wash in, and cook with, is reading a science text that states the idea that a liquid such as water takes the shape of any container into which it is poured (see Reproduction Page 34). This idea probably contains very little new information for the student, who has seen water take the shape of a glass, a cooking pot, or a bathtub. This stored information is then used by the student to understand the idea that a liquid is shapeless. But suppose the student continues to read and comes across the idea that water is made up of tiny particles called molecules that are in constant motion. This idea is new to the student and does not easily fit into his or her existing shema for water (see Reproduction Page 35). In order to understand this property of water the student needs more information that his or her science teacher can provide through the use of models, drawings, and experiments. After the teacher has explained the concept of molecules, the student ought to be able to add the information to an existing schema or develop a new schema that includes the molecular nature of water.

Conclude this activity by reviewing the concept of a schema, the hypothetical unit for storing memories in the brain. The following statements and questions may be used for this review and to determine if students have understood the idea:

- Explain the term *schema*.

- Give three examples of information that is contained in your schema for dogs.

- It was suggested in the presentation above that the idea that liquids are shapeless is an easier concept for students to understand than the idea that liquids are made up of molecules in constant motion. Do you agree with this suggestion? Try to explain your answer using the word "schema."

- Give examples of information contained in your schema for concrete concepts such as apples, chairs, or cars.

- Give examples of information contained in your schema for more abstract concepts such as honesty, peace, or government.

2. Though the term "schema" is probably new, most students are familiar with the term "background information" and these two terms are essentially synonymous. Some researchers seem to prefer schema because it helps them to conceptualize a more specific unit in the brain. Once students understand the idea that information gained from their experience is stored in an organized fashion in their minds, the next step in the process is to show how these schemata or stored background experiences can be used effectively by readers and students.

Both common sense and some of the findings from recent research suggest that reviewing what is already known helps students learn new information. Science teachers trying to explain the molecular nature of liquids might ask students to think back to the process of making Kool-aid, then explain that molecular movement is what really accounts for the dissolving process. Even without stirring, the sugar eventually disperses. Science teachers might follow this explanation by performing the simple experiment of putting a drop of ink into a beaker of water and instructing students to notice the way in which the ink becomes dispersed throughout the beaker even though the mixture is not stirred. Experiments and explanations convey new information to students so they can expand their knowledge structure. References to common past experiences and knowledge already acquired help prepare students to receive and organize the new information into an existing schemata.

After you have presented the above example to students, tell them that the purpose of the following activity is to help them realize that reviewing what is already known about a topic can help them understand and remember information they subsequently read. Then explain that they will be reading a selection about the Vietnam War. Before handing out the passage, "Bill's Dilemma: American Intervention in Vietnam" (Reproduction Page 36), ask them to write down any three things that come to their minds about the war. If they have trouble getting started, ask them questions such as:

- When was it fought?

- Who was involved?

- Why was it fought?

- Do you know any Vietnamese people?

Stress that any bit of information they remember is appropriate. As a group, briefly discuss some of the ideas individual students have written down. Next have students read Reproduction Page 36 and write answers to some or all of the questions. After a discussion of their answers and some of the issues presented in the selection, conclude the activity by focusing on the following ideas:

- Writing down three things about the Vietnam War ought to have caused students to recall thoughts and feelings they have about this topic.

- These thoughts and feelings brought from stored past memories to present awareness ought to make the reading easier and more interesting.

- Instead of becoming interested and activating prior knowledge while reading, the review before reading should prompt active involvement from the moment the first word is read.

3. Another approach to demonstrating the value of reviewing a topic before reading is to have students read a selection after they have done some thinking about the topic and then read a second selection without prior review. A comparison of the two reading situations ought to reveal some differences in the ways students think about the two selections.

Duplicate Reproduction Pages 37 and 38. Distribute copies of "Light Conditions Needed by Indoor Plants" (Reproduction Page 37) face down. Instruct students to spend one minute mentally reviewing what they know about indoor plants and light conditions. Signal them when the minute is up and tell them to begin reading the passage carefully. After they finish reading, instruct them to turn the page over and write five important ideas they remember from the passage on the back side of the page without referring back to the passage.

Next, distribute "How the Bicycle Works" (Reproduction Page 38). Instruct students to begin reading immediately and to write five important ideas they remember from the passage on the back of the page when they have finished.

Conclude this activity by discussing the differences students perceived in their thinking while reading material when they had had a chance to review the topic beforehand compared to reading the passage without a review. Some discussion starters might be as follows:

- Could you detect a difference in your thinking/reading behavior when you had a chance to review the topic ahead of time?

- Was it easier to write down five important ideas when you had a chance to review?

- Did you know more about one topic than the other? Do you for example know more about indoor plants than bicycles?

- How did the background experiences or stored memories about the topic affect your ability to review, to understand the passage as you read it, and to write down five ideas?

4. "Building an Awareness of Background Experiences" (Reproduction Page 39) is a paragraph that uses very simple language to describe the process of getting dressed; yet the passage is difficult if not impossible to understand because the reader is never told what is being described. The purpose of this exercise is to provide an opportunity for students to struggle through the process of understanding a passage when they are not given the information they need to find the appropriate schema or stored memories.

Instruct students to read Reproduction Page 39 carefully. After everyone has finished reading, ask them to write down what they think the passage is about. Ask students who are positive that they have the correct answer to raise their hands. (Usually, few if any students seem very sure of their responses.) Then tell students to reread the passage and think about the following two questions:

- What kind of general process is being described?

- What possible procedures could follow these steps?

When everyone has finished rereading and thinking about the questions, begin a discussion of students' ideas about the meaning of the passage. First, focus the discussion on the type of procedure being described (that is, the process of putting something together in an ordered fashion.) Next, encourage students to think about the steps in the procedure. During the course of this discussion someone will more than likely state the correct answer, which is that the paragraph describes the process of getting dressed.

Finally, ask students to read the paragraph one last time. After this final reading discuss how the reading and thinking were different when students knew what the paragraph was about. As part of this discussion, point out that the two questions they were asked to keep in mind when rereading were designed to help students:

- Focus their attention on the most important ideas in the paragraph.

- Use the knowledge they already have about steps taken in various procedures.

5. "How to Use the Information You Already Know" (Reproduction Page 40) gives some suggestions for students to follow when they are reading difficult material and finding many new ideas. After you have distributed copies of this reproduction page, discuss the suggestions, using the following comments as a guide. Encourage students to write notes in the spaces provided on the reproduction page.

- *Suggestion 1.*: Think about your own thinking as you read.
  Comment: The ability to think about your own thinking is probably one of the most important skills you can acquire. People who are aware of their own mental processes can make decisions about using this knowledge in an effective manner.

  A logical first step in developing this awareness while reading is to ask yourself: "Do I already know this information? How well do I know it? How much of this information is new to me?" These questions may seem simple and obvious, yet it usually takes a special effort to ask them while reading. Readers who know what they know and do not know are in a good position to apply reading and study strategies efficiently.

- *Suggestion 2.*: Actively search through the information.
  Comment: Recall the example given earlier about the schema for water. This showed how information gained from previous experience can be helpful when learning new information.

- *Suggestion 3.*: Use the learning aides provided in the text.
  Comment: Using these aides takes effort and independent thinking. Slow down your reading rate and spend time studying the examples and illustrations. You may find it necessary to reread several times a passage that explains and illustrates new ideas.

- *Suggestion 4.*: Seek out additional written resources.
  Comment: The ability to recognize that an idea is new to you and to seek out more information from written resources is a sign of an independent learner. Successful students in high school and college have this ability to recognize new information and have the motivation to follow through to find the assistance they need to understand and learn the new material.

Topic 2. Reading Is Reasoning

1. Since Thorndike[2] defined reading as reasoning long ago, educators and writers have used numerous terms to describe the mental processes readers use in

---

2. E. L. Thorndike, "Reading as Reasoning: A Study of Mistakes in Paragraph Reading," *Journal of Educational Psychology* 8 (1917): pp. 323–332.

order to comprehend printed material. Though some of these terms seem to describe discrete processes, the meanings of many overlap. "Drawing conclusions" or "making judgments" are terms that can be subsumed under the term "evaluation," for example, and a reader can reach a conclusion or make a judgment after either analyzing or synthesizing ideas. A variety of terms like these are defined and taught in reading instructional materials. The precise term used does not seem to be as important as conveying to students that some type of careful, deliberate thought is necessary in order to understand ideas an author is trying to communicate.

"Reading Is Reasoning" (Reproduction Page 41) consists of a list of terms commonly associated with the reading comprehension process. Distribute copies of this page to students and ask them to quickly write a definition for each term in the space provided. Suggest that they may work either as individuals or in small groups. Indicate that several terms may have the same or similar definitions. Stress that the purpose of the activity is to prompt students to think about the variety of mental processes readers use. After they have finished writing, discuss some of their definitions.

2. "Charles" is a short story by Shirley Jackson that induces readers to consciously infer, analyze, and synthesize. The story is an interesting one. The experience of reading it and discussing the events of the story ought to help students develop a greater awareness of the processes involved in reading comprehension.

"Charles" is about Laurie, a kindergarten boy, who comes home and tells his parents about Charles, a boy in his class who blantantly and frequently misbehaves. Laurie's mother worries about the effect Charles may have on her son. Finally, through a series of carefully developed inferences, the reader is led to the inescapable conclusion that Laurie and Charles are the same little boy. This story is often published in literature anthologies and is included in *Topics For The Restless*, a Jamestown Press publication (See Appendix A for a listing of publishers' addresses.)

Distribute copies of this story to students. When everyone has finished reading, discuss the story, emphasizing the points in the story where the reader is required to read thoughtfully. The following questions may be used as a starting point for the discussion:

- At what point in the story did you realize that Laurie and Charles were the same person?

- What are some of the clues Jackson gives that indicate that Laurie has made up the character Charles?

- What was the very first clue given?

- One important clue is given during the incident when Laurie came home late and tells his mother that all the children stayed after school to watch Charles, who was being kept after school for yelling. List the steps involved in the process of coming to the conclusion that Laurie made up this story to explain his own lateness.

- What piece of information provides the conclusive evidence that Charles and Laurie are one and the same?

3. The nature of poetry requires that a reader interpret, search for deeper meanings, and respond to words at different levels of thought. "Interpretive Reading," "Beat! Beat! Drums!" by Walt Whitman on Reproduction Page 42, is a poem about how the beat of drums symbolizing the call to war pulls people away from what they naturally do. The purpose of this activity, as in Activity 2 above, is to encourage students to think about the thought processes they use as they read. In the short story "Charles" the author used inferences to lead the reader to a specific conclusion. The interpretations and inferences the reader makes in "Beat! Beat! Drums!" lead to more open and expansive thought. Distribute copies of Reproduction Page 42 and read the poem aloud while students follow along silently. Then discuss the poem using the following questions as a guide:

   • What is the idea that comes across in the poem?

   • Can the drums be seen as a symbol of war?

   • What is the poet saying about the force of war?

   • How does the poet feel about war?

   • Could the poem describe how people in a small American city today might react if they fully realized that a war was coming?

   • What would have to be changed to make the poem timely?

   • What does it mean to think interpretively?

4. An important type of thinking that occurs spontaneously for many individuals as they read is *imaging* or the formation of mental pictures. Though some research indicates that the formation of images improves comprehension (Levin)[3], there are also indications that some very effective comprehenders form few mental pictures as they read (Witte)[4]. There seems to be some agreement though that readers enjoy reading more when the material prompts them to form mental images (Irwin and Witte).[5]

   Distribute copies of "Imaginative Reading: 'The Charge of the Light Brigade' by Alfred Tennyson" (Reproduction Page 43.) Read the poem aloud and encourage students to allow their imaginations to form images of the events that happen in the poem. Following the oral reading, ask students to share any especially vivid images they may have had or use the following questions to initiate a discussion:

   • Describe the most vivid image you had as you read and listened to the poem.

   • What would "the valley of Death" look like?

   • Does the line: "Forward, the Light Brigade!" prompt an image?

---

3. J. Levin, "Inducing Comprehension in Poor Readers: A Test of a Recent Model," *Journal of Educational Psychology* 65 (1973): pp. 19–27.
4. P. Witte, "An Investigation of the Imaging Behaviors of Good and Poor Fourth Grade Readers with Easy and Difficult Text," (Technical Report 455, Wisconsin Research and Development Center for Individualized Schooling, Madison, 1978), pp. 52–64.
5. J. W. Irwin and P. L. Witte, "College Readers' Mental Imagery, Comprehension, and Attitude with Abstract and Concrete Expository Material," *Reading World* 20 (1980): 35–43.

- In addition to visual images, does the poem prompt any sound, smell, or tactile images?

- Can you imagine "the jaws of Death" or "the mouth of Hell?"

- Does reading the poem result in one total mental picture?

5. The texts used in content area courses such as science and social studies are written to convey information and to help students learn concepts. Facts, definitions, illustrations, and examples are all used by textbook authors to help students gain a fully formed notion of the concepts basic to a content area. With this type of material, the first task confronting the reader is to identify the concept being taught. Next, the reader must give some attention to the type of reading/thinking strategy that would be most effective. "Content Area Comprehension Strategies" (Reproduction Pages 44, 45, and 46) consist of passages selected from science and social studies texts. Two statements follow each passage, requesting the student to write the main concepts presented in the selection and to identify an appropriate strategy for comprehending the passage. Distribute these pages and request that students read each passage and write responses. When students have completed this task, discuss their work.

6. Reproduction Page 47 consists of an article entitled "Some Bones of Contention," reprinted from *Time* magazine. The dispute presented in the article is whether researchers have the right to study America's past by examining the buried remains of members of ancient Indian tribes, or whether the Indians have the right to insure a peaceful, respectful burial for their ancestors.

    The ability to evaluate critically what has been read is another important aspect of reading comprehension. The purpose of this activity is to provide students with an opportunity to read about two opposing viewpoints and then to evaluate each viewpoint based on the information that is presented. After students have read "Some Bones of Contention," write the two following statements on the chalkboard:

- Scientists have the right to study the remains of past civilizations. The Indians do not have a strong case for interfering for the following reasons:

- The Indians have the right to insure that their dead remain respectfully buried. The scientists do not have a strong case for exhuming and keeping Indian remains for the following reasons:

As students supply reasons to support each statement, write them down on the chalkboard. After a number of reasons have been stated for each side, ask the class to decide which viewpoint has the stronger argument.

7. *Reading for Understanding* (RFU) developed by Science Research Associates (SRA) (see Appendix A for a listing of the publisher's address), is a reading comprehension program consisting of cards each containing ten short, unfinished paragraphs and a choice of conclusions from which the student is to select the most logical one. The purpose of the program is to develop the ability to analyze ideas, draw correct inferences, and grasp the full meaning of what is read. Students record answers in a record book and check their own work with an answer key booklet. There are three levels of RFU: RFU General (grades 3.0–14.0), RFU Junior (2.5–11.0), and RFU Senior (6.0–14.0).

Most teachers are familiar with the RFU program and many students have used it. RFU cards can make a contribution toward helping students develop their ability to reason while reading. The cards must not be overused and students should be encouraged to work with cards that challenge them and to discuss their responses to the items on the cards with other students. The following procedure seems to encourage both meaningful thinking and student interaction:

- Administer the Placement Test to determine the level at which each student should be working, or suggest that students select some cards, quickly read one or two items on each card, and then work through a few cards that appear to be at the correct level. Emphasize that it is acceptable to make one or two errors on a card. If a student completes a card rapidly and makes no errors, then that card is not a thinking challenge.

- After students have established their level, ask those who are working at similar levels to sit in a group.

- Direct students to complete one card and to score their own responses.

- Then ask students to exchange cards and to complete and score a card that another person in the group has done.

- Tell the students who have done the same card to compare and discuss their responses. Stress that they are to pay particular attention to the items scored as incorrect. If one student has an item correct but another has it incorrect, tell the student with the correct response to explain his or her reasoning to the other student.

8. *Preparation for the Miller Analogies Test* (see Appendix A for a listing of the publisher's address) is a practice book designed to help students prepare for a test. It is often used as a screening tool for college and graduate school admission. The book contains eight-hundred questions set up in an analogy format, (for example, scissors is to cut as hammer is to [a. dig b. drive c. pound d. drill]). The beginning section of *Preparation for the Miller Analogies Test* contains suggestions for methods for responding to analogy items and a discussion of various types of analogies. Following this are eight practice tests, an answer key for each test, and a section that explains each answer. The items in this practice book are difficult and challenge the more capable students in a developmental reading course. Working with the book will help them develop their ability to understand relationships and to identify the key elements in an idea. The following procedure describes one way *Preparation for the Miller Analogies Test* can be used:

- Read the section entitled "6 Important Tips" with students. Point out that these tips can be applied to other test-taking situations.

- The next section, "Various Types of Analogies," includes a description of forty different types of analogies. Select several of these examples and discuss them with the class. Suggest that the class read through the rest of the section on their own.

- Select one practice test and allow students one hour or one class period to complete it. Few students will finish in this amount of time, so tell them to work carefully and not to feel pressure. Remind them that this is a learning activity not a testing situation.

- On the following day, allow students to work in small groups to complete the test.

- When the groups have finished, have the entire class discuss items that were difficult for most students.

9. *The Watson-Glaser Critical Thinking Appraisal* is described in Chapter 2 of this guidebook as a diagnostic instrument (see Appendix A for a listing of the publisher's address). However, this test can also be used as a teaching tool as well as for diagnosis. Instead of administering the *Watson-Glaser* as a test and adhering to strict time limits, use it as a basis for a teacher-directed class activity. Use the procedure described below:

   A. Explain that the test contains five subtests: inference, recognition of assumptions, deduction, interpretation, and evaluation of arguments.

   B. Tell students to be sensitive to differences in their thought processes as they take each of the five different subtests.

   C. Beginning with Test 1, Inferences, read through the directions with the class.

   D. Instruct students to complete the sixteen items in Test 1. When they have finished, read the correct answers to them.

   E. Discuss any items that gave a number of students difficulty.

   F. Repeat steps C, D, and E with each of the four remaining subtests.

Topic 3. Applying Comprehension Skills

1. The ability to determine which idea is most important and which ideas are subordinate to other ideas is essential if a reader is to understand and mentally organize printer information. This process of "main-idea-getting" can be considered a global strategy if the reader is involved in studying long passages such as chapters in a textbook; but determining the main idea also involves some specific skills that can perhaps be taught best through studying paragraphs and short passages. In Chapter 5 of this guidebook ("Developing and Using Study Strategies") the process of identifying main ideas is presented from a more global perspective. However, at some point in a reading course, students generally need instruction in the specifics of main-idea-getting; or at least a review. That is the purpose of this and the following two activities.

   Some authors attempt to instruct students to identify the main idea according to its location in a paragraph. They suggest that readers look for a topic sentence, which they say is often found at the beginning of a paragraph. If readers cannot find it there these authors recommend looking in the middle or at the end of the paragraph next. Unfortunately, most real-world material does not conform to neat patterns. Sometimes a main idea is not directly stated.

There are paragraphs that do not seem to have even an inferred main idea. Many authors use several sentences or the entire paragraph to state the most important point. Often, the main idea simply unfolds as the passage is read. The reader must assimilate ideas from a number of places in the passage in order to determine *the* main idea of a selection.

"Determining the Main Ideas of Paragraphs in a News Magazine Article" (Reproduction Pages 48 and 49) is an activity designed to help students learn a process for evaluating the ideas in a paragraph in order to determine the key or the central point.

First, distribute copies of Reproduction Page 48, consisting of an article entitled "Bloodsuckers from France," reprinted from *Time* magazine. Direct students to read the article carefully and to attempt to identify the central ideas as they read. Next, distribute copies of Reproduction Page 49, which contains the same article except that marginal notes have been added to direct the reader's attention to the organization of ideas in the paragraphs. Discuss the notes on Reproduction Page 49 using the following comments as a guide:

- *Paragraph 1:* The last sentence appears to be the one that states the key idea. The preceding sentences merely inform the reader that the article is about bloodsuckers or leeches and presents some interesting background information that may cause the reader to associate leeches with the field of medicine.

- *Paragraph 2:* This paragraph follows a straightforward organizational pattern. The main idea is stated in the first sentence and the following sentences present supporting ideas.

- *Paragraph 3:* The bracketed sentence in the middle of Paragraph 3 seems to come closest to a main idea statement, which could then be followed by the supporting details listed on Reproduction Page 49. Ask students if they agree with this organizational plan or if they can suggest other possibilities.

- *Paragraph 4:* This paragraph concludes the article with the presentation of two closely related main ideas.

After the article and the comments on Reproduction Page 48 and 49 have been covered, continue the discussion by asking the following questions:

- How do you define "main idea"?

- How do you identify the main idea of a paragraph?

- Do you look in a specific location?

- What kinds of questions do you ask yourself to help determine the main idea?

2. This activity is similar to Activity 1 above except that the passage is an excerpt from a high school physics text and deals with the topic of gravity. The purpose of this activity is to develop skill in determining the main ideas of paragraphs by analyzing the ideas presented, and also to develop the awareness that the main ideas are found in different locations in a paragraph and are developed in a variety of ways. Distribute copies of Reproduction Page 50, "Determining the Main Ideas of Paragraphs in a Physics Text" and instruct students to:

A. Read the selection carefully.

B. Identify the main ideas by underlining them.

C. Restate the main ideas and write these restatements in the margins, as for Activity 1.

D. Note how the main ideas are developed in the selection.

Distribute copies of Reproduction Page 51 and discuss student responses, using this page as a guide. Conclude the activity by discussing the following ideas:

- Did the question stated in the heading help you focus on the main idea of the entire passage?

- How were the main ideas developed in this selection?

- Were the main ideas developed differently than in the article "Bloodsuckers from France"? What was the difference?

- Which was better written, "Bloodsuckers from France" or "What Does Gravity Do?"?

3. "Determining the Main Ideas of Paragraphs in a Social Studies Text" (Reproduction Page 52 and 53) can be used as a variation of Activities 1 and 2. Again, the purpose of this activity is to provide practice in identifying main ideas. Distribute copies of Reproduction Page 52 and ask students to read it carefully. Then distribute copies of Reproduction Page 53. Discuss this page using the following comments as a guide:

- Reproduction Page 53 is a worksheet to be used for the purpose of analyzing the passage on Reproduction Page 52.

- The first three paragraphs of Reproduction Page 52 have been analyzed and the results written on Reproduction Page 53. After these analyses have been discussed, complete Reproduction Page 53 by writing an analysis for each of the last four paragraphs on Reproduction Page 52.

- There is no one correct way of analyzing all paragraphs in terms of main and supporting ideas. Due to differences in background experiences and in the ways in which individuals think, one person may consider an idea to be the most important in a paragraph while someone else would choose another. Yet if the printed word is to have value as a means of communication, there must be some agreement regarding which ideas are important and which are less so.

As the first three paragraphs on Reproduction Page 52 are discussed, keep the ideas mentioned above in mind.

- The first and second sentences in Paragraph 1 seem to convey one idea, which is that East Germany supplied most of prewar Germany's food and that this factor caused problems for West Germany after the country was divided. Except for the last sentence, which states a simple fact, the entire paragraph is used to convey this main idea.

- The main idea of Paragraph 2 is stated in the first sentence. The rest of the sentences in Paragraph 2 explain why this statement is true. The relationship between the mean and the supporting ideas in this paragraph is easy to see.

217234

- When the subordinate clause "once the chief centers of government, culture, and commerce for all of Germany" is set aside, the first sentence conveys the main idea of Paragraph 3. The information in the subordinate clause and in the last sentence support the main idea.

- Now complete Reproduction Page 53 by writing an analysis of each of the four remaining paragraphs on Reproduction Page 52.

After students have finished writing their analyses you might want to discuss their responses as a class or collect and grade their papers. For a concluding discussion, instruct students to compare all three passages: "Bloodsuckers from France," the selection from the physics text, and the selection from the social studies text. Then ask the following questions:

- In which passage were the main ideas easiest to identify?

- What are some of the ways in which main ideas were presented? (Answers should include such ideas as: Main ideas were presented in several sentences. The location of the main ideas in a paragraph varied.)

- What should you look for when attempting to identify the main idea?

4. The purpose of this activity is to provide a way for students to gain a different perspective on the process of main-idea-getting by writing a paragraph. Writers must organize their thoughts by deciding how they will present the central idea and what information they will use to support that idea. Putting the focus on writing instead of reading ought to cause students to do some additional in-depth thinking about what a main idea is and how one idea can be used to support another.

Begin this activity by asking students, "Which came first, reading or writing?" The impulsive answer many students give is that reading came first. A response to that answer is to say, "How can anyone read unless something has first been written?" Of course, there is no answer to the question of which came first but the discussion can cause students to think about the relationship between reading and writing. This kind of thinking is essential if students are to gain insight from the following activity.

Instruct students to write a paragraph about the first time they performed an activity, such as the first time they drove a car, rode a bike, or their first day in high school. Explain that this paragraph is to have one main idea stated in the first sentence and then developed through a succession of supporting ideas. "A Writing Approach to Understanding the Concept of Main Idea" (Reproduction Page 54) can be reproduced and distributed to structure this activity. The following comments may be used to explain Reproduction Page 54.

- Quickly write down five first-time experiences you have had.

- Take a few minutes to think about these experiences. Decide which would be most interesting and the easiest to describe in written form.

- Based on this experience, write a topic sentence to serve as an organizer for the rest of the paragraph. A sentence such as: "The first time I drove a car was a nerve-wracking experience" provides an effective organizational framework because the supporting ideas then consist of incidents that demonstrate why this first-time experience was nerve-wracking.

- Using just a few words for each one, list the supporting ideas you will use to develop your main idea.

- Write the entire paragraph. Use the information you have written on Reproduction Page 54 as a guide.

   To conclude the activity, ask students if they would define "main idea" differently now that they have thought about it from the perspective of a writer.

5. Rewriting a sentence or paragraph using different words while retaining the same meaning is called *paraphrasing*. The ability to write paraphrases is technically not a comprehension skill, yet paraphrases written by students can be an accurate measure of how well they understand what they read. Writing paraphrases can also prompt students to become actively involved in comprehending. Paraphrasing requires the reader to:

A. Translate word symbols into ideas.

B. Think about these ideas by associating them with information that is already known or an established schema (see Topic 1 of this chapter for an explanation of this term).

C. Select word symbols that accurately combine the newly read information with the already known.

D. Write the resulting paraphrase.

   Introduce this activity by explaining the process of paraphrasing using the four steps listed above. You might want to write these steps on the board and request that students rewrite them in their notes. Next distribute copies of Reproduction Page 55 "Writing Paraphrases". Instruct students to read each sentence or passage carefully and then to rewrite it using their own words, rearranging the words and sentences as needed. When they have finished writing, ask several students to read their responses to each item. Compare these paraphrases and discuss their accuracy. You might want to write several paraphrases of the same item on the board for a detailed comparison and discussion.

6. "Paraphrase Practice" (Reproduction Pages 56 and 57) contain a complete article and suggestions for paraphrasing key ideas in that article. In a realistic reading or studying situation, readers paraphrase to assist in understanding and remembering. Reproduction Page 56 consists of a newspaper article that describes a National Academy of Science report on the current misuse of exams as a means of selecting people for jobs or admitting them to a college. A number of ideas discussed in the article ought to be of interest to high school students: according to the report cited in the article, no single test score should be used to make important educational decisions, and intelligence tests may convey false notions about what intelligence is.
   Distribute Reproduction Page 57. Tell students to first number each paragraph on Reproduction Page 56 and then to write a paraphrase according to the directions given for each item on Reproduction Page 57. Collect "Paraphrase Practice" when all students have completed the work and make written comments on their responses.

7. Numbers and letters that indicate a sequence; words that indicate a change of direction such as *but* or *however*; and terms such as *finally* and *in conclusion* provide useful guides for the reader. Thinking about the meaning of these words can result in more effective comprehension. Too often, readers simply skim over an *and* or a *but* without realizing their implications.

   Both Walter Pauk in *How to Study in College* and Edward Spargo in *The Now Student* include comprehensive listings of pivotal or signal words, along with discussions of how they are used and why they are important. Both of these books are easy to obtain (the publishers' addresses are listed in Appendix A). Both of these books, used separately or together, provide a valuable resource. Not only do they present the topic of signal or pivotal words well, but they include many other activities and ideas that can be used in a high school reading course.

   After you have discussed this topic with students using the resources mentioned above as a guide, have them apply what they have learned from your presentation. To provide such an opportunity, select and reproduce a current newspaper or magazine article and have students circle signal or pivotal words.

8. In addition to the two resources mentioned above, there are a number of other published materials that can be used to provide instruction in specific comprehension skills. Brief descriptions of materials that effectively supplement the activities described in this chapter can be found under "Other Resources" in the "Resources for Teaching" section at the end of this chapter.

ASSESSING LEARNING EXPERIENCES

The extent to which students have achieved the objectives of the "Learning Experiences" can be measured by having students submit many of the activity sheets for evaluation.

For an overall evaluation of student understanding of the comprehension process, have students discuss the following, either individually or in groups, orally or in written form:

1. Their own reading/thinking processes.

2. Schema theory and its relationship to reading.

3. Strategies for using information that is already known.

4. Strategies for determining the main idea of a paragraph.

5. Paraphrasing.

RESOURCES FOR TEACHING

Below is a selected list of resources useful for teaching the concepts and topics of this chapter. It is divided into two categories: "Books, Pamphlets and Articles" and "Other Resources." Addresses of publishers can be found in the alphabetical list in Appendix A.

Books, Pamphlets, and Articles

Abartis, Cassarea, and Collins, Cathy. "The Effect of Writing Instruction and Reading Methodology Upon College Students' Reading Skills." *Journal of Reading*, 1980, *23*, 408–413. A report of a study demonstrates that writing instruction can improve college students' reading skills.

Campbell, B. G. Aspects of Meaning. *Journal of Reading*. 1980, *24*, 46–53. The idea is discussed that meaning is not a single entity but that there are different types and levels of meaning such as grammatical, rhetorical, and functional. The ideas in the article are presented in a way that can be useful to teachers.

Christ, Frank L. *SR/SE Resource Book*. Chicago: Science Research Associates, Inc. 1969. A collection of excerpts from various reading and study skills manuals is offered. The selection on attitudes, interests, and habits is particularly useful in a developmental reading course.

Danks, Joseph, and Pezdek, Kathy. *Reading and Understanding*. Newark, Del.: International Reading Association, 1980. This pamphlet presents an in-depth discussion of the relationships between reading comprehension and listening comprehension and a discussion of how meaning is developed in sentences. It would be of interest to teachers who want to improve their own understanding of the comprehension process.

Guthrie, John T. (Ed.) *Cognition, Curriculum, and Comprehension*. Newark, Del.: International Reading Association, 1977. This collection of articles deals with many aspects of the comprehension process and includes models for incorporating comprehension instruction into the school curriculum. The book is organized so that each article is followed by a critical comment written by an expert in the area. Particularly strong articles in the book focus on the developmental aspects of reading comprehension.

Klein, Marv. "A Stab at Teaching Comprehension of the Conditional." *Journal of Reading*, 1975, *19*, 154–159. This article explains the importance of understanding the conditional or the use of language to express tentativeness, and explains why this language skill is an important one for good comprehenders. The article is thoughtfully written and includes some good suggestions for teaching

students to think carefully about cause and effect relationships as they read.

Langer, Judith A. "From Theory to Practice: A Prereading Plan." *Journal of Reading*, 1981, *25*, 152–153. This article discusses recent research concerning the relationship between background information and comprehending content area materials. A detailed plan is given for assisting students to organize and use what they already know before they begin to read.

Stevens, Kathleen C. "Can We Improve Reading by Teaching Background Information?" *Journal of Reading*, 1982, *25*, 326–329. This is a report of a study that demonstrates that teaching background knowledge of a topic can improve reading comprehension.

Stotsky, Sandra. "The Role of Writing in Developmental Reading." *Journal of Reading*, 1982, *25*, 330–339. The idea is elaborated that teaching writing skills enhances the development of reading skills. The author explains how teaching such writing skills as dictation, precis writing, paraphrase writing, and sentence combining can help readers improve their comprehension.

Waller, Gary T. *Think First, Read Later! Piagetian Prerequisites for Reading*. Newark, Del.: International Reading Association, 1977. A strong point is made for viewing reading as a thinking process. The author describes the stages of Piagetian thought, shows how these phases can be related to reading, and cites research that backs up his contentions.

Other Resources

College Reading Skills and Comprehension Skills Series. Jamestown Publishers, 1974. *College Reading Skills* was designed for college students who want to improve their reading skills. However, it works well with high school students because the materials are of high interest, on current topics, and well written. With teacher direction and aid, moderately delayed readers at the high school level can benefit from the materials. Three books that include comprehension and skill exercises are available on each of these levels.

The *Comprehension Skills Series* is available on two levels, junior and senior high. Each booklet provides instruction in a specific area, such as the ability to make inferences or to draw conclusions.

Reading Laboratory Series. Science Research Associates (SRA), 1982.

Primary	Intermediate and Secondary	
1a (1.2–3.0)	IIa	(2.0–7.0)
1b (1.4–4.0)	IIb	(2.5–8.0)
1c (1.4–5.0)	IIc	(3.0–9.0)
	IIIa	(3.0–11.0)
	IIIb	(5.0–12.0)
	IIa	(8.0–14.0)

According to the publishers, the Reading Laboratory Series can be used with a minimum of teacher direction. However, teacher direction is necessary in a remedial situation. The labs include activities in the areas of comprehension, vocabulary development, phonic and structural word attack, spelling, rate improvement, listening, and work/study skills.

Reading Skill Builders Kits. Reader's Digest Educational Division, 1977.
Primary Kit (1.0–4.0)
Intermediate Kit (2.0–6.0)
Advanced Kit (4.0–9.0)

Each Skill Builder Kit contains multiple copies of Skill Builders on at least five different reading levels. There are twelve or more different Skill Builders to choose from. They work well with individuals or small groups.

The kit also contains answer keys and a master manual to help the teacher select stories and exercises.

Reading for Understanding. Science Research Associates (SRA), 1978.
RFU General (3.0–14.0)
RFU Junior (2.5–11.0)
RFU Senior (6.0–14.0)

Each kit contains cards containing ten short, unfinished paragraphs and a choice of conclusions from which the student selects the most logical one. The main purpose of the series is to develop the ability to analyze ideas, draw correct inferences, and grasp the full meaning of what is read. Students record answers and progress in a Student Record Book and check their own work with an answer key booklet.

New Specific Skills Series. Barnell-Loft, Ltd., 1982.
Grades 1–12.
The Specific Skills Series is a nonconsumable reading program designed to develop eight crucial reading skills on the elementary and secondary level. The eight skills include: working with sounds, following directions, using the context, locating the answer, getting the facts, getting the main idea, drawing conclusions, detecting the sequence. One reading skill on one reading level is presented in each booklet.

5

Developing and Using Study Strategies

For years, reading educators have been encouraging content area teachers to become involved in helping their students develop effective reading and study methods. In a recent review of the literature concerning reading instruction at the postelementary level, Witte and Otto[1] indicate that content area teachers are concerned about their students' reading abilities, and some are in fact incorporating reading and study skills instruction into their courses. However, Witte and Otto conclude that, in general, content area reading programs have not been effectively integrated into the postelementary curriculum. Content area teachers still feel that their instructional time is limited and that their focus is on content rather than process. Many express alienation from the techniques of teaching recommended by reading educators.

The overall goal of this study unit is to teach not only study skills and strategies, but also to teach students the process of applying these skills and strategies to their content area courses. Activities that introduce and explain general study methods are followed by activities that require applying the methods to actual content area material. A number of the activities (such as the study skills project or keeping a class log) require an ongoing involvement with one of each student's current content area courses. This approach to study skills will not only have an effect on the way students learn from the printed material in their courses, but will also encourage communication between reading teachers and content area teachers and demonstrate the relevancy of the approaches recommended by reading teachers.

---

1. P. Witte and W. Otto, "Reading Instruction at the Postelementary Level: Review and Comment," *Journal of Educational Research* 74 (1981): pp. 148–158.

PERFORMANCE OBJECTIVES

As a result of the learning activities in this chapter students will:

1. Realize that the skills taught in the reading course can be applied in content area courses.

2. Understand how to use the following study approaches:

    A. Prereading strategies

    B. Underlining

    C. Writing marginal notes

    D. Notetaking and summarizing.

    E. Student questioning.

    F. Outlining.

    G. Graphic overview.

3. Select the most appropriate study technique for specific materials and specific learning tasks.

4. Complete a study skills project requiring students to:

    A. Keep a class log for a particular content area course.

    B. Apply some or all of the study techniques listed in Objective 2 above to a content area course.

LEARNING EXPERIENCES

Topic 1: The Study Skills Project

1. Although this project can be used at any time during the course, introducing it midway through the course and prior to instruction in specific study skills has a number of advantages: 1.) The first portion of the reading course can be used to help students develop word learning and comprehension skills in order to have a basis for working on the project; 2.) In most schools students will have received their quarterly grades, which will help them select the most appropriate course for the study skills project; and 3.) Introducing this project before actual study skills instruction gives students a format for immediately applying the skills within content area courses.

    The following steps describe how to set up the study skills project:

A. Explain that the purpose of the study skills project is to demonstrate that grades can improve when organized reading and study strategies are applied to content area courses.

B. Duplicate Reproduction Page 58, "Study Skills Project," and have students write down the courses they currently are taking and the grades received in these courses following the most recent grading period. (See Activity 2 below for students who have difficulty selecting a course.) Explain the reading course requirements for the study skills project. Set a beginning date and a date due: six to eight weeks seems to be a reasonable period. Stress that each student must turn in a completed log for that period of time. (See Activity 3 below for a description of how to keep a class log.) Next, explain that students will be expected to include in the project a demonstration of the ways they applied the study skills taught in the rest of the unit to this selected course. You may want your students to apply all the study techniques described in this chapter, or you may decide to have students apply only some of them. Instructions for applying each study skill to the content area course selected for the study skills project are given in the last activity for many of the topics below.

As part of this introductory activity, distribute copies of Reproduction Page 59, "Applying Study Skills," which is designed to help structure student work on the project. Explain to students that they can use this sheet when they are applying a specific study skill to the course they select.

C. Set aside one period a week for in-class work on the study skills project. This gives you as the teacher an opportunity to monitor and work with students as they are applying the study methods they have been taught.

Tell students that your role as the teacher is to show them how to use the various study strategies and to help them evaluate the effectiveness of the approaches they use. Stress that you want them to learn to evaluate their own learning. Suggest that you would like to provide a model for the kind of dialogue about thinking and learning that they should be having with themselves. Let them know during the class work period you might ask them questions like: "Is this approach working?" "Would another study method be more effective?" "Does this outline reflect the important ideas in the chapter?" Indicate that you want them to learn to ask themselves these kinds of questions.

D. Collect the projects on the date due and grade or comment on them. Also, ask students to indicate whether or not they have been receiving better grades in the course they selected for the study skills project. If possible, ask them to report back when they receive a final grade for the course.

2. Some students may have difficulty deciding on a content area course for the study skills project. In a number of cases these students may have selected courses in areas such as art, vocational education, or physical education, which require little or no reading. Have these students select a topic that interests them for this project—any subject from auto mechanics to glass blowing is acceptable as long as they can find some written material about it. After you have approved their selected topic and the printed materials they have found, indicate that they will be expected to apply to these materials the study strategies they are taught. The reading course requirements for these projects can be modified by having students keep a log for the time they spend on the project and by having them turn in outlines, notes, and other material to demonstrate

that they have applied organized study procedures to the task of learning more about a topic that interests them.

3. A daily record of class activities and assignments does help students remember what has happened during a class period and also helps them organize their study efforts. For this reason, keeping a daily log or record of the course chosen for the study skills project is essential. This is a simple task yet it requires some thought and discipline. At first it is probably a good idea to check the students' logs often; later, students should have developed the habit of keeping up the log without being reminded. The following guidelines may be useful for setting up the log keeping activity:

   A. Duplicate Reproduction Page 60, "Sample Log—American History," and give a copy to each student. Explain that the purpose of the log is to help students remember and organize their work for the course.

   B. Discuss the sample and emphasize the importance of making comments in the log about the class or the assignments. Their own personal remarks can help students become aware of how well they understand material that is presented and how much they need to study.

   C. Tell students to make a note in the log whenever they have been able to apply an insight, a skill, or an approach learned in the reading course.

   D. Check the logs daily for the first week. Stress the importance of making personal comments.

   E. Check the logs once every week or two for the duration of the study skills project.

4. "Course Analysis Form" (Reproduction Page 61) and "Textbook Analysis Form" (Reproduction Page 62) are intended to prompt students to analyze their learning attitudes and aptitudes for the course they have selected for the study skills project. Their responses on these two forms can also assist you to help students decide on the type of study strategy most effective for a particular course.

   Have students bring the appropriate text to class on the day you plan to have them fill out these forms. The course analysis form can be filled out quickly, but urge students to work carefully as they fill out the textbook analysis form. After students have completed them, collect the forms for an informal evaluation of their responses or else have students file them in their reading folders for reference as the study skills project progresses. A concluding discussion for this activity might focus on several questions such as:

   • Does your attitude toward a course reflect how well you perform in the course?

   • Do you understand class lectures and discussions but have difficulty reading the textbook? Or vice versa?

   • Why do you think it is difficult for you to learn from some teachers and some books?

   • What can you do when learning becomes difficult?

Topic 2: Prereading Strategies

Many of the activities for this topic and others that follow in this chapter require the use of a content area textbook containing chapters with introductory statements, headings, subheadings, illustrations, summary statements, and activities. Prior to introducing these topics, obtain a class set of a science, social studies, or other appropriate subject area text. Most postelementary school resource centers have supplementary texts that can be used for this purpose; even a slightly dated text will work. Using these types of texts for reading course activities not only helps students to learn effective study methods but also demonstrates how study methods can be directly applied to the texts students use every day.

If you are not able to obtain a class set of a content area text, Reproducton Page 68, "Memory and Thought," (a section from *Understanding Psychology*,[2] a high school psychology text) can be used to provide an opportunity for students to apply study skills. The selection chosen from *Understanding Psychology* is the beginning portion of a chapter entitled "Memory and Thought," which deals with how people take in and store information. The ideas presented reinforce many of the concepts concerning reading, thinking, and studying that are taught in the reading course. The headings and subheadings are reproduced just as they appeared in the original text, although the illustrations and pictures have not been included. A number of the activities that follow in this chapter are based on this selection. If you intend to use this material rather than or in addition to a content area text of your own choosing, Reproduction Page 68 can be reproduced and distributed as part of your introductory study skills activities.

The material from *Understanding Psychology* is at an appropriate reading level for most students in a developmental reading course, but it would probably be too difficult for students in a corrective or remedial reading course. To provide a textual basis for teaching some of the study techniques described in this chapter to very poor readers, a portion of a unit entitled "Exploring Our Nation" from *Exploring World Regions*,[3] a middle school social studies text, is included in this guidebook (see Reproduction Page 69, "A Heritage of Change"). Similar to the material from *Understanding Psychology*, Reproduction Page 70 is a reproduction of the text, including headings and subheadings but excluding pictures and illustrations.

1. The objective for this activity is to encourage students to develop the habit of preparing their minds for a topic before they begin indepth reading. As part of the introduction to the activity, remind students of the learning experiences described in Topic 1 of Chapter 4 which involved students in the process of reviewing the information they already know about a subject prior to reading.

   Distribute copies of the content area text you have chosen to use for this study skills unit. Tell students to read the title and several introductory paragraphs. Next, page through the chapter as they follow along with you. Point out the major headings, subheadings, illustrations that seem particularly interesting, and study aids such as questions, summaries, or lists of technical terms included in or at the end of the chapter. Then distribute copies of "Previewing a Chapter" (Reproduction Page 63) and ask students to write responses to the

2. A. Levine, *Understanding Psychology*, [2d ed.] (New York: Random House, 1977), pp. 51–71.
3. H. Gross and D. Follett, *Exploring World Regions*, (Newton, Mass.: Allyn and Bacon, 1975): pp 76–81.

four items without looking back at the chapter. When students discuss their responses to these items, either as a class or in small groups, encourage them to share the facts they know or thoughts they have about the topic of the chapter. Tell them that the purpose of question #3 on Reproduction Page 63 is to cause them to review information they already know so that their minds are ready to receive new information.

Students may read the chapter after this exercise or do several more pre-reading activities.

2. Distribute copies of Reproduction Page 68. Since a complete chapter is not included in these pages, students will only be able to apply some of the pre-reading strategies.

Suggest that students use the following procedure to preview Reproduction Page 68.

A. Read the introduction carefully. (The first two paragraphs of "Memory and Thought" provide an interesting overview of the subject and should help the reader to begin organizing the information that is to come.)

B. Read the major subheadings and note that they were mentioned in the introduction.

C. Read the short paragraphs that follow the two major subheadings of this section.

D. Read the rest of the headings and try to remember which headings come under other more important ones.

E. Briefly review what you already know about how people think and remember.

3. Anderson and Armbruster,[4] researchers at the Center for the Study of Reading at the University of Illinois, have done an extensive review of the research on studying. In their discussion, they point out that studying involves reading in preparation for performing some type of task. Students read to prepare for a class discussion, to perform a lab experiment, and most often they read in order to pass some type of test or exam. According to Anderson and Armbruster, the more students know about the type of test they will be given before they study, the more effective their studying will be. If, for example, good students know that they will be tested on the details presented in a chapter, they will study to remember details. On the other hand, if effective students think a teacher will test their understanding of general concepts, they will spend more time organizing the information they read and focusing on the central ideas.

Students often do not take the time to think about the kinds of tests their teachers give. As a result, they do not select appropriate study methods. The first part of Reproduction Page 64, "Types of Tests," is an explanation of the kinds of reading and study behaviors required to perform effectively when

---

4. T. H. Anderson and B. B. Armbruster, "Reader and Text—Studying Strategies" (Paper presented at a conference on Reading Expository Text, The University of Wisconsin–Madison, 1980), pp. 3–6.

taking specific types of tests. The second part of Reproduction Page 64 is designed to encourage students to think about the types of tests their teachers have given them.

Following completion and discussion of "Types of Tests," stress that, before they actually begin reading a chapter, students ought to think about the types of tests a particular teacher gives. Remind students of this activity as they proceed through this unit on study skills. Explain that mental preparation for the type of evaluation given by a particular teacher should become an essential part of studying.

4. Many postelementary content area teachers do not rely solely on one text but include many supplementary materials such as newspapers and magazine articles in their reading assignments. Often these articles are not organized for high school readers. They have few headings or subheadings, and pictures and illustrations are included to attract attention rather than to provide explanations. "Previewing Articles Without Headings" (Reproduction Page 65) offers some suggestions for previewing when an author provides few guidelines.

   Pass out copies of Reproduction Page 65 and instruct students to read and then briefly discuss the suggestions.

5. "Applying Previewing Skills" (Reproduction Pages 66 and 67) contain, respectively, a copy of an article that appeared in *Time* magazine and illustrations of how to apply previewing skills.

   Pass out copies of Reproduction Page 66. Instruct students to preview the article using the suggestions described on Reproduction Page 65. Discuss the information students learned from the preview. Ask questions such as:

   - What was the main point of this article?

   - Could you detect an organizational pattern?

   - What are some ideas that caught your attention?

   Finally, distribute copies of Reproduction Page 67 and have students compare their verbal answers with the comments on this sheet.

   A variation of this activity would be to distribute copies of Reproduction Pages 66 and 67 at the same time and show students how to preview using Page 67 as a model.

6. The Study Skills Project, the first topic discussed in this chapter offers an opportunity for students to apply the study skills they learn. To determine if students have acquired skill in previewing ask them to preview a chapter or a reading from the course they have selected for their project. One tangible demonstration of ability to use previewing would be to have students fill out Reproduction Page 63, "Previewing a Chapter," using material from their selected content area cause. Or students could take brief notes on Reproduction Page 59 following the suggestions for previewing given on Reproduction Page 63. After students have previewed using one or both of these approaches, you may want to collect and check their work. If students seem to have mastered the skill, return their papers with a reminder to include this previewing exercise in the study skills project.

Topic 3. Underlining

1. Underlining is one of the least time-consuming and most popular of study approaches. The technique is easy to use and allows students to distribute their attention evenly over a passage. For this reason, the underlining approach is probably most effectively used when the material is well organized, fairly easy to understand, and the student is reading to remember supporting details as well as main ideas. Yet, underlining is an approach that can be easily misused if students do not actively involve themselves in a process of deciding which ideas are important enough to warrant a line or a highlight. To introduce underlining to your students you might have them write the points mentioned above as answers to the following questions:

   • When is underlining an effective study technique to use?

   Answer: a. when the material is well organized

   b. when the material is easy to understand

   c. when the student wants to remember supporting details as well as main ideas

   • How can underlining be misused?

   Answer: Underlining can be misused if a student draws lines under ideas without thinking about their real importance to the passage.

2. The first two paragraphs of the subsection entitled "Selective Attention" from the "Memory and Thought" selection (Reproduction Page 68) can be used to demonstrate the underlining technique. On Reproduction Page 70, "Selective Attention," the important ideas in the two paragraphs have already been underlined. Either have students underline ideas they think are important and then check their responses using Reproduction Page 70 as a guide or simply read and discuss Reproduction Page 70. The reasons for underlining some sentences and not others are given below. These comments can be used as a basis for the class discussion. Each sentence in the first two paragraphs is numbered; these numbers correspond to the following statements:

   1) The first sentence is underlined because it contains a definition of selective attention.

   2) Sentence 2 is underlined. It gives a concrete example that illustrates the definition.

   3) & 4) The comparison between selective attention and tuning in a television set is developed in both sentences 3 and 4. More information is given in sentence 4 than in sentence 3; therefore sentence 4 is underlined.

   5) A clear illustration of what the author is trying to say in sentences 3 and 4 is provided in sentence 5. Sentence 5 is underlined.

   6) Another example of the idea explained in sentence 5 is given here. Since no new information is given, sentence 6 is not underlined.

   7) See 6) above.

8) Because this sentence includes a complete definition of selective attention as well as a summary of the illustrations given in the two paragraphs, it is underlined.

3. This activity is similar to the one described above but it is adapted for poor readers. The material from the text *Exploring World Regions*,[5] described earlier, is the textual basis used to provide underlining practice for corrective or remedial classes.

 Following an introduction to the underlining technique and using the suggestions given in Activity 1, instruct students to underline the important ideas in the first three paragraphs of the section entitled "A Heritage of Change" (Reproduction Page 69). Using Reproduction Page 71 as a guide, check and discuss student responses. Or you might want to guide students' underlining of the important ideas in the first paragraphs and then have them do the underlining in the last two paragraphs on their own. The rational for underlining some sentences and not others is given below:

1) The same idea given in the heading is repeated in sentence 1. It is not underlined because it contains very little new information.

2) The heading "A Heritage of Change" is explained in the sentence, so sentence 2 is underlined.

3) A simple fact is stated in sentence 3. The idea appears to be important but not enough information is given to warrant an underline.

4) The idea that half of our population moves every five years explains more fully the fact given in sentence 3. Therefore, sentence 4 is underlined.

5) Sentence 5 is underlined because it contains the important general idea that there is evidence of change all around us.

6) The first specific example of the change mentioned in sentence 5 is given in sentence 6, which is therefore underlined.

7) Sentence 7 is not underlined because it merely gives another example similar to the one stated in sentence 5.

8) See 7) above.

9) Sentence 9 is underlined. The main idea of the second paragraph is stated in it.

10) The idea stated in sentence 10 supports the main idea stated in sentence 9. Assuming the reader understands and remembers this idea, the example given in sentence 10 ought to be easily recalled. Sentence 10 is not underlined.

11) Next is a heading in bold type, needing no further emphasis. Notice though that this heading does give the main idea of the paragraph, which is that there was a progression of changing the land from wilderness to farms and then to cities.

---

5. Gross and Follett, *Exploring World Regions*, pp. 76–81.

12) & 13) Sentences 12 and 13 are underlined because the ideas given in the heading are restated and explained in them.

14), 15) & 16) More examples of the ideas stated and explained in the heading and in sentences 12 and 13 are given in sentences 14, 15, and 16. They are not underlined.

17) A new idea is stated in sentence 17; sentence 17 is underlined.

18) Sentence 18 is underlined because it contains an example of the ideas stated in sentence 17.

19) A second example of the idea presented in sentence 17 is given. Sentence 19 is not underlined.

Topic 4: Writing Marginal Notes

1. A system for writing notes in the margins of text can help the reader understand and remember key ideas. Like underlining, this approach can only be used with handouts that students may keep or if students own their books and thus can write in them. In most cases high school students do not own their texts, so these learning experiences apply only to handouts. But for those students who intend to go on to college or some other type of post-high school training where students are expected to purchase their texts, the following exercises ought to provide some meaningful practice.

   To introduce the marginal note approach to studying and learning from text, indicate that the technique, as mentioned above, is limited to books students own or to articles they may keep. Then explain the following three-step procedure for writing marginal notes.

   1. Preview the text using one or several of the procedures described under topic 2 of this chapter.

   2. Read the text carefully; stop to write notes when appropriate. (Specific suggestions for writing notes are given on Reproduction Page 72, "Writing Marginal Notes.")

   3. Review marginal notes prior to taking a test on the material.

   Now distribute copies of Reproduction Page 72 and discuss the suggestions with students.

2. "A Newsmagazine Article with Marginal Notes" (Reproduction Page 73) consists of a newsmagazine article that discusses the thinking ability of animals. The article has been marked with marginal comments and notes to aid in comprehension. Reproduction Page 73 can be used to provide an example of how the suggestions given on Reproduction Page 72 can be applied.

   Distribute copies of "A Newsmagazine Article with Marginal Notes." Ask students to read the article first without paying attention to the notes. Then either as a whole class or in small work groups have students study the marginal notes and relate them to the content of the article. Conclude the activity with a class discussion of the article and the marginal note writing study technique. The questions below can be used to focus the discussion:

- Give several examples of the so-called thinking behavior of animals.

- What are some of the misconceptions we have about animal thinking?

- Give some examples of behaviors that show that animals can process information and make judgments.

- Did the marginal notes help you organize and remember the content of the article?

- The marginal notes often consist of a paraphrase of a statement within the article. Did you notice how this was done?

3. Reproduction Page 74 contains marginal notes and comments for the first portion of the "Memory and Thought" selection (Reproduction Page 68), including the introduction and the material on selective attention and feature extraction. These pages may be used to evaluate student responses at the conclusion of this activity.

   To help students learn to write marginal notes, distribute copies of these pages of "Memory and Thought" or direct students to turn to them if you have already given them copies of the entire selection. Using the procedure described in Activity 1 above, first have students preview these pages. (Note: students may have already underlined the selective attention portion of this material if they did Activity 2 under Topic 3 of this chapter.) Next have students mark the text, writing comments in the margins and noting the important ideas. After students have marked the text themselves, have them compare their marginal notes with one another in small groups. Stress that marginal notes should reflect the individual's own response to the text. There are no definite correct or incorrect marginal comments, yet there should be some agreement among students concerning the key ideas and concepts presented in the selection. Finally, distribute copies of Reproduction Page 74 and have students silently read through the marginal notes and comments. Ask students if their own notes are similar to those on these pages. Encourage them to discuss differences and similarities.

4. This activity is based on the material from "A Heritage of Change" (Reproduction Page 69) and is a variation of Activity 3 above but designed for corrective or remedial classes. Following a procedure similar to the one described in Activity 3, have students preview the selection. Then distribute copies of Reproduction page 75, which includes the same text as page 69 except that notes have been written in the margins. Discuss these comments with the class, relating them to the text. Next have students write marginal comments on Reproduction Page 69. When they have finished writing, distribute copies of Reproduction Page 75. Discuss the comments on Reproduction Page 75 with the entire class and have students compare these comments with their own.

5. In "Organizing the Course", the first chapter of this guidebook, it was mentioned that articles from local newspapers can be reproduced and used for instruction in a reading class. To provide additional opportunities for your

students to apply the marginal notetaking technique, select an article of current interest from a newspaper. Make copies, and distribute them to your class. Have students preview the article. Then have them read and write notes following the suggestions given on Reproduction Page 72. Discuss the article by encouraging students to share their marginal notes and comments with the rest of the class.

6. Writing marginal notes is a study technique that students can directly apply to their high school content area courses. If you have set aside one day a week for students to work on the study skills project (Topic 1 of this chapter), encourage students to use this time to write marginal notes on any handouts or other consumable printed materials their content area teachers may have given them. Tell them that they may use Reproduction Page 59 as a cover page for the handout. Remind students that they can use marginal notes to draw attention to those portions of text that their teacher stresses and that might provide the basis for exam questions.

Topic 5: Notetaking and Summarizing

1. Explain to students that notetaking and summarizing are treated under one topic because similar thought processes and reading behaviors are used for both study techniques. In order to use these methods successfully, students ought to read a passage carefully, mentally organize the information, and then, using their own words, write notes about the important ideas expressed in short passages or paragraphs and write summaries of longer sections or chapters.

The process of taking notes and writing summaries is time-consuming. These study methods are most appropriate to use if the students must read and learn from texts that have difficult major ideas. As Anderson and Armbruster[6] suggest in their extensive review of the research on study strategies, writing a note or a summary may cause the reader to think deeply about an idea presented in text. If the idea is difficult for the reader to understand, this time is well spent; but if the idea is easily comprehended or seems obvious, the reader would probably remember the information without expending the time and effort required to write notes or summaries. These suggestions of Anderson and Armbruster can be taken one step further. If students know that a particular teacher will test them on many specific ideas and facts, notetaking and summarizing techniques are *not* good choices of study strategies. But if students expect a teacher to give an essay exam, notetaking and summarizing are logical study methods to use. The process of thinking through ideas and then paraphrasing them is similar to the behavior required when students take essay exams.

At this point, it might be helpful for students to compare briefly the marginal note technique with the notetaking and summarizing techniques.

A. Writing marginal notes allows the reader both to process difficult ideas by writing paraphrases in the margins and also to highlight specific ideas and details by drawing arrows, numbering, or writing brief notations. The mar-

---

6. Anderson and Armbruster, "Reader and Text—Studying Strategies," pp. 21–50.

ginal note study technique is limited, however, to handouts and materials that are consumable; it is not workable with most high school texts.

B. The study techniques of writing notes and summaries can easily be used with high school textbooks, but when using these techniques the tendency is to process the larger ideas at the expense of details and more specific information.

Conclude this introductory discussion by reviewing the following ideas:

• Notetaking and summarizing require similar thought processes and study behavior.

• To write useful notes and summaries, read, think about, and then rewrite the important information in your own words.

• Write notes for short passages and write summaries for longer sections or chapters.

• Taking notes and writing summaries are time-consuming study techniques. For this reason, use them when the material contains complex and difficult ideas rather than when studying texts that have listings of ideas and examples or many details and facts.

• The process of writing notes and summaries is good preparation for taking essay exams.

2. The purpose of this activity is to help students attain awareness that notetaking and summarizing are more appropriate for some kinds of material than for others. For this activity arrange for students to have copies of both "Memory and Thought" (Reproduction Page 68) and "A Heritage of Change" (Reproduction Page 69). Follow the steps given below for a guided discussion designed to build this awareness.

A. Remind students of the suggestions for using the notetaking and summarizing techniques given in Activity 1 above.

B. Instruct students to preview and then carefully read several paragraphs in both "Memory and Thought" and "A Heritage of Change."

C. Ask students the following questions:

1) Which article contains the most difficult ideas?

2) Which article contains listings of ideas, examples, or details that are easy to understand?

D. Point out that the "Memory and Thought" article contains difficult ideas, while ideas that are easy to understand are presented in "A Heritage of Change."

E. Finally, ask students to explain how notetaking or summarizing might help them understand the "Memory and Thought" selection.

3. "Applying Notetaking Skills" (Reproduction Page 76) consists of an article reprinted from *Time* magazine. The article attempts to explain why the question posed by pro-choice supporters and anti-abortionists alike is impossible to

answer: "When does life begin?" The idea developed in the article is a complex one. Reading the article several times and thinking carefully about the content each time seems to be necessary in order to comprehend the message. If students expect to be tested on the content of the article, notetaking is a good study choice.

Ask students to read this article carefully. Then ask them as part of a class discussion to explain what the authors mean by "The Unresolvable Question." Following a brief discussion of the main topic of the article, tell students that you will write a brief note on the chalkboard or on an overhead transparency to summarize the main point of each paragraph. Emphasize that you want the class members to supply the content for these notes.

After the notes have been written, distribute copies of Reproduction Page 77, "Applying Study Skills," which consists of notes for the *Time* article. As a class, compare and discuss the notes on the chalkboard or transparency with the notes on Reproduction Page 77. There may be differences between the class notes and those on page 77 but these differences ought to be a source for further discussion (The comments on Reproduction Page 77 represent this author's impression and are not intended to be the final word.) Point out to your students, though, that these notes were written as an example of how they can use this page to write the notes they will be including in their study skills project.

4. After students have completed Activity 3 above, have them divide into small groups of three to five students. Ask each group to write a brief summary of the *Time* article on Reproduction Page 76 and to select one student to read the summary aloud to the entire class when the group has finished writing. Before summaries are read, instruct the class to listen carefully to determine if each group has included the essential ideas. A summary of the *Time* article also appears on Reproduction Page 78, "Applying Study Skills." A final activity might consist of asking students to compare their summaries with the summary on this page.

5. Notetaking and summarizing are both study skills that require practice. In the initial stages of learning these skills, students need guidance in terms of selecting the appropriate important ideas for notetaking and summarizing and constant reminders to write the ideas *in their own words*. If you have obtained a class set of a content area text to use as a basis for study skills applications (as suggested in the introduction to Topic 2 of this chapter), you may at this point want to choose a chapter or section of this text to provide notetaking and summarizing practice.

Have students read the section or chapter; then ask them to write notes, either individually or in small groups. After you have checked or discussed their notes, instruct students to write a summary of the same section.

6. Reproduction Pages 77 and 78 are examples of how students can use Reproduction Page 59 to apply the notetaking and summarizing techniques to the course chosen for their study skills project. On the day selected to be used for student work on this project, distribute several copies of Reproduction Page 59 to each student. Provide individual assisstance to students as they work at applying these skills.

Topic 6: Student Questioning

1. The mental processes involved in generating effective study questions are similar to those involved in writing good notes and summaries. The student must read, think through the ideas, and then write questions that reflect this in-depth thought. Like notetaking and summarizing, the questioning technique seems to be most effective when used to help students understand and retain difficult key ideas rather than when used to organize and recall details and facts. Used in the first-mentioned manner and for that purpose, self-generated questions ought to help students learn and remember from printed material. If students turn a heading or a subheading into a question by using words like *who, what, which,* or *why,* or by some other simple syntactical maneuver, the questioning technique may not be effective. When used thoughtfully, however, the process of generating questions may be more helpful for some readers than notetaking or summarizing because an unanswered question arouses curiosity; also, the question-and-answer format can help the reader organize information.

   There are several approaches to the self-questioning technique. One is to preview the article first by reading the title, the introduction and/or the first paragraph, and then the last paragraph. The second step is to write the questions. Next, the article is read and, finally, the student writes answers to the questions. A second approach is to read the article carefully first and then write questions. A second reading may be needed to locate and write specific answers. Anderson and Armbruster[7] cite a study in which the results indicated that writing questions after reading the entire passage did help students perform significantly better on a posttest than did students who only read the passage. Particularly with difficult passages, this practice of reading a passage thoroughly before writing questions would seem to be a good idea.

   The purpose of the following activity is to demonstrate how information in the title, the introduction, and the first and last paragraphs of an article can be used to generate questions. The article "Fast Shuffle for Card Counters?" appeared in *Time* magazine. Card counting, or a mathematical system used to beat the odds in favor of the house at gambling casinos, is the topic of the article.

   Distribute copies of Reproduction Page 79, "Using the Questioning Study Technique," which contains the article and Reproduction Page 80, "Applying Study Skills," which contains questions generated from a preview of the article as well as answers resulting from a careful reading. Tell students to preview the article by reading the title, introduction, and first and last paragraphs, and then to read the questions on Reproduction Page 80. Briefly discuss these questions and ask students if they can think of others. If they do, encourage them to write them on the bottom of Reproduction Page 80. Now instruct students to read the article carefully and to follow this by reading the answers to the questions appearing on Reproduction Page 80. Discuss any questions or comments students might have about this process of generating questions.

2. Your students may have already read and studied portions of "Memory and Thought" if they performed some or all of the activities described above. Since

---

7. Anderson and Armbruster, "Reader and Text—Studying Strategies," pp. 30–32.

this passage is relatively difficult, it might provide a good opportunity for students to practice the technique of generating questions after reading an entire passage. Ask students to read the entire selection and then, have them write questions either individually or in small groups. Discuss these questions as a class. Draw attention to those student-generated questions that demonstrate that the writer really thought about the ideas. Then either decide on a master list of questions, instructing all students to answer the same ones, or allow students to answer only those questions that they or their group generated. Reproduction Page 81, "Applying Study Skills," consists of questions based on the heading, subheading, and some information found in the "Memory and Thought" text. Answers to these questions are also included. Students may compare their responses to this page after they have finished writing answers to their own questions.

3. To provide additional practice in applying the questioning technique, select and duplicate an article, preferably one from the front page of your local newspaper. Front page articles often tend to be difficult, especially if the reader has not been following that particular news topic and therefore has little or no background information. Ask half of your class to write questions based on a preview of the article while the other half of the class writes their questions based on a careful reading of the entire article. After the questions are completed, have the two groups of students discuss and compare their questions. The following questions can be used to initiate the discussion:

   - Are the questions based on the preview different from those generated after reading the entire article?

   - Which set of questions is the most thoughtful?

   - Which set of questions will be the best study aid?

   - Which set of questions will be easiest to answer?

   - Which approach—writing questions after a preview or writing questions after reading carefully—do you prefer?

   Following this discussion have students write brief answers to their questions.

4. Distribute copies of Reproduction Page 59 to students on the day set aside for work on the study skills project. Explain that students may use either approach: questions based on previewing or questions based on a careful reading. Ask them to indicate on the blank line after "Study Technique" which approach they will apply to their content area course material. Remind students that the questions they write should be thoughtful and should help them organize the information in the selection they are reading.

Topic 7: Outlining

1. Outlining is a study technique that seems to have many advantages. When using the technique in a meaningful manner, students have a format for processing main ideas and difficult concepts in an in-depth manner, recording

facts and supporting details and representing the overall organization of the passage. The disadvantage of outlining is that it takes time and, like notetaking, summarizing, and questioning, is not worth the effort if the material to be studied is easy to understand. But unlike notetaking and summarizing, outlining does help students organize facts and details in a fairly efficient manner. Therefore if material has difficult ideas as well as facts and details the student needs to remember, outlining is a better study choice than notetaking, summarizing, and questioning.

After explaining the advantage and disadvantage of outlining, distribute copies of "Suggestions for Outlining" (Reproduction Page 82). Have students read these suggestions and then briefly discuss them.

2. Reproduction Page 83, "Outlining a Newsmagazine Article," consists of a reprint of an article about the recollections of people who died or were close to death but somehow recovered to tell about the experience. Reproduction Page 84 is an outline of the article. Instruct students to read Reproduction Page 83. Then distribute copies of the outline and ask students to match the statements in the outline with the corresponding statements in the article. Next to the first paragraph, for example, students would write Roman numeral I because the information in this paragraph provides the basis for the first outline statement. As students are doing this matching, ask them to pay attention to how the statements in the outline represent attempts to summarize the information in the article by using paraphrases. Reproduction Page 84 can be used to check student responses in this activity.

3. Poor readers especially may need extensive training in order to use the outlining technique effectively. Without training they may simply be inclined to use the outline format without thinking through the ideas presented. After discussing Reproduction Page 82 ("Suggestions for Outlining"), provide practice for these students by distributing copies of "A Heritage of Change" (Reproduction Page 69). If these students have already read this material as part of an activity described earlier in this chapter, ask them to reread these pages to refresh their memories. If they have not read "A Heritage of Change," urge them to read it carefully or ask for volunteers to read the passage aloud to the entire class. Then using Reproduction Page 85, "Outline of 'A Heritage of Change,'" as a guide, write the two main subdivisions on the chalkboard:

   I.   The History of America shows that the country has been constantly changing.

   II. There are many examples of change that have occurred in America.

   Tell students to rewrite these headings on a separate sheet of paper and then ask them to complete the outline on their own. Explain that they will need to refer back to the text often. When students have completed this assignment, distribute copies of Reproduction Page 85 and have them compare their responses with those on this page.

4. If you have selected a content area text to use as a basis for teaching students to apply study skills (see introduction to Topic 2 of this chapter), you may want to provide additional practice by instructing students to outline a short chapter or section from this text.

After they have read the selected portion of this text, have students work in small groups to establish the main subdivisions of the outline. Then ask them to work individually to complete the outline. To check their individual work, request that students return to these groups to compare outlines with one another.

5. When students are working on their study skills project, remind them that the outlining procedure is particularly useful for material that contains difficult ideas and important facts and supporting details. Assist them to select a portion of text appropriate for outlining and encourage them to think through the content of the text and to carefully plan their outline.

Topic 8: Graphic Overview

1. Like outlining, the graphic overview is another study technique that students can use to deal with the overall organization of a passage. A graphic overview, as the name suggests, is a way of transforming linear prose into visual form so that students have an overall view of the ideas in a passage and the ways in which they are related. The idea of a graphic overview is not new. The terms *mapping* or *networking* are sometimes used to describe the approach.

   To introduce the graphic overview to students, make a transparency of Reproduction Page 86, "Sample of a Graphic Overview" or duplicate it and distribute copies. Explain that this sample overview was constructed by a high school student to represent the ideas in one chapter of a biology text. Point out that the main topic, "Origin and Evolution of the Human Species," which in this case was the chapter title, is written in the center. The secondary categories or main subtopics are written on the lines that branch off the center box. After this, the important facts and ideas that support the secondary categories are written on lines branching from the first set of lines. In this way, the student created an overview of an entire chapter on one page. By looking at the graphic overview the student can see how ideas are related while reviewing the important ideas presented in the chapter.

   After students have had an opportunity to read through the information given in the graphic overview on Reproduction Page 86, explain that the headings and subheadings of content area texts often provide the information needed for the secondary categories. While it often makes sense to use these headings for the graphic overview, remind students that they ought to think carefully through the printed information while they are constructing the overview: mechanically transposing the headings from a text to the format of a graphic overview will not help them learn the information. Conclude by reviewing the three steps involved in the process of constructing a graphic overview:

   • Decide how to state the main topic of the passage and then write it in a central box, circle, or other figure.

   • Determine the secondary categories and write then on lines coming from the central figure.

- Finally, select the supporting details and important facts to remember from the passage. Place them on a second set of lines branching off from the secondary categories. If further subdivisions are needed, a third set of branching lines may be added.

2. "Graphic Overview of 'Memory and Thought'" (Reproduction Page 87) is an example of an overview that is based primarily on the headings and subheadings of the chapter. Two of the secondary categories, "Retrieving Information" and "Central Processing," are included on the graphic overview because these topics are part of the chapter in the original text, although they are not part of the reproduction pages of this guidebook.

   Distribute copies of Reproduction Page 87 to students and explain that this type of overview is easy to construct and can be used to provide prompts as students review for a test. For example, students might study the overview and then attempt to recall from memory the four secondary categories and the important ideas under these categories. This type of graphic overview provides a representation of the large chunks of information given in a passage and shows how these chunks are related.

   "Graphic Overview of Storing Information" (Reproduction Page 88) is a detailed representation of one of the secondary categories presented on Reproduction Page 87. In this case, the secondary categories came from the headings but the important supporting ideas came from the text. A careful, thoughtful reading of the text was necessary in order to decide which ideas ought to be included in the graphic overview and the process of constructing the overview was helpful in terms of understanding such concepts as how short-term and long-term are related (that is, memory must be stored in short-term memory before it can become a part of long-term memory.)

   This second type of graphic overview (Reproduction Page 88) can be used as a more detailed review aid and, probably more important, this graphic overview is based on a careful reading of the text and so it can help students understand and organize difficult ideas and concepts.

   To conclude this discussion of these two types of overviews and their respective purposes, stress the following points:

- A general graphic overview based on headings and subheadings within a chapter can be used:

   a. To gain an overall impression of the content and organization within a chapter.

   b. As a guide for reviewing a chapter prior to taking a test.

- A more detailed overview that is partly based on headings but primarily based on information given in the text can help students understand difficult ideas and reorganize information mentally so that they can learn it more effectively.

3. Reproduction Page 73 consists of a newsmagazine article concerning the thinking abilities of animals. This article is part of an activity designed to help students learn how to write marginal notes. The article can also provide a basis for developing a graphic overview. In particular, practice with this article ought to help students learn how to construct an overview of passages without headings or subheadings.

First have students read the article carefully, or review it if they have read it previously. Then, as part of a class discussion, direct students to decide on a statement to write in the central figure of the overview. A question such as "Do Animals Think?" would be appropriate. Select the secondary categories. These might include:

• Difficulty scientists have when they attempt to measure animal intelligence.

• Animal use of tools.

• Animal language behavior.

• Animal ability to make judgments.

Instruct students to write the important supporting ideas under the secondary categories on their own. When students have finished this task, have them compare their work in small groups.

4. If your students seem to need more directed practice in order to understand and apply the graphic overview procedure, use the content area text you selected to provide this additional practice. Since the construction of a general graphic overview using headings and subheadings is a fairly simple task, place most of the emphasis on having students develop more detailed graphic overviews to help them understand and organize the concepts presented in the text.

5. Distribute copies of Reproduction Page 59 on the day selected to be used for work on the study skills project. Encourage students to construct both a general type of overview to be used as a review aid and a detailed graphic overview, where the focus is on helping the reader understand the content of a written passage.

Topic 9: Selecting and Using Study Techniques to Prepare for Tests

1. As part of your concluding activities for this unit on study skills, stress to students that there is no magic formula for learning in any study approach: to be used successfully, all require concentration and active involvement with the material. Almost any study technique can be effective if students read carefully and then use the format of a specific study approach to help think through and organize the information.

    To review the study approaches presented in this chapter, list them on the chalkboard and ask students to briefly explain the procedure involved for each. The approaches are listed and described below to assist you in directing this discussion. You might ask students to record the information below in their own notes after it has been discussed.

Study Approach	Procedure
Prereading Strategies:	• Review what you already know about the subject.
	• Think about the type of test your teacher will give on the material.

	• Preview the article by reading the title, headings, introductory, and final paragraphs. Try to establish in your mind the main point and the organizational structure of the material.
Underlining:	• Read and then think through the information.
	• Draw lines under the ideas you have decided are essential.
Writing Marginal Notes:	• Preview first and then read carefully.
	• Use abbreviations, numbers, or letters to mark important ideas and the details that support them.
	• Writes notes in the margins using your own words to explain difficult ideas, pose questions, or make comments.
Notetaking and Summary:	• Read carefully.
	• Think about the information given.
	• Write the important ideas in your own words.
Student Questioning:	• Preview or read carefully.
	• Write thoughtful questions. Finding the answers to these questions ought to help you understand and retain difficult ideas.
Outlining:	• Preview the passage.
	• Read the passage carefully.
	• Write the main headings for your outline.
	• Reread to complete the outline with important facts and supporting details.
Graphic Overview:	• Preview and read.
	• Write the main topic in the central figure.
	• Write the secondary categories on lines drawn from the central figure.
	• Write important facts and supporting details on a second set of lines branching from the secondary categories.

2. "Some Suggestions for Using Particular Study Approaches" (Reproduction Page 89) summarizes information given in this chapter concerning choosing which study approach to use when studying a particular type of material before taking various forms of exams or tests.

You may want simply to discuss the information given on this reproduction page with your students, asking them to take notes, or you may want to distribute copies and then discuss the suggestions. Whichever approach you choose, explain that these are only suggestions, not definite statements about which approach is best for a specific purpose. Some of the evidence presented by Anderson and Armbruster,[8] as well as common sense, seems to indicate that these suggestions are valid. However, individual difference among the reading and learning abilities of students and the unique characteristics present in all written materials make it impossible to say that any one approach is best for a specific kind of material.

3. Reproduction Page 90, "Selecting Study Strategies," consists of an example of how students might analyze a reading assignment in order to select a study strategy. The first part of Reproduction Page 90 consists of a sample showing how a reader might veiw the assignment in terms of the:

- Type of material.

- Purpose for reading.

- Difficulty level of the material.

- Type of test to be given on the material.

   After students have studied the sample, ask them to fill in the second part of the reproduction page by referring to a reading assignment given to them in one of their content area courses.

4. For the final activity of the study skills unit, explain that the purpose of the study skills project was to provide a format for students to use to apply the study strategies taught in the reading course. It is hoped that this type of direct application helped students realize that reading and studying in an organized manner results in improved grades on tests and better performance on all types of class assignment, such as written reports and themes. You might want to add that there are no quick and easy ways to prepare for texts and no tricks to test-taking. The most effective approach is to study regularly in the way students have done as part of the study skills project, and to review the study notes several times prior to actually taking a test.

   When students have completed the study skills project, including demonstrations of how they applied all or some of the study strategies described in this chapter and also including a daily log for the course they selected, distribute copies of Reproduction Page 91, "Study Skills Project." Ask students to fill out the sheet by listing the strategies they used and the grade they expect to receive in the course at the end of the current grading period. Finally, instruct them to write a paragraph stating which approach they found to be most effective and to explain why.

---

8. Anderson and Armbruster, "Reader and Text—Studying Strategies," pp. 1–19.

ASSESSING LEARNING EXPERIENCES

The extent to which students have mastered the concepts and skills presented in the chapter can be measured by having students submit for evaluation the study skills project or the final products of almost any of the activities suggested earlier. The study skills project in particular ought to provide an in-depth assessment of students' understanding and ability to apply the various study strategies taught. The following list can be used to evaluate the project:

Log

Was it kept daily?

Did students make comments that show they attempted to apply study skills?

Application of Study Strategies

Did students attempt to use a variety of strategies?

Were the applications of study strategies thoughtfully done?

Did students use the class time allocated for the study skills project constructively?

Were students able to write paragraphs showing that they attempted to think about which study strategy worked best for them?

Did students' grades in the courses selected for the study skills project improve?

RESOURCES FOR TEACHING

Below is a selected list of resources that can provide further background for teaching the concepts and topics of this chapter. Addresses of publishers can be found in the alphabetical list in Appendix A.

Bean, Thomas, and Pardi, Rick. "A Field Test of a Guided Reading Strategy." *Journal of Reading*, 1979, 23, 144–147. The authors of this article describe a guided reading strategy that relies mainly on previewing or surveying a chapter prior to reading and then organizing the information gained from the survey. The authors explain how this can be done through a class discussion approach.

Estes, Thomas, and Vaughan, Joseph. *Reading and Learning in the Content Classroom.*

Boston: Allyn and Bacon, 1978. Prereading activities, study guides, and group discussions are among the approaches recommended in this text for helping students learn from the material they read. Ten model lessons are also included to demonstrate how effective reading strategies can be applied to content area texts.

Hansel, T. "Stepping Up to Outlining," *Journal of Reading*, 1978, 22, 248–252. The results of a study are reported in this article, showing that students who were taught a step-by-step procedure for outlining out-performed students who were not trained in the same method. In addition to this report, a detailed description of the procedure for teaching students to outline is included.

Hill, Walter. *Secondary School Reading: Process, Program, Procedure*. Boston: Allyn and Bacon, 1979. This text represents a comprehensive approach to reading instruction at the secondary level. Also, several chapters are devoted to descriptions of how reading instruction ought to be executed in developmental and corrective reading classes. Many suggestions for teaching a variety of study skills are included in these chapters.

Johns, Jerry L., and McNamara, Lawrence. "The SQ3R Study Technique: A Forgotten Research Target." *Journal of Reading*, 1980, *23*, 705–708. An important point is made in this article. The effectiveness of SQ3R has not been demonstrated empirically even though the technique is widely used and generally assumed to be effective.

Moore, Mary. "C2R: Concentrate, Read, Remember." *Journal of Reading*, 1981, *24*, 337–339. C2R is a study approach that encourages students to examine their own learning styles and then choose a study strategy that is best suited to this style. The author of this article relates many study problems to the inability to concentrate, and then offers a variety of solutions.

Norman, Maxwell, and Norman, Enid. *How to Read and Study for Success in College*. 2d ed. New York: Holt, Rinehart and Winston, 1976. This book represents a comprehensive approach to reading and studying. Detailed descriptions of many basic study techniques are included as are quizzes to evaluate student learning.

Pauk, Walter. *How to Study in College*. 2d ed. Boston: Houghton Mifflin, 1974. This book is a basic guide for studying a variety of content area materials. Topics such as notetaking, preparing for exams, and building memory skills are presented in detail.

Smith, Ellen, and Standal, Timothy. "Learning Styles and Study Techniques." *Journal of Reading*, 1981, *24*, 599–602. The results of the study reported in this article showed that learning style, not study technique, was the best predictor of student achievement on a reading comprehension test. The discussion of learning styles and study techniques presented in this article provides some valuable insights into student reading and learning behaviors.

Singer, Harry, and Donlan, Dan. *Reading and Learning from Text*. Boston: Little, Brown, 1980. Of all the available texts that deal with reading and studying at the secondary level, this one provides the most complete presentation of strategies designed to help students learn from content area texts. Specific suggestions for constructing reading guides and other types of textual aids are included.

Tierney, Robert; Readence, John; and Dishner, Ernest. *Reading Strategies and Practices: A Guide for Improving Instruction*. Boston: Allyn and Bacon, 1980. This book is a resource for a variety of reading and study strategies. Methods such as SQ3R, the cloze procedure, and the structured overview are included. The way in which these approaches and strategies are presented makes them particularly suitable for the very poor reader at the secondary level.

6

Teaching Rate Flexibility

Many people are lured into speed-reading courses because they have the notion that they will be able to greatly increase their reading rate. Indeed, advertisements for some speed-reading courses boast that graduates have attained reading rates of one thousand, ten thousand, and even more words per minute. Yet the results of studies of eye movement patterns indicate that eight hundred words per minute is about the maximum speed anyone can attain and still read every word.[1] Speeds beyond that can be attained only if the reader skips words. But can a skipping procedure legitimately be called reading? The terms "skimming" or "scanning" would seem to be more appropriate.

According to the research, the rate at which good readers read and comprehend material usually varies between two hundred and four hundred words per minute, depending on the purpose for reading, the difficulty of the material, and the reader's skill and background knowledge. When reading to prepare for an exam, even a highly skilled reader might read only two hundred words per minute. This same reader, though, might read a popular novel at a rate of six hundred words per minute, or ten thousand words per minute when skimming the front page of a newspaper.

The approach taken in this guidebook is that most high school students can improve their reading efficiency in two ways: 1.) They can learn to adjust their reading rate to suit their purpose for reading and ability to understand, and 2.) They can develop their ability to concentrate while reading. This type of approach will not produce students who claim to speed read at rates higher than one thousand words per minute, but it ought to result in students who know how to read flexibly and with concentration.

The first topic in this chapter includes background information that can be used to introduce students to the idea that rate flexibility—not speed—results in efficient reading. Activities for developing skimming and scanning skills are also included under this topic. The second topic concerns rate of comprehension. The activities are designed to encourage students to concentrate fully when reading. Even though this unit on

---

1. E. J. Gibson and H. Levin, *The Psychology of Reading* (Cambridge, Mass.: MIT Press, 1976), pp. 539–549.

reading rate appears last in this guidebook, the order of presentation is not meant to suggest that it ought to be the final skill taught. In fact, the first topic in this chapter might well be presented early in the course, directly following some of the initial diagnostic work; the activities presented under Topic 2 of this chapter can be done once every week or two so that students are involved in a structured program for developing their rate of comprehension and their ability to concentrate.

PERFORMANCE OBJECTIVES

As a result of the learning experiences in this chapter, students will be able to:

1. Realistically understand the concept of reading rate.
2. Learn that rate flexibility, not speed, is the key to efficient reading.
3. Skim when appropriate.
4. Improve their ability to concentrate when reading.

LEARNING EXPERIENCES

Topic 1: Developing Reading Flexibility

1. The purpose of this activity is to teach students that improving reading rate means training the brain, not the eye. Common sense tells us that reading is a complex mental activity, not just a simple physical action. Moving the eyes over a page does not result in comprehension. Rather, the brain must be poised and ready to grasp the information on the printed page, organize it, and file it away for future use.

   According to studies cited by Gibson and Levin,[2] readers spend only about 6 percent of the time in eye movements and 94 percent in fixation pauses. Reading occurs only when the eye is fixated or paused, not when it is moving. In the early stages of learning to read, the reader has chaotic eye movements. Pauses are frequent. Usually only one word is picked up per pause and the eye often regresses or goes back to reread words. By the fourth grade, most good readers have developed the eye movement patterns they will have as adults. They can pick up three to four words per fixation, regressions are few, and pauses are brief.

   The results of studies like these have lead some people to believe that training eye movements ought to result in improved reading. Gibson and Levin address this issue directly, firmly routing such an idea. Their remarks are worth quoting:

   > Nowhere has the confusion between correlation and causality been more obvious than in the clinical implications drawn from the research on eye move-

---

2. Gibson and Levin, *The Psychology of Reading*, p. 354.

ments. Since good readers had long saccades, [eye movements between fixations], fewer fixations, fewer regressions, and shorter pauses, it was hypothesized that poor readers could be assisted by getting them to move their eyes in those ways. But to no avail. The eye movement patterns reflected efficient mastery of extracting information from text, not the other way around.[3]

Further studies cited by Gibson and Levin also show that the length of pauses increases as the material becomes more difficult for the reader. This lends further support to the idea that reading is thinking, not just a quick look at words.

Summarize the above information for students, stressing that increased reading rate results from training the mind to concentrate and actively organize information. Then, to help students understand eye movement patterns and the idea that reading occurs only during the pauses, ask them to closely observe another student as he or she reads. The following procedure can be used to organize the activity:

A. Ask students to select a brief passage either from a textbook they may have with them or from a book or magazine in the reading classroom.

B. Instruct students to select partners and to position themselves directly opposite one another.

C. Tell students to have one member of each pair silently read the selected passage with his or her head held so that the other partner can observe the eyes of the reader.

D. Next, have the partners switch roles so that the observer is now the reader and the reader is the observer.

E. Discuss the student observations. Be sure that they noted that quick eye movements were followed by brief pauses. If students do not mention it, ask if they observed the longer sweeps that were made when the eye returned to the left side of the page to begin reading a new line of print.

F. Conclude this activity by stressing that the reading and thinking required for comprehension to take place occurred during the time when the eyes paused.

2. "Speed Readers Don't Read; They Skim" by Ronald Carver[4] (Reproduction Page 92) includes a detailed description of Evelyn Wood Reading Dynamics, one of the most popular speed-reading courses. Even though this article was written sometime ago (1972), Carver's description of the course is still accurate. The only real difference is that the price has gone up considerably from the $175 mentioned in the article. In the process of describing the Evelyn Wood Course and explaining why the faults it claims to correct are not really faults, Carver conveys a great deal of worthwhile information about the reading process. A careful reading of this article ought to help students set realistic expectations for improving their reading rate and help them learn more about the reading-thinking process. The article, however, is long and contains some information that might be difficult for students to understand. To assist them,

3. Gibson and Levin, *The Psychology of Reading*, p. 359. Square bracketed comment by this author.
4. Ronald P. Carver, "Speed Readers Don't Read; They Skim." *Psychology Today* (October, 1972), pp. 84–105.

comments and questions have been written in the margins. The following procedure may be used to help students benefit from the article and the marginal comments and questions:

A. Distribute copies of Reproduction Page 92 and explain that the purpose for reading the article is to:

    1.) Learn about speed-reading courses—what they can and cannot do, and

    2.) Learn more about the reading-thinking process.

B. Preview the article by reading the marginal comments and questions with students.

C. Instruct students to read the article carefully.

D. Distribute copies of Reproduction Page 93, "Worksheet for 'Speed Readers Don't Read, They Skim.'" This page contains the same questions that are written in the margins of the article. Tell students they are to write answers to these questions, referring back to the article when necessary.

E. Collect Reproduction Page 93 when students have finished. Grade or comment on their work.

F. Return student papers and discuss their responses.

3. One of the claims made by advocates of the Evelyn Wood Reading Dynamics course is that graduates can double or triple their reading rates with no loss of comprehension. In his article (see Activity 2 above), Ronald Carver explains how he found that people who had not read a passage scored almost as well on a test as those who had read that passage. The reason was that many of the test questions were not passage-dependent. In other words, some readers could answer some questions on the basis of their own general knowledge and common sense notions. Their ability to answer the question did not depend on their having read the passage.

    To be fair to the Evelyn Wood course, it ought to be noted that many commercially available reading instructional materials, including some standardized tests, contain comprehension questions that are not text- or passage-dependent. Of course, it is difficult to write, on any large scale basis, questions that are totally text-dependent. Attempts to do so often result in questions dealing with the details and even the minutiae of a passage. There is nothing wrong with using background information or general knowledge to answer questions. Higher level thought processes such as inferencing and evaluating require the use of that which is already known. Intelligent, efficient readers always use whatever information is available to them when studying, working to improve reading rate, and certainly when they are taking standardized tests. (See Chapter 4, Topic 1 for a further discussion of the importance of using background information). The problem occurs when the developers of courses and materials maintain that their methods have resulted in significant reading growth and support their claims by using comprehension questions that are not text-dependent. The consumers of such courses and materials are then led to place their confidence in the method rather than in their own ability to learn and think.

As an extension of Activity 2 above and to encourage students to have confidence in their own knowledge and thinking ability, perform an experiment similar to Carver's. Have students answer comprehension questions without first reading the passage on which they are based.

Materials common to most high school reading labs or classrooms will work for this activity. What is needed is a large number of brief reading passages followed by multiple choice comprehension questions. A number of popular reading kits and timed-reading booklets have these characteristics. The following procedure can be used to organize the experiment:

- Ask students to select any one passage from the book or kit you are using. Encourge each student to select a different passage.

- Instruct students to turn to the question portion of each comprehension exercise and to begin answering the questions without first reading the passage.

- When all students have finished answering, ask them to correct their work.

- Ask several students to report the number of items that were scored as being correct. (This author's experience has been that, without reading the passage, students report anywhere from two to seven correct out of a possible ten items when using the types of materials mentioned above.

- Select a passage on which a student has scored five or more correct and discuss the passage with the class. Read each item aloud, followed by the answer choices, and ask students to explain how their background knowledge helped them answer the question.

- Conclude this activity by explaining to students that this ability to answer questions without reading shows how important it is to think about what they already know and to use this information even when they have read the material. Stress that this experiment is not intended to disparage or discount the value of the material used. In order to provide students with an opportunity for ample practice, publishers of some types of reading instructional materials use the multiple choice question format. These types of questions can be quickly and objectively scored and, when carefully written, can prompt thoughtful recall of the passage read. The point is that some questions are not very carefully written and are not based solely on the text. But instead of criticizing the materials, teachers and students can use these non-text-dependent questions to expand their ability to use their prior knowledge.

4. In his article entitled "Speed Readers Don't Read; They Skim," Ronald Carver criticizes speed-reading courses that claim to teach people to read rapidly when all that is really taught is a skimming procedure. Throughout his discussion, though, Carver was careful to point out that skimming is a valuable skill when used appropriately. The purpose of this activity is to provide an opportunity for students to skim[5] and to learn when to use this skill. The activity is divided into

---

5. The terms *skim* and *scan* are commonly used to describe rapid reading approaches. In some reading instructional materials, skimming is presented as reading rapidly to gain an overview and scanning is described as a way of finding specific facts quickly. But according to *A Dictionary of Reading and Related Terms* (Theodore L. Harris and Richard E. Hodges, [coeditors] Newark, Delaware: International Reading Association, 1981, pp. 285 and 298.), there is very little real difference between the primary meanings of the two words. Both are defined as a process of reading rapidly and selectively but with a purpose. Based on this reference, the term "skim" is used to describe rapid, selective, purposeful reading in this activity but the word "scan" could have been used just as well.

two parts. The first involves students in the process of skimming a newpaper article. The second part consists of an explanation of the skimming process and the purposes for skimming. Hopefully the experience of skimming an article in the first part of the activity will enable students to understand and contribute to the discussion of skimming, which is the second part of the activity.

Part One

Begin the activity by explaining to students that they will have one minute to skim a newspaper article that contains approximately seven hundred and fifty words. During the one minute, they are to find the main idea of the article and the essential supporting ideas.

Distribute copies of "Skimming Practice" (Reproduction Page 94) to students, face down. Instruct students to turn the page and begin skimming when the signal is given. Stop students after one minute and discuss what they have learned from the article. Some key points that ought to be mentioned are as follows:

Main Idea

Hurricanes are more dangerous today because of increased development of land vulnerable to hurricanes.

Supporting Ideas

- Poor building codes, out-of-date evacuation plans, and overdevelopment may result in a major disaster.
- Where six thousand people once lived there are now tens of thousands of people.
- There are now seventy thousand people in the Florida Keys and escape routes are poor.
- The real danger is the "storm surge" or high water.
- Barrier islands are only a few feet above sea level and could be quickly covered as a result of a storm surge.

Part Two

After discussing the content of the article, continue this activity by asking students what they did when they skimmed. Allow the discussion to be open-ended. Then distribute "Procedures for Skimming" (Reproduction Page 95). Explain each step in the process, relating it to the hurricane article by asking students if they had used the step on their own. Encourage students to write notes and comments in the space provided. Conclude the discussion of skimming procedures by asking students if they can think of any steps that could be added or of any other changes that might improve the list of skimming steps.

"When to Skim" (Reproduction Page 96) contains five suggested purposes for skimming. Distribute copies of this page to students and discuss the suggestions. Ask students to think of specific instances in which they might employ each suggestion. Instruct them to write these instances in the space provided.

5. To help students gain further insight into the skimming procedure, ask them to compare their reactions to an article they have skimmed to their reactions when they have carefully read a similar passage. The following procedure can be used to organize this activity:

A. Choose two selections that are approximately 2,000 words in length. Both should be of a similar type (fiction, nonfiction, essay, newspaper article, etc.) Jameston Publishers' *College Reading Skills* series contains many appropriate passages (See Appendix A for a listing of publishers addresses). Also, stories from nearly any literature anthology could be used.

B. Assign one reading to one half of the class and the second reading to the other half.

C. Tell students they will have two minutes to skim their assigned selection. Signal them when to begin skimming and when to stop.

D. As soon as the two minutes are up, instruct students to write down ten ideas, facts, or impressions resulting from skimming the article. If the selection includes comprehension questions, ask students to complete these also.

E. Now ask students to exchange articles and carefully read the article that the other members of the class had skimmed in step C of this activity. Allow students as much time as they need to complete this step.

F. When students have finished reading, repeat step D. Have them write ten things they remember from the article and complete any comprehension questions that are included.

G. Instruct students to self-correct the comprehension questions and ask them to compare their scores from the passage skimmed with their scores from the passage carefully read.

H. Then tell students to compare their list of ideas remembered from the article skimmed with the list of another student who read the same article and to compare their list made after reading an article with someone else who skimmed it.

I. Finally, use the questions listed below to initiate a discussion of these student comparisons:

   a. Was there a difference between the comprehension scores on the article that was skimmed and the article that was read? If so, which was higher? Would you have expected a difference? (This author's experience has been that there is little difference between the scores of the skimmers and the readers.)

   b. Was there a difference in the list of ten ideas between the students who skimmed an article and those who read the same article? Which person seemed to have the most complete and accurate list?

   c. Which technique, skimming or reading, was most satisfying? (Some students indicated to this author that they did not like skimming because of the time pressure. After some discussion, though, the conclusion was reached that in a normal skimming situation there would be no overt time pressure—students could skim or read carefully, if they chose, in response to their own judgments about the importance and interest of the material.)

Conclude this activity by asking students to reflect on the differences they felt when skimming and when reading and to write a brief paragraph describing their reactions to the two procedures. They may want to include a brief discussion of when it is most appropriate to use each of the two techniques.

Topic 2: Improving Rate of Comprehension

1. The ability to concentrate—to focus attention—is basic to all learning and essential for efficient reading. Often when students read slowly or comprehend poorly, the reason for the problem is that they are not concentrating. When they read, their minds drift to other thoughts; they reread the same sentences several times; or they simply stare at the words. This kind of behavior seems to be particularly prevalent among students who lack confidence in their own ability to be good readers and good students.

   This activity[6] requires students to focus their attention on reading and on answering comprehension questions for brief three-minute periods. It serves as a good warm-up procedure for all students prior to timed-reading exercises and encourages active involvement on the part of poorly motivated students. Just about anyone can be talked into doing just about anything for only three minutes!

   Most postelementary schools have the *Reading Laboratory Series* published by Science Research Associates (SRA). (See the "Resources for Teaching" section of Chapter 4 for a description of this material and Appendix A for a listing of the publisher's address.) The primary lab is appropriate for students in a corrective reading course and a combination of intermediate and secondary labs works well in developmental reading courses. Each lab contains both a series of single cards, each with a brief passage followed by comprehension questions, and double-folded cards with longer passages. *Use the single cards only for this activity.* Place the SRA Labs in a convenient location in the classroom and proceed as follows:

   A. Instruct students to select three or four cards from the beginning section of the lab and to take an answer key.

   B. Tell students they will be given exactly three minutes to read the passage and answer all the comprehension questions. Explain that the three minute period is just about the right amount of time if students have selected a card that matches their reading ability. If the card is too easy, they will finish before the three minutes are up. If the card is too difficult, time will be called before they have completed it.

---

6. The idea and the general procedure for this activity is based on the work of Bernice Bragstad, Reading Specialist at LaFollette Senior High School, Madison, Wisconsin.

C. Direct students to select one card. Give the signal to start and call time at the end of three minutes. During the three minutes, note those students who finish early. Encourage them to try a more difficult card the next time.

D. Tell students to correct their responses. Stress that one or two items scored incorrect is not an indication of a problem but rather that the card does provide a challenge.

E. Compliment students on their concentration. Point out to them that this intense work for three minutes is what concentration feels like. Emphasize how much they accomplished in such a short time span.

F. Call on several students to explain what they learned from the card they read. Too often students perceive working with materials such as SRA labs as just exercises, not as opportunities to learn. The SRA cards contain well-documented information on a wide variety of interesting topics. Reading the cards ought to help students increase their store of knowledge about the world. But this will happen only if someone such as a teacher expresses an interest in what students are learning and periodically makes an effort to discuss the content of the cards.

G. Instruct students to select another card. Encourage them to take a more difficult card if they finished the first one early or an easier card if they ran out of time. Those students who finished in three minutes and scored 80 percent or better on the comprehension questions ought to continue with the sequence. Repeat steps C, D, E, and F for the second card.

H. After doing three or four cards, students usually have found the section of the lab that will present a challenge but not cause frustration.

I. Conclude this activity after the third or fourth card. Direct students to write the color and number of the card they last used on their folder so they will know where to begin the next time the activity is done.

J. The three-minute rate-card procedure usually provides a stimulus for students. They become active and involved in concentrated reading. A good follow-up is a timed reading. The procedure for that is described below.

2. There are a number of published materials that can be used for timed readings. Most contain passages of counted words, comprehension exercises, and charts for determining rate of reading. Below is a listing of some of these materials that can be used effectively in a high school reading course. The addresses for the publishers of these materials can be found in the Appendix A.

Hy Cite Corporation

Speed Way

Rate development exercises, passages selected to be of timely interest, and comprehension questions are included. This book is most appropriate for advanced students in a high school reading course.

Holt, Rinehart, and Winston:

How to Read and Study for Success in College

In addition to discussions of general reading and study strategies, this book contains timed readings followed by comprehension questions. These readings are a challenge to most advanced students.

Jamestown Publishers:

Timed Readings

These consist of eight books (grade six to college level), each containing fifty four-hundred word selections followed by questions.

Reading Drills

Contains thirty thousand word selections ranging from grade seven to grade ten, followed by a variety of comprehension drills, including factual recall and inference-type questions.

The Now Student

Topics such as "Learning to Concentrate" and "How to Take Notes" are covered in twenty-five timed-reading selections. Comprehension tests consisting of fill-in-the-blank statements (modified cloze procedure) follow each passage.

The timed-reading procedure described under Topic 5, Chapter 2 of this guidebook can be used with any of the above materials. In Chapter 2, this procedure was presented as one of the initial diagnostic activities done to assess students' strengths and weaknesses. Specific directions were given for timing the reading and recording rates and comprehension scores on the Reading Rate Graph (Reproduction Page 21).

Follow this same procedure for continued timed-reading activities, instructing students to record rates, scores, and dates on the reading rate graph. After each new recording, ask students if their reading rate has improved. If it has not, ask questions such as:

• Was the material more difficult this time?

• Were you less interested in the topic?

• Were you unable to concentrate fully for some reason?

If a particular series of published materials only provides the number of words in each passage but does not include a chart that students can use to convert their reading time to number of words per minute, use the following procedure:

• Convert the total time in minutes and seconds to seconds only by multiplying the number of minutes by 60 and adding the number of seconds. For a time of 3 minutes and 40 seconds a student would multiply 3×60 and add 40 for a total of 220 seconds.

• Divide this total number of seconds into the number of words in the selection. If the selection is for example 1,500 words long, divide 220 seconds into 1,500. This equals 6.8 or the number of words read in a second.

- Multiply the words read per second by 60 to convert words read per minute: $6.8 \times 60 = 408$ words per minute.

As mentioned earlier in this chapter, it works well to do reading rate activities once every two weeks. The combination of three or four three-minute rate-cards plus one timed reading activity takes about one period of a typical high school day.

3. "Determining Reading Rate for All Types of Materials" (Reproduction Page 97) contains a list of steps that can be used to convert any type of material into a timed-reading activity. As a teacher you can use this procedure to organize an activity that helps students compare their reading rate on informational material (such as a textbook) with their rate on recreational reading materials (such as short stories or novels). Reproduction Page 97 can also be distributed to students and used to instruct them in the process so they can work toward improving their rate on materials they select themselves. Do mention to students, though, that the procedure described on Reproduction Page 97 results in an approximate number of words read. To get an exact number, each word must be counted, a time-consuming process to say the least.

ASSESSING LEARNING EXPERIENCES

The extent to which students have mastered the concepts and skills of the topics in the chapter can be measured by having them submit material from almost any of the activities.

Other evaluation activities might include:

1. Ask students to participate in a group discussion of the pros and cons of taking speed reading courses.

2. Write responses to the following questions:

   - What is the difference between reading and skimming?

   - When should you read?

   - When should you skim?

   - What is the advantage of skimming?

   - What is the advantage of reading?

3. Keep a record, including a rate chart, of recreational materials read during a one-week period.

RESOURCES FOR TEACHING

Below is a list of resources that provide useful background information for teaching the concepts and topics of this chapter. Addresses of publishers can be found in the alphabetical list in Appendix A.

Cranney, A.; Brown, B.; Hansen, Dorothy; and Inouye, D. "Rate and Reading Dynamics Reconsidered," *Journal of Reading*, 25, 6, 1982, pp. 526–533. The authors describe a study designed to evaluate the effectiveness of the technique taught in the Evelyn Wood

Reading Dynamics course. The article is written in response to the many criticisms made of the Evelyn Wood course. Results are reported that seem to indicate that graduates of the course do have superior reading skills in some aspects of reading rate and comprehension.

Flynn, Peggy. "Speed Is the Carrot," *Journal of Reading, 20*, 8, 1977, 683–687. This article describes a course for low-achieving college freshmen. The article is very readable, explaining how skimming practice and the resulting high reading rates can be used to motivate students to work toward improving their reading performance. The ideas presented in the article can be easily applied in a high school setting.

Lucas, Diana-Dee. "Reading Speed and Memory for Prose," *Journal of Reading Behavior, 11*, 2, 1979, pp. 221–233. This presents the results of a detailed study of the effects of increased reading rate on recall. The findings indicate that both fast and slow readers made about the same number of recall errors and both gained a general impression of what the text was about. The fast readers, however, had more difficulty picking up the relations that are implicit in the text.

Miller, Phyllis. "Considering Flexibility of Reading Rate for Assessment and Development of Efficient Reading Behavior" in Samuels, J. (ed.), *What Research Has To Say About Reading Instruction*. Newark, Del.: International Reading Association, 1978, pp. 72–83. Reading rate assessment and the development of efficient reading behavior are discussed in depth. According to Miller, three factors determine rate flexibility: the reader, the text, and a factor interacting between the reader and the text. Each of these factors is discussed in detail. The article is well organized and includes information useful for understanding the process of rate improvement. The pros and cons of current instructional materials for rate improvement are discussed, as well as principles applicable to instruction.

Schachter, Sumner. "Developing Flexible Reading Habits," *Journal of Reading, 22*, 2, 1978, pp. 149–152. Schachter explains how such materials as phone books, newspapers, and content-area textbooks can be used to help students develop flexible reading habits. Suggestions are made for teaching even very young children to skim and scan, and specific ideas for developing instructional materials for high school students are given.

Spache, George E., and Berg, Paul C. *The Art of Efficient Reading*. 2d ed. New York: Macmillan, 1966. Part I of this book "Flexibility in Reading," includes discussions of how to preview, skim, and scan as well as exercises that can be used to provide practice in each of these skills. The book also covers such topics as study skills, vocabulary growth, and applying reading skills. The section on reading flexibility is a good resource for teachers wanting to develop their units on reading rate.

APPENDIX A

Addresses of Producers of Resources

Allyn and Bacon, Inc.
7 Wells Avenue
Newton, MA 02159

American Guidance Service
Publisher's Building
Circle Pines, MN 55014

Barnell Loft Ltd.
958 Church Street
Baldwin, NY 11510

Bobbs-Merrill Co.
4300 West 62nd Street
Indianapolis, IN 46206

Charles E. Merrill Publishing Co.
1300 Alum Creek Drive
Columbus, OH 43216

Economy Company
P.O. Box 25308
Oklahoma City, OK 73125

Educational Testing Service
CTB–McGraw-Hill
2500 Garden Road
Monterey, CA 93530

G & C Merrian Co.
47 Federal St.
Springfield, MA 01101

Harcourt Brace Jovanovich
7555 Caldwell Avenue
Chicago, IL 60648

Harper & Row/J. B. Lippincott, Publishers
2530 Crawford Avenue
Evanston, IL 60201

Holt, Rinehart & Winston
901 North Elm Street
Hinsdale, IL 60521

Houghton Mifflin Company
1900 South Batavia Avenue
Geneva, IL 60134

Humanics Inc.
Liberty Drawer 7970
Ann Arbor, MI 48107

Hy Cite Corporation
340 Coyier Lane
Madison, WI 53713

International Reading Association
800 Barksdale Road
P.O. Box 8139
Newark, DE 19711

Jamestown Publishers
P.O. Box 6743
Providence, RI 02940

Little, Brown and Company
34 Beacon Street
Boston, MA 02114

Macmillan Publishing Company
866 Third Avenue
New York, NY 10022

McGraw-Hill Book Company
1221 Avenue of the Americas
New York, NY 10036

MIT Press
28 Carleton Street
Cambridge, MA 02142

Planem Press
P.O. Box 3088 Steinway Station
Astoria, NY 11103

Prentice-Hall Books
Educational Division
Englewood Cliffs, NJ 07632

The Psychological Corporation/Harcourt
Brace Jovanovich
755 Caldwell Avenue
Chicago, IL 60648

Random House, Inc.
2970 Brandywine Road
Suite 201
Atlanta, GA 30341

Reader's Digest/Educational Division
Pleasantville, NY 10570

Scholastic Book Services
904 Sylvan Avenue
Englewood Cliffs, NJ 07632

Scott Foresman and Company
1900 East Lake Avenue
Glenview, IL 60025

Simon and Schuster, Inc.
1230 Avenue of the Americas
New York, NY 10020

Science Research Associates
155 North Wacker Drive
Chicago, IL 60606

William C. Brown
2460 Kuper Blvd.
Dubuque, IA 52001

APPENDIX B

Reproduction Pages

The pages that follow have been provided to facilitate the reproducing of exercises, sample exercises, and materials needed for activities suggested in the preceding pages. Each page is perforated to make removal from this book easier. Once removed, a page can be used in several ways:

1. For projection with an opaque projector. No further preparation is necessary if the page is to be used with an opaque projector. Simply insert it in the projector and the page can be viewed by the entire class.

2. For projection with an overhead projector. The Reproduction Page must be converted to a transparency for use on an overhead projector. Overlay the Reproduction Page with a blank transparency and run both of them through a copying machine.

3. For duplication with a spirit duplicator. A master can be made from the Reproduction Page by overlaying it with a special heat-sensitive spirit master and running both through a copying machine. The spirit master can then be used to reproduce more than one hundred copies.

CONTENT OF THE READING COURSE

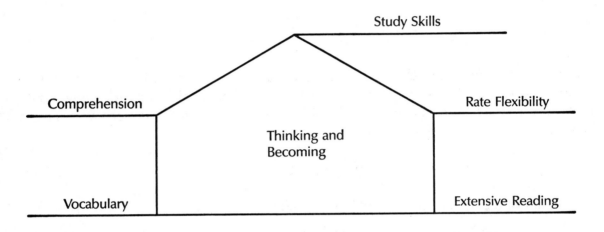

Study Skills

Comprehension

Rate Flexibility

Thinking and
Becoming

Vocabulary

Extensive Reading

STUDENT INFORMATION SHEET

Fill out this sheet as completely as you can.

Today's date   _____

Name   _____

Grade   _____

Age   _____

1. List the courses you are taking this semester. Star those that you think might be difficult.

   _____

   _____

   _____

   _____

   _____

   _____

   _____

2. What do you plan to do after you graduate from high school?

3. Describe your reading ability.

4. Describe yourself as a student:

   Do you study?

   How do you study?

   Do you think that you are a good student?

5. What do you hope to learn in this course?

WHY TAKE A READING COURSE?

Our Next Disgrace: Why Johnny Can't Log On

By Eric Zorn
© Chicago Tribune

① *Ann Arbor, Mich.*—You can call him Johnny: long-suffering mascot of national illiteracy; standardbearer of our collective disgrace; blot on western culture.

② He can't read well, his writing is getting worse and he's about to be victimized by one of the most dramatic undertakings in the history of civilization: the Information Revolution, a watershed in human development to compare with the Industrial Revolution 150 years ago and the invention of the printing press in 1440.

③ During the projected Information Revolution of the next 20 years, Johnny will be overrun by those marching to the muted, staccato drumbeats of clicking electronic keyboards.

④ Those whose jobs involve the processing and communication of information—as opposed to those who work in industry, agriculture, service, etc.—now account for more than 50 percent of the work force, according to Commerce Department surveys. That number is expected to reach 65 percent by 2000, when the home and marketplace will be flooded with "message units," from video shopping lists to home computer reference libraries.

⑤ The common person supposedly will have access to the equivalent of 10,000 mental slaves. Money will be made and business conducted by buying, selling and trafficking in information and its complicated delivery systems.

⑥ The already evident truth will become more obvious: Power, for individuals and nations, is knowledge.

⑦ Where will that leave Johnny, the person who does not have a functional ability to read or write any language?

⑧ He will find there are fewer jobs for unskilled workers. His world will be highly complex and interconnected, and daily life will demand control of sophisticated cable and computer technology; he will be unable to take advantage of this vast technology with his so-so skills.

⑨ Self-styled experts will speculate endlessly why Johnny can't log on.

---

⑩   Parents, educators and politicians now face a particularly pressing crisis in literacy. The national ability to read and write capably is either declining or stagnating—depending on which studies you read—at the same time that the emerging Information Revolution is compounding the problem by placing greater demands for literacy on all people.

⑪   To be a leader of future civilizations, a nation must have a highly literate population. Today's estimates on the number of functionally illiterate Americans—those who cannot read a want ad, bus schedule or label on a medicine bottle—run as high as 25 million; another 34 million are barely capable of simple reading tasks.

⑫   Despite these depressing statistics, most educators say the real crisis of literacy in the 1980s is not in basic reading skills. We're doing a better job on that score, they say. Young Johnny can sound out words on a page.

⑬   This type of reading may suffice in the Industrial Age, but it will not pass muster in the Information Age. The core of the crisis is that Johnny isn't being taught what to do with words once he reads them. He isn't being taught to think, to interpret, draw inferences or criticize. He doesn't know how to create images and use his imagination. Such disabilities are going to be tragic in the Information Revolution.

⑭   Rudolph Flesch, the celebrated scold who ushered in an era of national handwringing with his 1955 expose, "Why Johnny Can't Read," says that America is rapidly becoming a semiliterate nation, and will "join the ranks of Third World countries like Zambia" within 10 years.

⑮   In his 1981 update, "Why Johnny Still Can't Read," (Harper and Row, $10.95) Flesch cites the precipitous drop in college entrance exam scores in the last 20 years and studies which show only 75 percent of the American population as functionally literate in today's society, and only 46 percent as "fully proficient" in everyday skills.

⑯   He blames the current situation on the continuing failure of American public schools to adopt a "phonics first" strategy for teaching children to read. Teaching phonics emphasizes the sounds of letters and letter-combinations within words, as opposed to the "Look-and-Say" method, reviled by Flesch, in which children are taught to recognize entire words at a glance.

⑰   "America is sinking into a morass of ignorance," he warns.

⑱   Roger Farr of Indiana University, director of the International Reading Association, agrees that phonics is an important part of teaching fundamental literacy, but calls Flesch "an empty windbag" on his criticisms of the American educational establishment.

⑲   "Recent studies of 9-year-olds show we are doing a great job today in teaching the basics," Farr argues. "We have, in fact, returned too far to these basics, neglecting the end goal of meaning, reaction and thinking. This shows up in tests of older students."

⑳   Farr blames undemanding, permissive high school curricula for this decline: In 1924, high school students read an average 1,750 pages of printed matter a term, about three times what they read today.

㉑   Others who have studied the problem say television viewing—five hours a day for the average school child—has created a nation of "image-lazy" non-readers. They say TV doesn't encourage the higher skills necessary for students to draw and process new information.

㉒   Declining facility with language also may have roots in the large number of one-parent families and sociopolitical changes that have taken women out of the home and put them in the work force. Johnny is no longer read to or exposed to "literacy" role models.

㉓   A result as well as a cause of semi-literacy has been the development of "The Cult of the Dumb," a society in which books, learning and writing skills are not valued as they once were. This attitude seems especially prevalent in lower economic classes, the same group educators warn is going to suffer the greatest losses in the Information Revolution.

㉔   To address these and other issues associated with the emerging problems of the new literacy, an international panel of educators, politicians and business representatives gathered recently at the University of Michigan in Ann Arbor. Speakers at the "Literacy in the 1980s" program stressed that the ability to have access to a body of information and communicate it to other people has become a life-survival skill, like as hunting was for a frontiersman.

㉕   Every year, the output of government forms increases 10 percent, regulatory documents become more complex, and the demand for unskilled laborers, now at 5 percent of the work force, diminishes.

㉖   The result, says Edwin DeLattre, president of St. John's College in Annapolis, Md., is a nation divisible into insiders and outsiders. "Insiders have access to ideas, events and progress," he says. "Outsiders are eternally strangers. If you want to know what it feels like to be an outsider, look at a printed page in a foreign language, or a science equation you do not understand."

㉗   One of the best ways to make Johnny learn to read and write well, says Sarah Power, former deputy assistant secretary for Human Rights and Social Affairs in the State Department, is to show him how such skills can help him get what he wants out of life.

㉘   Speaking on "The Politics of Literacy," Power outlined the connection between the prestige, influence and wealth, and ability to use a language well. She said that two out of three illiterates worldwide are women, and a disproportionate number are poor and black.

㉙   "And powerlessness means victimization," adds textbook author William Coles of Pittsburgh University. "Bad language is a ticket down the river. We've got to teach people how not to be losers."

㉚   If Alvin Toffler, Ben Bagdikian, John Wicklein and other contemporary writers are correct, however, the next generation of students will plug in, log on and broadcast out.

㉛   In the most controversial and provocative speech at the Michigan conference, Paul Strassman, vice president of Xerox Corp., plumbed history and the outer limits of scientific research to describe the new educational strategies which teachers must employ to meet the challenge and the Information Age.

㉜   "Those who just get by in one culture do not survive in the subsequent cultures," he insists. "Those who know vocabulary and grammar today must be taught coding, programming, flow diagrams and the syntax of artificial intelligence."

㉝   In a highly interactive world bursting with information traveling along fiber optic wires and through connected computers, literacy no longer will be a concern solely of the academic world.

㉞   As Paul Strassman said, "To take care of the education of our children is going to be an awesome task."

PERSONAL BOOK LIST

On the following blanks, make a list of books that you would like to read during free reading time. Your list must include at least one biography or autobiography and one book that is nonfiction.

Title	Type of Book	Number of Pages in Book	Number of Pages Read

READING IMPROVEMENT PLAN

Standardized Test Scores

Name of test _____

Subtests	Raw Score		Stanine		%	
	Pre	Post	Pre	Post	Pre	Post
_____	___	___	___	___	___	___
_____	___	___	___	___	___	___
_____	___	___	___	___	___	___
_____	___	___	___	___	___	___
_____	___	___	___	___	___	___

Vocabulary

Name of test or inventory

Results or area where improvement is needed

_____   _____
_____   _____
_____   _____

Comprehension

Name of test or inventory

Results or area where improvement is needed

_____   _____
_____   _____
_____   _____

Study Skills

Name of test or inventory

Results or area where improvement is needed

_____   _____
_____   _____
_____   _____

Rate of Comprehension

Name of selection	Words/minute	Comprehension score
_____	_____	_____
_____	_____	_____

STRUCTURAL ANALYSIS ASSESSMENT

Name _____

Date _____

I. *Identifying Meaningful Word Parts*
Draw lines between the meaningful parts of the following words:
Examples: mis/taken   un/eat/able
1. outstanding
2. replacement
3. telescope
4. psychology
5. bibliography
6. photogenic
7. homogeneous
8. judgment
9. inspection
10. auditorium

II. *Using Meaningful Word Parts*
A definition is given for a prefix and a root word in each item below. Then the prefix and root are combined to form one commonly used word. Using the definition given for each word part, write a definition for the combined word.
Example: "Mono" means one and "chrom" means color.
Monochromatic = *something that has or consists of only one color.*
1. "Poly" means many and "gam" means marriage.
Polygamy = _____
2. "Zo" means animal and "logy" means the study of.
Zoology = _____
3. "Psych" means mind and "logy" means the study of.
Psychology = _____
4. "Trans" means across and "fer" means carry.
Transfer = _____
5. "Post" means after and "pon" means place or put.
Postpone = _____
6. "Micro" means small and "scope" means see.
Microscope = _____
7. "Sym" means with or along and "path" means feeling.
Sympathy = _____
8. "Mono" means one and "lith" means stone.
Monolith = _____
9. "Con" means with and "junct" means join.
Conjunction = _____
10. "A" means not or no and "the" means God.
Atheist = _____

III. *Using Suffixes*

Fill in the blank in each sentence below by adding the correct suffix to the bracketed word that follows each sentence.

1. The way he walked onto the stage was _____. (comedy)
2. This is not a _____ sentence. (meaning)
3. The _____ of hydrochloric acid was too concentrated. (solved)
4. This is the 93rd _____ session. (legislature)
5. Their clothes and the concrete dust on their shoes suggested that they were _____ men. (construct)
6. His story was a _____ of the truth (distort)
7. What type of _____ does this vehicle use? (propel)
8. The quality of her acting caused people to say she was an excellent _____. (perform)
9. He walked to the front of the room with great _____. (reluctant)
10. That dog is just not _____. (train)

		% Correct
I.	Identifying Meaningful Word Parts	_____
II.	Using Meaningful Word Parts	_____
III.	Using Suffixes	_____

USING CONTEXT CLUES

Read each of the following sentences or brief passages. After you have read each one, write a definition of the underlined term using your own words.

1. All the nerves leading to and from the brain and spinal cord are the *peripheral nerves*. They connect the nervous system with the rest of the body.[1] _____

    _____

    _____

2. The term *professional* is usually reserved for those careers which require specialized training at the college level or beyond.[2] _____

    _____

    _____

3. A human being has a very long period of physical and mental development, called childhood, in which to grow and learn what others of the group already know. It takes many years to complete this process of *enculturation*.[3] _____

    _____

    _____

4. Eight chief minerals are used for the production of special kinds of steel. They are known as *ferroalloys* and are used to "season" a batch of steel to give it special characteristics.[4] _____

    _____

    _____

---

1. Charles Heimler and Charles Neal (Consultant), *Principles of Science: Book Two*, 4th Ed. (Columbus, Ohio: Charles E. Merrill, 1980), p. 80.
2. Beatrice Paolucci, Theodoria Faiola, and Patricia Thompson, *Personal Perspectives* (New York: McGraw-Hill, 1973), p. 176.
3. Preston E. James and Nelda Davis, *Global Geography* (New York: Macmillan, 1981), p. 35. Reprinted with permission of Macmillan Publishing Company. Copyright © 1981, Macmillan Publishing Co., Inc.
4. Ibid, p. 154.

5. A pair of parentheses is called a *symbol of inclusion* or a grouping symbol because it is used to enclose, or include, an expression for a particular number. In the expression "2 × (5 + 6)," the parentheses group the numerals "5" and "6" together with the symbol +, and thus show that the sum of 5 and 6 is to be multiplied by 2.[5]

_____

_____

_____

6. *A bill of lading* is completed for each freight shipment moving by rail, truck, or ship. This form provides space for the shipper to supply a full description of the shipment and to give basic shipping instructions, such as routing, to the carriers. Weight data should be as accurate as possible. The rate, if given, refers to rate per hundred pounds as set forth in official freight rate tariffs.[6] _____

_____

_____

7. Because Sumerian scribes used a pointed stick, called a styles, most of the signs were combinations of wedge shapes. The Latin word for "wedge" is *cuneus* so we call the writing of the Sumerian *cuneiform*.[7] _____

_____

_____

8. Insurance companies require applicants for life insurance policies to meet certain standards for *insurability*. That is, the companies inquire whether or not applicants measure up to particular standards of health.[8] _____

_____

_____

5. Mary Dolcani and William Wootan, *Book One: Modern Algebra Structure and Method,* Revised Edition (New York: Houghton Mifflin, 1975), p. 4.
6. Fred Ancher, Raymond Bricker, and Jeffery Stewart, Jr., *General Office Procedures,* Fourth Edition (New York: McGraw-Hill, 1975), p. 452.
7. Anatole G. Mazour and John M. Peoples, *Men and Nations,* Second Edition (New York: Harcourt Brace Jovanovich, 1968), p. 39. Copyright © 1968 by Harcourt Brace Jovanovich, Inc. Reprinted by permission of the publisher.
8. Kennard Goodman and C. Lowell Harriss, *Economics* (Boston: Ginn, 1963), p. 231.

9. If a force causes a body to move, *work* is done. In science, work is defined as a force acting through a distance.[9] _____

_____

_____

10. Our bodies can manufacture their own vitamin A if given the right raw materials. This is *carotene*, which is found in green and yellow vegetables.[10] _____

_____

_____

11. A *point* is represented on paper by a dot. Dots vary in size with even the smallest having some area. A point in mathematics has no size, it has position only. Thus, no mention is ever made of the size of a point.[11] _____

_____

_____

12. *Finishing* is whatever is done to a fabric after it becomes a fabric. Finishing may involve applications of heat, pressure, or chemicals. Special finishing adds a desirable quality that the fabric would not otherwise have. Fabrics finished with chemicals may be resistant to moths and mildew.[12] _____

_____

_____

9. Charles Heimler and Charles Neal (Consultant), *Principles of Science: Book One*, Fourth Edition (Columbus, Ohio: Charles E. Merrill, 1980), p. 97.
10. Beatrice Paolucci, Theodoria Faiolo, and Patricia Thompson, *Personal Perspectives*, p. 126.
11. Ray Jurgensen, Alfred Donnelly, and Mary Dolciani, *Modern School Mathematics Geometry* (New York: Houghton Mifflin, 1972), p. 18.
12. Beatrice Paolucci, Theodoria Faiolo, and Patricia Thompson, *Personal Perspectives*, p. 208.

13. *Organic compounds* always contain carbon. They are often parts of living things. Plants, animals, your body, food, wood, and most fuels are made of organic compounds.[13] _____

_____

_____

14. Certain plants—called *halophytes*—are adapted to soils with a high salt content.[14]

_____

_____

_____

15. A *wave* is a disturbance that transfers energy from point to point. Some waves, such as sound waves, must travel through matter. Other waves such as radio and light waves can travel through a vacuum. All waves carry energy from one place to another.[15] _____

_____

_____

---

13. Charles Heimler and Charles Neal, *Principles of Science: Book One,* p. 35.
14. James Otto and Albert Towle, *Modern Biology* (New York: Holt, Rinehart and Winston, 1977), p. 306.
15. Charles Heimler and Charles Neal, *Principles of Science: Book One,* p. 67.

VOCABULARY CONCEPTS ASSESSMENT

Pretest _____

Posttest _____

Select the phrase that best completes each of the following statements. Write the letter that corresponds to your answer on a separate sheet of paper.

1. Phonic analysis is the process of
   a. dividing sentences into phrases and clauses.
   b. sounding out words by associating the correct sounds with the letters in the word.
   c. looking for the meaningful parts within a word, such as prefixes, roots, or suffixes.
   d. analyzing the sentence or sentences in which a word is used to determine the word's meaning.

2. Structural analysis is the process of
   a. dividing sentences into phrases and clauses.
   b. sounding out words by associating the correct sounds with the letters in the word.
   c. looking for the meaningful parts within a word, such as prefixes, roots, or suffixes.
   d. analyzing the sentence or sentences in which a word is used to determine the word's meaning.

3. Contextual analysis is the process of
   a. dividing sentences into phrases and clauses.
   b. sounding out words by associating the correct sounds with the letters in the word.
   c. looking for the meaningful parts within a word, such as prefixes, roots, or suffixes.
   d. analyzing the sentence or sentences in which a word is used to determine the word's meaning.

4. When readers come to an unknown word, the first word-identification strategy or strategies to employ is (are)
   a. phonic analysis
   b. structural analysis
   c. contextual analysis
   d. look up the word in a dictionary
   e. both a and b
   f. both b and c
   g. both c and d

5. When readers come to an unknown word, the word-identification strategy or strategies they ought to resort to after all others have been tried is (are)
   a. phonic analysis
   b. structural analysis
   c. contextual analysis
   d. look up the word in a dictionary
   e. both a and b
   f. both b and c
   g. both c and d

6. The approximate number of words in the English language is
   a. over 3 million.
   b. about 2 million.
   c. about 100 thousand.
   d. about 10 thousand.

7. One of the most effective ways to develop your vocabulary is to
   a. learn lists of words found in vocabulary self-help books.
   b. study lists of prefixes, roots, and suffixes.
   c. study and attempt to learn new words encountered while reading.
   d. read and study dictionaries.

8. Most of the words in the English language are
   a. used by just about everybody.
   b. associated with specialized fields.
   c. no longer used by anyone.
   d. should be learned by just about everyone.

9. The average person knows about _____ words.
   a. 1 million
   b. 2 thousand to 4 thousand
   c. 2 million
   d. 30 thousand to 60 thousand

10. Structural and contextual analysis are most often used to
    a. identify words that are part of a reader's listening and speaking vocabularies.
    b. identify words that are not part of a reader's listening and speaking vocabularies.
    c. determine how a word sounds.
    d. locate unknown words in a dictionary.

PARAPHRASING ASSESSMENT

Read each item below carefully. Some ought to be familiar to you. Then rewrite each item using your own words. Try to demonstrate that you understand the meaning of the statement by using as many of your own words as possible. Changing only one or two words is not an acceptable paraphrase.

1. Where ignorance is bliss, tis folly to be wise. (Thomas Gray)

2. Tis better to have loved and lost than to never have loved at all.

3. Sticks and stones can break my bones but words will never hurt me.

4. Life isn't all it's cracked up to be.

5. No man is an island, entire of itself; every man is a piece of the continent, a part of the main. (John Donne)

6. Too much of a good thing is still too much.

7. If wishes were horses then beggars would ride.

8. When the one great scorer comes to mark against your name, it matters not if you won or lost: it's how you played the game.

9. Winning's not the most important thing; it's the only thing! (Vincent Lombardi)

10. You can't make a silk purse out of a sow's ear.

AN IMAGERY INVENTORY

1. In terms of size and natural resources, the United States is one of the great nations of the world.[1]

2. Grandma kept pointing to yellow chrysanthemums but my mother said they reminded her of football games and that she preferred something all white, in a graveyard container.[2]

3. And in a freak of war, one wild shot missed the moon and hit an incoming formation of space ships that carried 15,671 Martian Imperial Commandos.[3]

4. Many psychologists have tried to teach chimpanzees to use language, but only recently have such efforts been successful.[4]

5. In the forest evening was already beginning to fall, and they walked in silence.[5]

6. Kennedy solemnly declared: "And so, my fellow-Americans: ask not what your country can do for you—ask what you can do for your country."[6]

7. Newfoundland is . . . poised like a mighty granite stopper over the bell-mouth of the Gulf of St. Lawrence . . .[7]

8. Most California rice is milled and marketed by grower-owned cooperatives, although significant amounts are handled by independent millers.[8]

9. Heat the pan and add 1 tablespoon of vegetable oil, garlic, and brown beans.[9]

10. The tears coursed down her cheeks—not freely, however, for when they came into contact with her heavily beaded eyelashes they assumed an inky color, and pursued the rest of their way in slow black rivulets.[10]

11. I open the window and feel the air, eat gratefully, sleep well.[11]

12. The factors governing the swimming of dolphins differ from those that pertain to ships because the hull of a ship is only partly submerged whereas the body of a dolphin is completely below the surface except during brief moments of respiration.[12]

13. In the dazzle of diamonds and the glow of California tans, Reagan saw a bright future for his Administration: "There isn't anything we can't do," he told the glittering crowd at the Sheraton, "and together we're going to do it."[13]

---

1. H. Bragdon and S. McCutchen, *History of a Free People* (New York: Macmillan, 1978), p. xi.
2. J. Blume, *Then Again, Maybe I Won't* (New York: Dell, 1971), p. 30.
3. K. Vonnegut, Jr., *The Sirens of Titan* (New York: Dell, 1959), p. 168.
4. A. Levine, *Understanding Psychology*, 2nd ed. (New York: Random House, 1977), p. 177. Copyright © 1974, 1977 by Random House, Inc. Reprinted by permission of CRM Books, a Division of Random House, Inc.
5. M. L'Engle, *A Wrinkle in Time* (New York: Dell, 1962), p. 41.
6. H. Bragdon and S. McCutchen, *History of a Free People*, p. 6.
7. F. Mowat and J. DeVren, *This Rock Within the Sea: A Heritage Lost* (Boston: Little, Brown, 1968), p. 6.
8. J. Rutgers and D. Brandon, "California Rice Culture," *Scientific American*, February (1981): p. 50.
9. B. Lee, *The Easy Way to Chinese Cooking* (Garden City, New York: Doubleday, 1963), p. 122.
10. F. Scott Fitzgerald, *The Great Gatsby* (New York: Charlie Scribner's Sons, 1925), p. 51.
11. J. Didion, *The White Album* (New York: Pocket Books, 1979), p. 171.
12. L. Mathews, *The Natural History of the Whale* (New York: Columbia University Press, 1978), p. 99.
13. J. Adler, M. Kasindorf, J. Whitmore, D. Weathers, J. Young, and J. Buckley, "Hitting the Ground Dancing," *Newsweek* February 1 (1981).

14. Flowing spaces abound in the open interior of his dynamically designed home.[14]

15. The time the crowd comes alive is when a man is hit hard over the heart or head, when his mouthpiece flies out, when the blood squirts out of his nose or eyes, when he wobbles under the attack and his pursuer continues to smash at him with pole-axe impact.[15]

16. Now you have to determine how much life insurance will accomplish your objective and how much you're willing or able to pay for it.[16]

17. The cabinets are oak plywood finished with urethane and the counter tops are genuine maple butcher block.[17]

18. Using Old World techniques developed by craftsmen in the twelfth century, Jim Bramstedt custom-designs stained glass windows, hanging sculptures, and lamps which bring the beauty of colored glass and light into everyday living.[18]

19. From a tin box on whose cover fading blue asters had been painted Amarante then removed a well-oiled revolver, an old, very heavy Colt Peacemaker.[19]

20. The present is passed over in the race for the future; the here is neglected in favor of the there; and the individual is dwarfed by the enormity of the mass.[20]

21. Because Walter is being claimed as a dependent on his parents' return and has unearned income of $1,000 or more and earned income of less than $2,300, he must use Part II of schedule TC.[21]

22. Moments later, Paul Huereman made the front end of two free throws and Thad Garner plucked his missed second shot off the board and scored off the rebound.[22]

23. An elementary teacher works every day in the classroom helping children learn to read—assigning workbook lessons, helping a student to sound out a word, asking a question that will clarify a meaning.[23]

24. Mosses are usually shade-loving plants of open woods, field, and river banks.[24]

25. Oscar Mayer and Co. will be sold to the General Foods Corp. of White Plains, New York, for $464 million if negotiations are completed, officials said Saturday.[25]

14. J. McCloskey (ed.), "You Can Do It—With A Good Builder," *Better Homes and Gardens Building Ideas* Spring (1981), p. 96.
15. N. Cousins, "Who Killed Benny Paret?" in *How to Read and Study for Success in College* 2nd ed., M. Norman and E. Norman (eds.). (New York: Holt, Rinehart & Winston, 1976), p. 246.
16. (Advertisement) Bankers Life Insurance *Newsweek* October 6, (1980), p. 5.
17. J. McCloskey (ed.), "Sensible Excitement," *Better Homes and Gardens Building Ideas* Spring (1981), p. 74.
18. M. Saart, "The Gothic Act of Stained Glass," *Wisconsin Trails*, 21 (1980), p. 30.
19. J. Nichols, *The Milagro Beanfield War* (New York: Ballantine, 1974), p. 71.
20. A. Lindbergh, *Gift From the Sea* (New York: Random House, 1974), p. 126.
21. Tax Computation Schedule (Form 1040) U.S. Tax Return 1980, U.S. GPO. 1980-0-313-444.
22. T. Butler, "Second-Half Slumber Dooms Badger Cagers," *Wisconsin State Journal*, 1 February 1981, sec. 2, p. 1.
23. R. Smith, W. Otto, and L. Hansen, *The School Reading Program* (Boston: Houghton Mifflin, 1980), p. 16.
24. F. Shuttleworth and H. Zim, *Non-Flowering Plants* (New York: Western Publishing, 1967), p. 9.
25. C. Martin and P. Fanland, "General Foods Seeking to Purchase Oscar Mayer," *Wisconsin State Journal*, 1 February 1981, sec. 1, p. 3.

IMAGERY RESPONSE FORM

Name _____

Date _____

Rate (1, 2, or 3) the vividness of the mental images evoked by each of the statements in Reproduction Page 10.

1 = Highly vivid, 2 = Somewhat vivid, and 3 = Not vivid.

1. _____   14. _____

2. _____   15. _____

3. _____   16. _____

4. _____   17. _____

5. _____   18. _____

6. _____   19. _____

7. _____   20. _____

8. _____   21. _____

9. _____   22. _____

10. _____   23. _____

11. _____   24. _____

12. _____   25. _____

13. _____

STUDY SKILLS SELF-ASSESSMENT

Pretest _____   Name _____

Posttest _____   Date _____

The list below is made up of statements that describe students who already know how to apply the reading and study skills taught in this course. Check those statements that you think accurately describe you. If a statement only partially describes you or your behavior, do not check it.

1. When material is difficult to understand, I read it more than once.   _____

2. After I finish reading a magazine or a newspaper article, I think about what the author has said and then decide if I agree or disagree with his or her point of view.   _____

3. I keep a notebook or a log for each of my courses so that I have a record of each day's activities and assignments.   _____

4. If it is possible for me to write directly on to a reading assignment, I often do so by underlining important ideas and writing notes and comments in the margins.   _____

5. When I come to a word I don't know, I make an effort to determine the meaning.   _____

6. Preparing an outline of a chapter helps me to think through the important ideas.   _____

7. I usually remember material I have studied.   _____

8. I usually preview a chapter to get the gist of it before I read it carefully.   _____

9. I know what is the best time of the day for me to study.   _____

10. I understand my own strengths and weaknesses as a student.   _____

11. I understand how to use a variety of study methods.   _____

12. I think that I am a good reader.   _____

13. I schedule my study time carefully.   _____

14. I think that I have a good reading vocabulary.   _____

15. Before I begin reading about a particular subject, I review what I already know. _____

16. I make good use of the study time I have during school. _____

17. When I come to a word I don't understand, I reread the passage and try to use the context to help me determine the meaning of the unknown word. _____

18. When I read something and do not understand it, I realize it immediately. _____

19. When I study, I use my time efficiently. _____

20. Before I begin to read, I organize my thoughts by developing questions I expect to be able to answer after I finish reading. _____

21. If I take notes while reading, I always make an effort to rewrite the author's ideas using my own words. _____

22. Before answering an essay question, I organize what I am going to write. _____

23. I am very aware of how I spend most of my time. _____

24. I study regularly, not just before tests. _____

25. I know when I have understood the material I have read. _____

26. I know what type of study approach works best for me. _____

27. I stop to review what I remember after reading each section in a chapter. _____

28. I set aside time to review for each course that I am taking. _____

29. I study charts, tables, graphs, and any illustrations when I read a chapter. _____

30. With some effort, I feel that I am able to read and understand most materials. _____

31. I am satisfied with my grades. _____

32. I know what types of tests my teachers give. _____

33. I try to predict the kinds of questions which will appear on exams. _____

34. I know how to rewrite an author's ideas using my own words. _____

35. I can concentrate well when I read. _____

36. When material is difficult to understand, I read it more slowly. _____

37. I realize that rapid reading involves the quickness of thoughts, not the speed at which my eyes move. _____

38. I understand that I should vary my reading rate depending on my purpose for reading. _____

39. When I come to a word I don't understand, I try to look for meaningful parts within the word. _____

40. I think that I have good study habits. _____

41. I frequently test myself to be sure I know the material. _____

42. I am able to understand the difference between what is important and what is unimportant when I am reading. _____

43. I understand that I should study differently depending upon whether I am taking a multiple choice test or an essay exam. _____

44. The thoughts and ideas I read have an influence on my own thoughts and behavior. _____

45. I realize that if the material is easy and I already know a great deal about the subject, I ought to try to increase my reading rate and push myself to read quickly. _____

46. If I have any time left during an exam, I check over my test to avoid errors. _____

47. Before starting a test, I plan how much time to use on each section of the test. _____

48. I realize that I may need to use a different study approach depending upon whether I am studying a science text or a social studies text. _____

49. I know how to skim. _____

50. I am able to identify the main ideas of paragraphs and passages. _____

RESPONSE EVAULATION

Circle the numbers of the items you checked in the self-assessment inventory under the categories below. Now count the total number of items you checked in each category and write down that total number.

Study Methods	General Reading	Time Scheduling	Rate	Taking Exams
1, 3, 4, 6, 7, 8, 10, 11, 15, 20, 21, 26, 27, 29, 31, 40, 41, 48, 49	2, 5, 12, 14, 17, 18, 25, 30, 34, 35, 39, 42, 44, 50,	9, 13, 16, 19, 23, 24, 28	36, 37, 38, 45	22, 32, 33, 43, 46, 47
Total _____	_____	_____	_____	_____

Using the chart on Reproduction Page 14, find your total score for each category in the column of numbers on the left hand side of the page. Then find the percentage score that corresponds to this total number under each category. Record this percentage score on the appropriate lines below. High percentage scores indicate that you think you have adequate skills in a particular category. Low percentage scores indicate that you think you have inadequate skills. Finally, draw a circle around the category in which your percentage score was the lowest.

Study Methods _____

General Reading _____

Time Scheduling _____

Rate _____

Taking Exams _____

PERCENTAGE SCORES FOR RESPONSES ON STUDY SKILLS SELF-ASSESSMENT

Number Circled	Study Methods	General Reading	Time Scheduling	Taking Exams	Rate
19	100%				
18	.95				
17	.89				
16	.84				
15	.79				
14	.74	100%			
13	.68	.93			
12	.63	.86			
11	.58	.79			
10	.53	.71			
9	.47	.64			
8	.42	.57			
7	.37	.50	100%		
6	.32	.43	.86	100%	
5	.26	.38	.71	.83	
4	.21	.29	.57	.67	100%
3	.16	.21	.43	.50	.75
2	.11	.14	.29	.33	.50
1	.05	.07	.14	.17	.25

WEEKLY SCHEDULE

Name _____

Time															
Sunday															
Monday															
Tuesday															
Wednesday															
Thursday															
Friday															
Saturday															

SAMPLE WEEKLY SCHEDULE

Name_____

Time	8:00	9:00	10:00	11:00	12:30	1:00	2:00	3:00	6:00	7:00	11:00		
Sunday	Gets up and spends time with fa,ou →				Eat	Misc.	Visit Friends	Drive Around	Eat and watch TV	Home Work, TV and Read	Go to Bed		

Day	8:00	9:00	10:00	11:00	12:00	1:00	2:00	3:00	3:15	4:00	5:30	6:00	8:00	11:00
Monday	Geometry	U.S. History	Study Time	Physical Education	Lunch	Music	English	Earth Science	Travel Home	Soccer Practice	Eat	Talk to friends Homework	Watch TV	Go to Bed
Tuesday				Study Time								Watch TV	Homework	
Wednesday				Physical Education						Soccer Practice		See some friends →		
Thursday				Study Time									Read and do homework ↓	
Friday	↓	↓	↓	Physical Education	↓	↓	↓	↓	↓	Soccer Practice		Go out with Friends →		
Saturday	Gets up and spends time with family →				Soccer Game →					→	↓	Go out with friends →		

TIME ANALYSIS OF A WEEK

Name _____

Date _____

Number of Hours Spent

Sleep   _____

Meals   _____

Job   _____

Travel time   _____

Class time   _____

Sports/scheduled recreation   _____

Additional scheduled activities   _____

Total hours: _____

Subtract "total hours" from 168, the number of hours in seven days. The result = _____.
This is the amount of unscheduled or free time you have.

What do you generally do with this time?

THE KALAHARI DESERT

In southwestern Africa there is a great stretch of dry land. The land is flat with no lakes or rivers. Vegetation is scarce. The plants and animals that live here have adapted to an environment with little water and high temperatures. This land is the Kalahari Desert. The Kalahari Desert covers part of South Africa, much of Botswana, and part of Namibia. These are three nations of southern Africa.

The plants of the Kalahari have adapted to the desert environment. Most of these plants are grasses and bushes. However, every now and then across the barren desert a huge, 200 foot baobob tree is seen. Its great, thick branches reach like stretching arms into the sky. The bark is thick and smooth, and sags in folds toward the bottom of the tree. The tree is adapted to the hot, dry climate because it is able to store water in the spongy wood of its huge trunk. Some of the other desert plants store water in large underground roots. Many rest as seeds until the rainy season. The seeds cannot germinate without water, but when the rain falls, the seeds can finally sprout.

Because plants such as these grow on the Kalahari Desert, animals that consume these plants are also able to survive. Antelope and zebras mainly eat the grasses. Insects, such as ants, are also plant eaters. The plant eaters are food for animal-consuming predators like lizards, snakes, lions, and leopards. Birds are also part of the food chains in the Kalahari Desert. Very large birds called vultures eat animals that are already dead.

The desert is without rain for almost 10 months of the year. A hot, dry wind blows across the desert most of the time. During the two cool months, June and July, the bushes and grass are covered with frost at dawn. Any water left standing freezes at night. Days warm slowly to around 80 degrees, but the cold returns at night.

Rains come at last to the Kalahari in December, January, and February. At this time, holes in the ground fill with water, and small ponds form. All of the desert life becomes active with the coming of the rains. The grass turns green and new leaves and blossoms appear on the bushes. Flowering plants add bright colors to the desert scene. Much of the plant life sprouts from seeds that have rested while waiting for moisture. These plants bud, blossom, and bear their seeds quickly, for the season is short. The animals of the kalahari graze on the new, tender plants brought to life by the long-awaited rains.

In March the drought, or dry time, returns. When the rains stop, the water holes start to dry up. They become slippery mud and then caked white earth. By June only little water holes which are deep in the ground and covered with long grass are left. These water holes are miles apart, and travel in the desert is nearly impossible when the water holes completely dry up in August. A time of waiting begins. All desert life awaits the rain.

To adapt to the desert environment, the animals, like plants, face the task of finding and storing water. Many birds, such as the ostrich, and grass eaters, such as the antelope, travel across the desert to water holes. When times are very dry they often seek water outside the desert.

Much of the need for water is met through food chains. Some plant eaters, such as insects, eat plants that have water stored in them. Predators, such as lions, can sometimes quench their thirst on the flesh and blood of prey.

Some desert animals seek a drink or store water in surprising places. Lizards and insects often lap dew at daybreak. Dew is tiny drops of water formed at night when it is cool. Desert tortoises carry extra body water around with them in two sacs under their upper shell. These sacs serve as two canteens for the tortoises.

People of the Kalahari

The Kalahari Desert is the home of people called Bushmen. The Bushmen are rather small people. As adults, they are four and one-half to just over five feet tall. The hot desert sun has darkened their skin to a copper brown color to protect them from sunburn. Over the years their skin becomes very wrinkled. The language spoken by these people is unusual. The tongue makes clicking sounds against the roof of the mouth to make words. These people once lived on rich grasslands of South Africa. In the struggle with cattle-raising peoples for this land, the Bushmen were driven north. They found safety on the Kalahari, and as a hunting and gathering people, still live as the earliest people on earth once did.

Because of the harsh desert conditions, the Bushmen do not plant crops or herd animals. Instead, they gather roots, berries, and nuts, and hunt animals. They are adapted to and are part of the food chains in the Kalahari. Like other animals and plants, they take only what they need from their environment. Their way of life does not upset or break the food chains. When the water holes in one place are dry and little food remains, the Bushmen must move to a new place. The food chains are able to renew themselves. In their search for food and water, these peole must move a great deal. They do not stay in one spot, but migrate from place to place. Such people are called nomads. The Bushmen do not change their environment for their own use. Like the antelope and the lion, they adapt to the desert environment.

Where food and water can be found, a band of about 20 Bushmen set up a *werf* which is their word for camp. A visitor could probably walk through the werf without knowing it because the small, cone-shaped houses made of sticks and grass look much like bushes. The Bushmen live in these *skerms* which give them shade during the day and shelter from the cool winds at night. Near the houses is a carefully placed row of ostrich eggshells, often decorated with carved designs of zigzags and diamonds, or animal pictures. The eggshells are important because they hold water. Each one is filled through a hole cut in the shell. The hole is then stopped up with grass.

Sometimes no skerms are built at all. A stick may be stuck into the sand to mark the spot where the band has decided to settle. Small holes are made in the sand for sleeping. These "sleeping nests," like the skerms, give protection from chilling winds at night.

Bushmen clothing, like Bushmen housing, is suited to the climate and the natural environment. A man wears only a leather breech cloth which is all the clothing needed in the hot environment. Over one shoulder, he carries a leather bag. In this is an ostrich eggshell and things like arrowheads, a skinning knife, a pipe, and tobacco.

A woman wears a big cape called a *karass,* and a small leather apron. The folds in the cape may be used to carry a baby, food, or firewood. Also tucked into the folds are her jewelry and makeup.

COMPREHENSION CHECK—THE KALAHARI DESERT

1. The Kalahari Desert is in
   a. southwestern Africa.
   b. northwestern Africa.
   c. southeastern Africa.
   d. central Africa.

2. The baobob tree is adapted to the desert environment because
   a. it requires little water.
   b. it stores water in its roots.
   c. it stores water in its trunk.
   d. it stores water in its leaves.

3. The two cool months on the desert are
   a. June and July.
   b. December and January.
   c. November and December.
   d. May and June.

4. Travel on the desert becomes nearly impossible when
   a. there are dust storms.
   b. wild animals search for food.
   c. the water holes dry up.
   d. during July and August.

5. Desert animals meet their need for water by
   a. traveling to water holes.
   b. eating other animals.
   c. eating plants that have water stored in them.
   d. lapping dew.
   e. all of the above.

6. The Bushmen, people who live in the Kalahari Desert,
   a. are large, tall people.
   b. survive by raising animals.
   c. are adapted to the food chains of the Kalahari.
   d. have changed the desert.

7. A *werf* is
   a. a stick house.
   b. a cape.
   c. a blowgun.
   d. a camp.

8. The Bushmen did not always live in the Kalahari. Once they lived
   a. alongside a large river.
   b. on rich grasslands.
   c. in the mountains.
   d. in the deep forests..

9. The best definition of a food chain would be
   a. the way in which animals obtain food for themselves.
   b. the way animals use plants and other animals to obtain water.
   c. a process by which the Bushmen survive on the Kalahari Desert.
   d. a process by which an animal becomes food for another animal which is in turn eaten by still another animal.

10. The Bushmen clothing
    a. is simple and suited to a hot environment.
    b. is made of cloth and woven grasses.
    c. is the same for both men and women.
    d. is decorated with beads and bits of eggshell.

READING RATES FOR *THE KALAHARI DESERT*

Reading Time	Words Per Minute		Reading Time	Words Per Minute
1:00	1260		4:40	270
1:10	1080		4:50	261
1:20	950		5:00	252
1:30	840		5:10	244
1:40	756		5:20	236
1:50	687		5:30	229
2:00	630		5:40	222
2:10	582		5:50	216
2:20	540		6:00	210
2:30	504		6:10	204
2:40	473		6:20	199
2:50	445		6:30	194
3:00	420		6:40	189
3:10	398		6:50	184
3:20	378		7:00	180
3:30	360		7:10	176
3:40	344		7:20	172
3:50	329		7:30	168
4:00	315		7:40	164
4:10	302		7:50	161
4:20	291		8:00	158
4:30	280			

Copyright © 1985 by Allyn and Bacon, Inc. Reproduction of this material is restricted to use with *A Guidebook for Teaching Reading,* by Pauline L. Witte.

READING RATE GRAPH

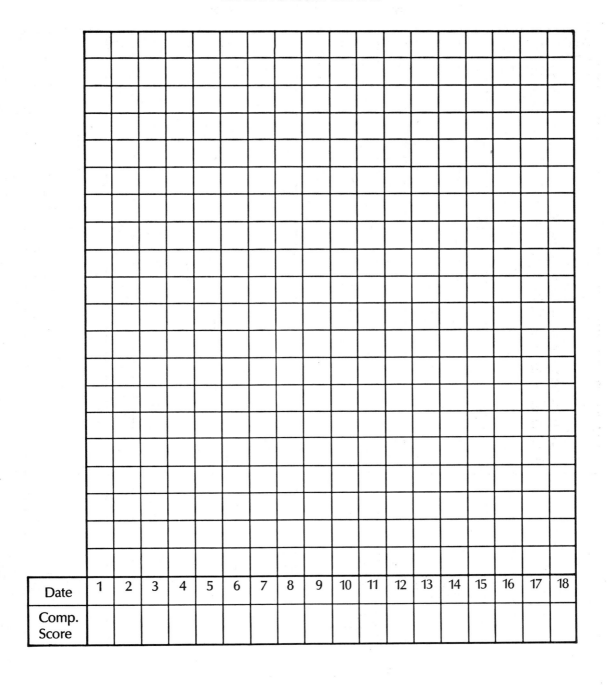

Date	1	2	3	4	5	6	7	8	9	10	11	12	13	14	15	16	17	18
Comp. Score																		

READING RATE GRAPH (DEMONSTRATION SAMPLE)

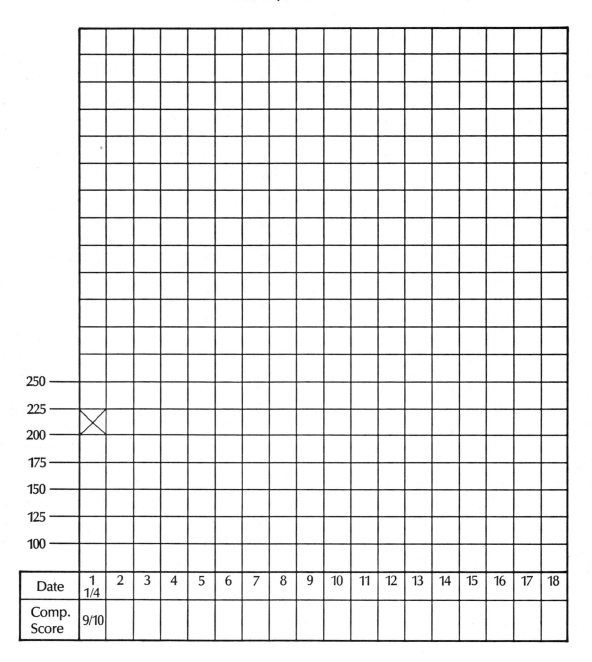

"MRS. JOE GARGERY"

My sister, Mrs. Joe Gargery, was more than twenty years older than I, and had established a great reputation with herself and the neighbours because she had brought me up 'by hand.' Having at that time to find out for myself what the expression meant, and knowing her to have a hard and heavy hand, and to be much in the habit of laying it upon her husband as well as upon me, I supposed that Joe Gargery and I were both brought up by hand.

She was not a good-looking woman, my sister; and I had a general impression that she must have made Joe Gargery marry her by hand. Joe was a fair man, with curls of flaxen hair on each side of his smooth face, with eyes of such a very undecided blue that they seemed to have somehow got mixed with their own whites. He was a mild, good-natured, sweet-tempered, easy-going, foolish, dear fellow—a sort of Hercules in strength, and also in weakness.

My sister, Mrs. Joe, with black hair and eyes, had such a prevailing redness of skin, that I sometimes used to wonder whether it was possible she washed herself with a nutmeg-grater instead of soap. She was tall and bony, and almost always wore a coarse apron, fastened over her figure behind with two loops, and having a square impregnable bib in front, that was stuck full of pins and needles. She made it a powerful merit in herself, and a strong reproach against Joe, that she wore this apron so much. Though I really see no reason why she should have worn it at all, she should not have taken it off every day of her life. . . .

My sister had a trenchant way of cutting our bread-and-butter for us that never varied. First, with her left hand she jammed the loaf hard and fast against her bib—where it sometimes got a pin into it, and sometimes a needle, which we afterwards got into our mouths. Then she took some butter (not too much) on a knife and spread it on the loaf, in an apothecary kind of way, as if she were making a plaister—using both sides of the knife with a slapping dexterity, and trimming and moulding the butter off round the crust. Then, she gave the knife a final smart wipe on the edge of the plaister, and then sawed a very thick round off the loaf; which she finally, before separating from the loaf, hewed into two halves, of which Joe got one, and I the other.

From Chapter II of *Great Expectations* by Charles Dickens

RECORDING NEW VOCABULARY WORDS

New Word _____

Sentence in which it was used _____

_____

Context Meaning _____

Dictionary Meaning _____

Write a sentence using the word _____

_____

New Word _____

Sentence in which it was used _____

_____

Context Meaning _____

Dictionary Meaning _____

Write a sentence using the word _____

_____

New Word _____

Sentence in which it was used _____

_____

Context Meaning _____

Dictionary Meaning _____

Write a sentence using the word _____

_____

WORD KNOWLEDGE ASSOCIATED WITH RECREATIONAL ACTIVITIES

Rejuvenated Putter Gives Levi New Life

Williamsburg, Va. (AP)—Wayne Levi overcame continued putting problems with a four-under-par 67 and took a one-stroke lead Friday in the second round of the $300,000 Anheuser-Busch Golf Classic.

"It's nice to be respectable again," Levi said after posting his 36-hole total of 137, five shots under par for two trips over the, 6,822-yard Kingsmill Golf Club course.

"I've been putting so bad . . . I've been so discouraged," said Levi, who has won a title in each of the past three seasons.

"It's been just an awful year for me. I'm a better player than that. But my putting has been so bad, I've gotten down on myself."

And those putting problems have not yet been solved, despite his position at that top of the field, Levi said.

"With any luck at all, I'd be leading by five or six shots," he said. "I've had a lot of spin-outs."

As an example, he pointed to the par-five 15th hole, where he hit a three-wood second shot five feet from the flag, then lipped out the eagle putt and settled for his fourth birdie of the day.

It was that birdie, however, that lifted him out of a tie and put him one shot in front of Bob Murphy, Howard Twitty and Jim Booros, tied at 138. Twitty matched Levi's no-bogey, four-under-par 67, while Murphy and Booros each recorded a second consecutive 69.

Ben Crenshaw, who won this title last year when the tournament was played in Napa, Calif., and former PGA champ John Mahaffey were another shot back at 139. Crenshaw had a 70 and Mahaffey included a eagle-three in his round of 67.

Bill Rogers, who won the British Open last weekend, shot another round of par-71 and was at 142, five back.

First-round leader Bob Gilder slipped to a 73 and was at 141.

Meanwhile Andy North of Madison, Wis., emerged with a 70 after Thursday's 73. His 143 total put himself six shots behind the leader.

Wisconsin State Journal, July 25, 1981. Used by Permission of the Associated Press.

WORD KNOWLEDGE NEEDED TO BE AN INTELLIGENT CONSUMER

Eating Better for Less

BUYING RED MEATS

When shopping for meat, you can use a basic rule of thumb if you don't have the chart for reference: for boneless and lean meats, expect 5 to 6 servings per pound; for meat with some bone or fat, 4 servings per pound; and for meats with large amounts of bone or fat, 2 servings per pound.

Steaks and chops are among the most prized cuts of meat. These cuts come mainly from the rib, short loin, and sirloin parts of the beef, veal, or lamb carcass, and the loin of pork. Since those portions or muscles get the least exercise, they'll be the tenderest after a minimum amount of cooking. They also tend to be the most expensive meats you can buy.

You can enjoy these tender cuts more often if you use the Meat-Buying Chart on page 110 to determine the best value for your money. Also take advantage of family-size packages of pork chips or thinly sliced sirloin steaks at special prices. Top round steak usually costs less per pound than eye of round steak.

Roasts can be a thrifty option, not only because they contain some of the more desirable steaks and chops, but also because the initial price per pound is usually lower than if you purchased the chops separately.

You can purchase a large family-size roast which will provide both the tender and less tender cuts. Divvy it up yourself to provide several different meals. For example, you can portion a pork roast into chops and bite-sized chunks for kabobs. A beef chuck blade pot roast can be divided 3 ways: use the blade and center meat portion for cubed meat for a stew, reserve the top blade section for a small pot roast, and cut up the center muscle for a beef pot pie or stir-fry.

Bony meat cuts such as beef, lamb, or ham shanks, ribs, pork hocks, and oxtail have a place in every budget. The bones and meat add a wonderful flavor to soups and stews, since all these cuts require long, slow simmering to make them tender. Though these cuts will yield only about 2 servings per pound, you can make the meat go further by supplementing it with small amounts of beans, lentils, or cheese.

Ground meats, whether beef, veal, lamb, pork, ham, or turkey, all provide 4 servings per pound. However, you'll find that the fat content will affect the price, particularly with respect to ground beef.

The fat content of ground beef is regulated by federal and state laws. By law, ground beef must be at least 70 percent lean. Some package labels will carry the statement "not less than X percent lean" (or no more than X percent fat), but this type of labeling is strictly voluntary.

Ground beef may be labeled ground chuck, ground sirloin, or ground round to show the cut of meat that was used. When fat content information isn't given, use this rule of thumb to help you judge the amount of fat present in the meat: ground chuck usually contains the most fat, and ground round the least.

The fat content of ground pork, veal, lamb, ham, and turkey is not governed by state law, but ground turkey, veal, and lamb are the leanest of the group.

VERSATILE VARIETY MEATS

To add a new dimension to menus, call on variety meats, because they're high on nutrition and low on waste. Liver, heart, kidney, and tongue are rich in iron and B vitamins and have virtually no bone and little fat. And since there's less demand for these cuts of meat, they're inexpensive enough for you to enjoy them often.

The beef variety meats are the best known and most popular; the veal, pork, and lamb counterparts are less common. Some retail stores do not stock heart, kidney, or tongue; you might have to special-order them. Tongue offers the most variety; you can buy it fresh, smoked, or pickled. Fresh tongue is cheapest.

POULTRY POINTERS

Poultry, whether it's fresh or frozen, will always be a smart buy. If your family is picky about the parts they like to eat, buy bonus packs of chicken pieces which usually contain extra legs, wings, or breasts. Use the bonier parts, such as the backs, necks, and wings, to make a rich stock for soups or stews.

REPHONIXED READING TEST

Reverse Announces Tu Nu Hi Performans Tenis Shus With Sumthing In Them Know Wun Els Haz

Nou thar ar tu Reverse Tenis Shus dezined around tha wa tha world's top tenis plaers pla tha gam.

Both hav tha yunek Reverse biofleks outer sol that maksamizes the fleksabilete and kantrol in yur forfut area—tha porshen uv yur fut on hevich yu pla tha most krushel part uv yur gam. So both shuz giv yu ekstra trakshan.

Plus, both giv yu tha kind uv kumftebel fit onle a Reverse kan bikaz thar mad on tha advanst Reverse last. So heven yu war them, yu get tha same kind uv inkrese endyurence they giv tha champeans.

Fecher for fecher they beet evre shu in thar klas. Tri on a par and se hou it fels to bee wun uv tha world's topp tenis plaers toda.

Comprehension Quiz

1. The Reverse bioflex sole is designed especially
   a. for long wear.
   b. to increase running speed.
   c. to add height to jumps.
   d. to maximize flexibility.
2. Reverse shoes give you a comfortable fit because
   a. they are made of leather.
   b. they are made very carefully.
   c. they are made on the advanced Reverse last.
   d. they are inspected before they leave the factory.
3. The portion of your foot on which you play the most crucial part of your game is
   a. the heel.
   b. the arch.
   c. the forefoot.
   d. the hindfoot.
4. Reverse has designed
   a. one new type of tennis shoe.
   b. two new types of tennis shoes.
   c. three new types of tennis shoes.
   d. four new types of tennis shoes.
5. When you wear Reverse Tennis Shoes you get increased
   a. strength.
   b. endurance.
   c. speed.
   d. hope.

BASIC CONCEPTS INVOLVED IN LEARNING TO READ:
LETTERS, WORDS, AND SENTENCES

Kindergartners are shown a sentence such as the one below. They are asked to draw:

1. an "x" on a letter.

2. a circle around a word.

3. a line under a sentence.

The sun is a star.

BASIC CONCEPTS INVOLVED IN LEARNING TO READ:
LETTERS-SOUND CORRESPONDENCE

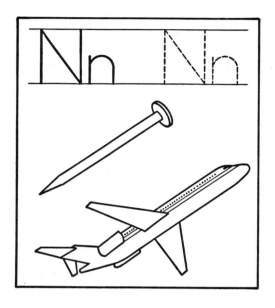

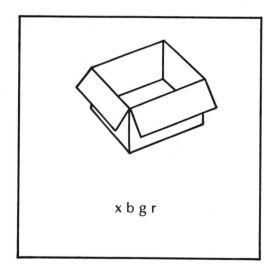

x b g r

x s ll d

CHOOSING WORD IDENTIFICATION STRATEGIES

Study the following list of words. Structural analysis can be used to identify the meaning of some of these words. Others can only be defined by reading them in context or by consulting an outside source such as a dictionary. Write SA on the blank in front of words that you can define through structural analysis.

1. _____ anthropology

2. _____ banal

3. _____ technocrat

4. _____ charisma

5. _____ lactate

6. _____ paradoxically

7. _____ insipid

8. _____ macho

9. _____ debilitating

10. _____ homeostasis

11. _____ derogation

12. _____ sublessee

13. _____ coeval

14. _____ spendthrift

15. _____ supersede

16. _____ familial

17. _____ hypothermal

18. _____ ornithologist

19. _____ cryophilic

20. _____ thermoregulatory

COMMON PREFIXES, ROOTS, AND SUFFIXES

Common Prefixes

Prefix	Meanings	Example
anti	opposite, against,	antibiotic
auto	self	autobiography
bi	two	bicycle
circum	around	circumscribe
de	down, separation	deflate
dis	negation, away	disapprove
ex	out of, off, away from	exhusband
hyper	over, above	hyperactive
hypo	below	hypothermia
il		illegal
im	not, non, un	immature
in		insecure
inter	among	interracial
intra	within, inside	intrastate
ir		irreparable
mis	wrong, ill	mistaken
non	not	nonproductive
post	after	posttest
pre	before	pretest
re	back, backwards, again	reinvest
semi	half	semicircle
sub	under, below	subway
trans	over, across	transcontinental
un	not, removal, contrary	unearth
uni	one, single	uniform

Common Roots

Root	Meanings	Example
aud, audit	hear	auditory
anthrop	man	anthropology
biblio	book	bibliography
bio	life	biorhythm
coput	head	capital
cred	to believe	credible
dem	people	democracy
dic, dict	say	dictaphone
fac, fic, fact	to make	manufacture
fin	end	finite
geo	earth	geography
jun, junct	join	junction
log	speech, word, study	anthropology
man	hand	manufacture
micro	small	microcomputers
mit, miss	send	missile
phon	sound	telephone
photo	light	photograph
sci	know	science
scrib, script	write	scribble
spect	look	spectator
tele	for	telephone
ven	come	convention
viv, vit	live, life	vital
voc	call	vocal

Common Suffixes

Noun Suffixes	Meanings	Example
sion	the act of	explosion
ity	state or condition	beauty
ance	quality	prominence
ment	agency or instrument	government
ness	condition of	kindness
ship	condition of	friendship
or	doer	actor
ant	person or thing as agent	attendant
ward	in the direction of	westward
ize	to subject to	rationalize
fy	to make	fortify
ate	combine, treat with	meditate

Adjective Suffixes	Meanings	Example
able	fitness, able to	usable
ive	nature or quality of	relative
al	belonging to	natural
ful	full of	beautiful
ish	of the nature of	bullish
less	without	useless
ous (-ious)	full size	gracious

TYPES OF CONTEXT CLUES

1. **Direct Definition**
   Peripheral nerves *are nerves that connect the brain and the spinal cord with the rest of the body.*

2. **Restatement**
   Peripheral nerves are nerves that connect the *nervous system, or the brain and the spinal cord,* with the rest of the body.

3. **Accompanying Description**
   All the nerves leading to and from the brain and spinal cord are the peripheral nerves. *They connect the nervous system with the rest of the body.*

4. **Comparison/Contrast**
   The peripheral nerves connect the brain and the spinal cord with the rest of the body *just as the veins and arteries connect the rest of the body with the heart and lungs.*

5. **Synonym**
   All the nerves leading to and from *the brain and spinal cord* are the peripheral nerves. They connect the *nervous system* with the rest of the body.

6. **Adjective Clause**
   The peripheral nerves are nerves that connect *the nervous system, which consists of the brain and the spinal cord,* with the rest of the body.

7. **Appositive**
   Peripheral nerves, nerves leading to and from the brain and spinal cord, connect the brain and the spinal cord to the rest of the body.

8. **Typographical**
   Peripheral nerves (nerves leading to and from the brain and the spinal cord) connect the brain and the spinal cord to the rest of the body.

SCHEMATA FOR WATER

SCHEMATA FOR WATER

A liquid such as water takes the shape of any container into which it is poured.

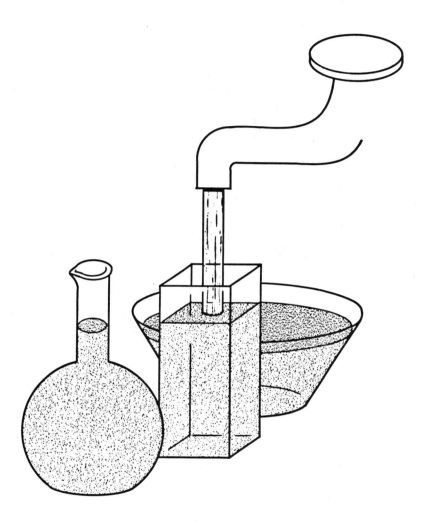

SCHEMATA FOR WATER

A liquid such as water consists of molecules that are in constant motion.

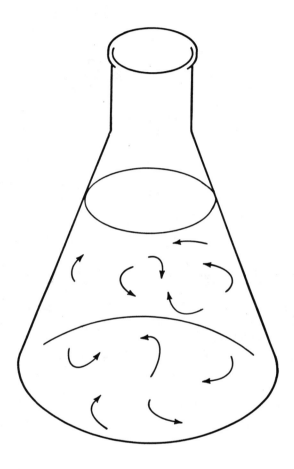

BILL'S DILEMMA: AMERICAN INTERVENTION IN VIETNAM

Read the story below and answer the questions that follow.

It is 1972. Bill, a freshman attending college fifty miles from the state capital, his hometown, is enjoying his college experiences and becoming very involved in campus life. This morning he and his roommate Joe were listening to the news and heard an uncomfirmed report that America had resumed heavy bombing in North Vietnam. Bill found this news very disturbing, for, as the months have passed, he has felt more and more uncomfortable about American presence in Vietnam. The latest new made him think about the events leading to this day.

Bill had never even heard of Vietnam until this war started. After World War II Vietnam had received its independence from France. Under the terms of the Geneva Agreement of 1954 two nations were formed, a pro-communist government in the North and a noncommunist government in the South. Elections were to be held at a later date to elect one government for all of Vietnam.

A man named Ngo Dinh Diem siezed power and later was elected president of South Vietnam. He refused to allow the reunification election on the basis of North Vietnamese aggressions. Many South Vietnamese hated Diem's government. The Viet Cong (procommunist South Vietnamese), supported by the North Vietnamese, began to attack areas in the South. Large areas of the country were taken over by the Viet Cong. Diem asked for American aid. President Kennedy had to make a decision. If he supported Diem, he would be supporting a government that was corrupt in many ways. If he refused to help Diem, communist forces would take control of the whole country. This spread of communism seemed the greater threat. Kennedy originally sent only military advisers to South Vietnam, but as the situation became critical American troops were sent to reinforce the South Vietnamese position.

The war rapidly escalated. In 1963 Diem was assassinated. Political stability was not restored until 1967 with the election of President Nguyen Van Thieu. By 1965 American planes were bombing strategic sites in North Vietnam. Ground fighting became intense. North Vietnam retaliated by giving full support to the Viet Cong in South Vietnam.

Because of rising opposition at home President Johnson ordered a halt to the bombings in 1968. The new president, Nixon, began a gradual withdrawal of American troops. U.S. troops were reduced from over 500,000 men in 1969 to fewer than 150,000 in 1972. That was why Bill found this morning's news so upsetting. He could not understand Nixon's decision to resume the bombing, to escalate the war once again. He thought that Nixon wanted to end the war.

Soon after hearing the news Bill called his father, a state congressman. His father had also heard the report and explained to Bill that President Nixon was using the bombings to exert pressure on the Viet Cong and North Vietnamese to accept cease-fire proposals. If this worked, the war would be over soon. Bill and his father have had long talks in the past about the Vietnam War. Bill's father has supported America's position in Vietnam on the grounds that it is absolutely essential to contain communism. If one country falls to communist control, others will soon follow. Although it disturbs Bill's father to hear of American casualties, this is the price America has to pay to keep the world safe from communist aggression.

From Tedd Levy and Donna Collins Krasnow, *A Guidebook for Teaching United States History; Mid-Nineteenth Century to the Present.* Copyright © 1979 by Allyn and Bacon, Inc. Reprinted by permission.

Bill finds this position harder and harder to accept. He has heard news stories about the thousands of innocent civilians killed by American, South Vietnamese, and North Vietnamese troops. Bill now feels that American support of Diem's corrupt government was wrong. If a majority of South Vietnamese wanted communist rule, then communism should have been allowed. U.S. interference in the governments of other countries makes a mockery of the American Declaration of Independence.

Bill's roommate Joe suddenly rushes into the room confirming American resumption of full-scale bombings in North Vietnam. Joe tells him of a rally planned for this afternoon in the state capital to demonstrate citizen opposition to the renewal of bombings. Joe wants Bill, as the son of a state congressman, to attend the rally, for Bill's presence will undoubtedly be noticed by the press and will focus more attention on the protest. Bill knows that he is strongly opposed to this new American decision but is still unsure about what to do. Bill loves his father and knows that his appearance at the rally could really hurt his father's political career, perhaps even jeopardize his reelection. And yet his father supports the government's position in Vietnam. If he doesn't stand up to his father, Bill is indirectly approving Americn intervention in Vietnam. He has to decide right away. The bus going to the rally is leaving in five minutes.

Questions

1. What is Bill's dilemma?

2. Of Bill and his father, which is the hawk and which is the dove?

3. Briefly, how would Bill's father justify Nixon's decision to resume heavy bombing of North Vietnam?

4. Briefly, why does Bill feel that American presence in Vietnam is wrong?

5. With whose position do you agree more—Bill's or his father's? Explain.

6. If you were Bill how would you resolve this dilemma? Justify your position.

LIGHT CONDITIONS NEEDED BY INDOOR PLANTS

Proper light conditions are a vital factor in growing green plants indoors. All plants require light to manufacture food and generally as light becomes brighter, more food is produced. Some plants, particularly those that are dark green, such as the snake plant with its large, sword-like, thick leaves, will survive in low light areas. But most indoor plants require at least a medium or high light level. Level or intensity is only one variable concerning light needed for plant growth. The two others are light quality and light duration. Light quality refers to the wavelength of light the plant receives. Both the sun and artificial lighting produce the two wavelengths, red and blue, that plants need. Sunlight is of course the best source of light, but artificial light can supplement natural light as well as serve as the sole source of illumination. The total amount of light a plant receives during a 24-hour period is called *light duration*. This is a product of light intensity and time. Extending the length of time during which a plant receives light can compensate for lower light intensity. Plants are a kind of living furniture that can enhance our indoor environment. Proper light conditions are needed to ensure their attractive growth.

HOW THE BICYCLE WORKS

The bicycle is said to be the most efficient means ever developed to convert human energy into propulsion. The rider supplies power by pushing two pedals which turn a sprocket or toothed wheel. A chain fits over the metal teeth on this wheel and extends to a smaller sprocket or toothed wheel on the rear wheel of the bike. When the large sprocket turns, the chain moves. This moving chain turns the small sprocket and the rear wheel. Today most bicycles have gears designed to make pedaling easier at certain times. Shifting into low gear when going up hill or riding against the wind makes pedaling easier, but the rider looses speed. Using a higher gear results in greater speed on level surfaces. Pedaling in high gear is slower but requires more force. Sprockets of different sizes are the gears of multispeed bikes. The rider shifts gears on a 3-speed bike by moving a lever on the handle bar. A mechanism called a *derailleur* shifts the chain from one sprocket to another on 10- and 15-speed bicycles. To shift a bike with derailleur gears the rider moves two levers on the down tube, which extends from below the handle bars to the pedals.

BUILDING AN AWARENESS OF BACKGROUND EXPERIENCES

The first and most important step in the whole process is to decide what you want the end result to look like. Then the next step is to place the inner most layer in the right places. Some people do this second step first because for them it is always the same no matter what they decide for the first step. It is important that this inner layer be arranged carefully. The whole process really consists of putting one layer on top of another. There is no set number of layers that need to be used. This decision is up to you. However, too many or too few layers can cause problems. You can also change your mind about any layer at any time during the process. A layer can be removed and replaced by another and no damage will be done. But changing your mind and changing layers does take time. Once you have completed the whole process you can decide if you like the way it looks.

HOW TO USE THE INFORMATION YOU ALREADY KNOW

1. Think about your own thinking as you read. When you come to an idea that is unfamiliar you should be aware enough to say to yourself, "Hey, this is all new to me!"

   Comment:

2. Actively search through the information in your mind that might be related to the new idea. Often concentrated thinking turns up some information that will aid understanding.

   Comment:

3. Take advantage of the models, illustrations, and examples that textbooks often provide. Using these textual aides takes effort and independent thinking, so slow down and perhaps reread the passage several times.

   Comment:

4. Seek out additional written resources such as dictionaries, encyclopedias, books, or other materials that could provide needed explanations.

   Comment:

READING IS REASONING

Write brief descriptions for each of the following terms in the space provided.

1. Interpret

2. Infer

3. Evaluate

4. Draw conclusions

5. Make judgments

6. Understand relationships

7. Translate

8. Analyze

9. Synthesize

10. Apply

11. Recall

12. Deduce

13. Induce

14. Understand

15. Imagine

INTERPRETIVE READING

Beat! Beat! Drums!

Beat! beat! drums!—blow! bugles! blow!
Through the windows—through doors—burst like a ruthless force,
Into the solemn church, and scatter the congregation,
Into the school where the scholar is studying;
Leave not the bridegroom quiet—no happiness must he have now
    with his bride,
Nor the peaceful farmer any peace, ploughing his field or gathering
    his grain,
So fierce you whirr and pound you drums—so shrill you bugles blow.

Beat! beat! drums!—blow! bugles! blow!
Over the traffic of cities—over the rumble of wheels in the streets;
Are beds prepared for sleepers at night in the houses? no sleepers
    must sleep in those beds,
No bargainers' bargains by day—no brokers or speculators—would
    they continue?
Would the talkers be talking? Would the singer attempt to sing?
Would the lawyers rise in the court to state his case before the
    judge?
Then rattle quicker, heavier drums—you bugles wilder blow.

Beat! beat! drums!—blow! bugles! blow!
Make no parley—stop for no expostulation,
Mind not the timid—mind not the weeper or prayer,
Mind not the old man beseeching the young man,
Let not the child's voice be heard, nor the mother's entreaties,
Make even the trestles to shake the dead where they lie awaiting the
    hearses,
So strong you thump O terrible drums—so loud you bugles blow.

From *Drum-Taps* by Walt Whitman.

IMAGINATIVE READING

The Charge of the Light Brigade

Half a league, half a league,
Half a league onward
All in the valley of Death
　　Rode the six hundred.
"Forward the Light Brigade!
Charge for the guns!" he said.
Into the valley of Death
　　Rode the six hundred.

"Forward, the Light Brigade!"
Was there a man dismayed?
Not though the soldier knew
　　Some one had blundered.
Theirs not to make reply,
Theirs not to reason why,
Theirs but to do and die.
Into the valley of Death
　　Rode the six hundred.

Cannon to right of them,
Cannon to left of them,
Cannon in front of them
　　Volleyed and thundered;
Stormed at with shot and shell,
Boldly they rode and well.
Into the jaws of Death,
Into the mouth of Hell
　　Rode the six hundred.

Flashed all their sabres bare,
Flashed as they turned in air
Sabring the gunners there,
Charging an army, while
　　All the world wondered.

By Alfred Tennyson.

Plunged in the battery-smoke
Right through the line they broke;
Cossack and Russian
Reeled from the sabre-stroke
   Shattered and sundered
Then they rode back, but not,
   Not the six hundred.

Cannon to right of them,
Cannon to left of them,
Cannon behind them
   Volleyed and thundered;
Stormed at with shot and shell,
While horse and hero fell,
They that had fought so well
Came through the jaws of Death.

Back from the mouth of hell,
All that was left of them,
   Left of six hundred.

When can their glory fade?
Oh, the wild charge they made!
   All the world wondered.
Honor the charge they made!
Honor the Light Brigade,
   Noble six hundred!

BACKGROUND INFORMATION

The *Charge of the Light Brigade* describes an attack made by a group of about 600 British cavalry men during the Crimean War. The Crimean War was fought between Russia and the allied forces of England, France, and Turkey. The war was caused by rivalries concerning who would control the Holy Places in Jerusalem. The men in the Light Brigade made a gallant but tragically useless attack on a strong Russian position. Less than a third of the men survived. The stupidity and personal rivalry of two high-ranking British officers were perhaps the chief causes of the tragedy.

CONTENT AREA COMPREHENSION STRATEGIES—CHEMISTRY

According to the atomic theory, matter is composed of minute particles called *atoms*. Substances may be divided into two classes. Substances composed of only one kind of atom are called elements. Examples are: sulfur, oxygen, hydrogen, nitrogen, copper, gold, and chlorine. If the particles of a substance are composed of more than one kind of atom, the substance is called a compound. The atoms in the particles of compounds are always bound together in definite ratios. Chemistry is a study of substances. The composition of the particles in a compound may be determined by a process called chemical analysis. Chemistry is somtimes defined as the science of substances and of the processes by which substances may be transformed into still other substances. Homogeneous materials which always have the same composition are called substances.*

Briefly explain the concept to be learned from this passage:

_____

_____

_____

_____

Refer to Reproduction Page 41 "Reading Is Reasoning." Select the terms from this list that you think best describe the reading thinking strategies most helpful to you as you attempt to learn the concepts presented in the passage above.

_____

_____

_____

_____

*From Robert C. Smoat, Jack Price, and Richard Barrett, *Chemistry a Modern Course.* (Columbus, Ohio: Charles E. Merrill Publishing Co., 1971) p. 43.

CONTENT AREA COMPREHENSION STRATEGIES—BIOLOGY

Fruits and Seeds

What would happen if seeds just fell to the ground and grew right next to the parent plant? All those seedlings would soon be competing with each other and the parent for sun, water, and minerals. Not many would survive to maturity.

Instead, many seeds are scattered some distance away from the plant that produced them. This is called seed dispersal. There are many means of scattering seeds. In some plants, dispersal is mechanical. In others, the dispersal is helped by agents like wind, water, or birds.

Mechanical dispersal happens in pods like the bean and pea. The pods often twist as they ripen and dry out. Eventually the strain makes them burst open, with enough force to throw the seeds some distance. When the fruits of the garden balsam, or touch-me-not, are ripe, they open at the slightest touch. They curl up violently. The seeds are often thrown several feet.*

Briefly explain the concept to be learned from this passage:

_____

_____

_____

_____

Refer to Reproduction Page 41 "Reading Is Reasoning." Select the terms from this list that you think best describe the reading thinking strategies most helpful to you as you attempt to learn the concepts presented in the passage above.

_____

_____

_____

_____

---

*From James H. Otto and Albert Toole, *Modern Biology*. (New York: Holt, Rinehart, and Winston, Publishers, 1977), P. 328.

CONTENT AREA COMPREHENSION STRATEGIES—SOCIAL STUDIES

The Caste System

No other people in the world have developed anything like the caste system of India. It began in northern India when the invading Aryans laid down rules to prevent intermarriage between themselves and the peoples they had conquered. By the beginning of the Epic Age, four distinct classes had emerged in Indian society: (1) at the top were the rulers and warriors, called Kshatriyas (Kshaht rih yuz). (2) Next came the priests, scholars, and wise men, called Brahmans. During the Epic Age, the Brahmans and the Kshatriyas changed positions, with the Brahmans becoming first. (3) Next came the merchants, traders, and owners of small farms, called Vaisyas (Vy syuz). (4) At the foot of the ladder were the Sudras, who were peasants bound to work the fields of large landowners.

A fifth group of people in Indian society was not even on the ladder. These people were the pariahs (puh ry uz). They were also called "untouchables," because it was thought that merely to touch them would defile other people; indeed, it was believed that even their shadows would defile a Brahman. Many of the conquered peoples were included among the pariahs.

As time passed, the original four groups were subdivided many times into the smaller groups called castes, and the caste system emerged. As society became more complex and new occupations were created, castes themselves were subdivided and new castes appeared.

Eventually there developed some 3,000 hereditary castes, each with its own fixed social position and rules about eating, marriage, labor, and worship. For example, a person could not eat or drink with someone of lower caste, nor could he render any service to a person of lower caste. He could work only at those occupations recognized for his caste. He could not marry outside his caste. A person who violated any of the rules could become an untouchable, or "outcaste."*

Briefly explain the concept to be learned from this passage:

_____

_____

_____

_____

Refer to Reproduction Page 41 "Reading Is Reasoning." Select the terms from this list that you think best describe the reading thinking strategies most helpful to you as you attempt to learn the concepts presented in the passage above.

_____

_____

_____

---

*From *Men and Nations*, Second Edition by Anatole G. Mazour and John M. Peoples, copyright © 1968 by Harcourt Brace Jovanovich, Inc. Reprinted by permission of the publisher.

CRITICAL EVALUATION

Some Bones of Contention

THE FIRST CALIFORNIANS ARE CHALLENGING ARCHAEOLOGISTS

In a meadow near Eureka, Calif., on the state's rocky northern coast, 50 Yurok Indians gathered for an unusual ritual. After three younger members of the tribe hollowed out a bit of earth, a Yurok leader reverentially placed seven bags in the hole. Ella Norris, 83, the tribe's oldest member, moved forward. Raising her eyes toward the sky, she said a prayer in English and in the language of her forebears: "We are sorrowful for the sacrilegious actions of the past. May these remains lie peacefully at rest forever."

The ceremony took place at Patrick's Point State Park, and for the Yuroks, a small tribe of California Indians, it was an especially important rite. After years of anguished protest, they had finally recovered the bones of their ancestors, plundered by scientists and amateur collectors, and reburied them in sacred soil. But for many California scientists, especially archaeologists and anthropologists, the ceremony had a different meaning: it was the latest episode in a continuing battle over the right of researchers to study America's distant past.

The reburial was the second staged by California's Indians, and may soon be followed by others because of a controversial state decision in September. Bowing to strong pressure from an Indian heritage group led by William Pink, 31, the state parks and recreation department agreed to allow the tribes to reclaim bones and artifacts from its collection in Sacramento. Curator Francis Riddell was in despair. "We're giving back what I spent 25 years excavating and preserving." The Yuroks reburied their bones in an unmarked plot to guard against future looters. The field at Patrick's Point, though it now belongs to the state, is part of an ancient burial ground that was long a favorite target for hunters of Indian relics. Says Yurok Tribal Chairman Joy Sundberg, 49: "White people came through this area in the 1920s and '30s and took everything Indian they could get their hands on. Every college, every souvenir hunter wanted Indian artifacts. Back then there was no way to stop them. Now we can at least try to protect our ancestors."

For archaeologists, who are often accused of grave robbing, the Indian war cries should come as no surprise. Only a few months ago, militant Orthodox Jews in Israel clashed with police during protests against excavations in an area of Old Jerusalem considered sacred ground, a medieval Hebrew cemetery. A year before his death, Egyptian President Anwar Sadat ordered Cairo's collection of mummies closed to the public, explaining that they were not merely objects of scientific or public curiosity but human remains and thus deserving of respect.

The complaints of American Indians have special poignancy. The culture of these conquered people was long regarded as inferior. When 19th century scientists first began to unearth the huge, artfully built prehistoric mounds found throughout the Midwest, they refused to believe that America's surviving Indians were the descendants of people who had such engineering skill. Some of this scientific racism still torments the Indian psyche. Walter Lara, 47, a leader in the Yuroks' fight for the return of the bones, says, "We're not property, and neither are our ancestors. Archaeologists don't dig up George Washington's body and put it on a shelf. But they do have the skull of one of our leaders, Captain Jack, sitting in a glass case in the Smithsonian."*

For their part, scientists fear that the action in Sacramento is only the first step in a systematic assault against other private and public Indian collections. Many also perceive an antiscientific bias in the Indians' campaign and a broader threat to all free inquiry. U.C.L.A. Archaeologist Clement Meighan, who is the chairman of a recently formed committee seeking to overturn the state's decision in the courts, even invokes the image of China's Cultural Revolution, during which centers of learning were shut down and scholars exiled to the countryside to do menial labor. Says Meighan: "Since many of these bones are over 2,000 years old, it's hard to imagine how any Indian in California can trace lineal descent [from them]."

Other archaeologists take a more sympathetic view of the Indians' aroused racial pride. Indeed, some are making a special effort to cooperate with Indian leaders. Under an agreement with the Sioux tribal council, for example, archaeologists have pledged to return after two years of study any bones removed from the newly discovered site of a massacre that took place at Crow Creek, S. Dak., 600 years ago. California's directive, though, contains no provision for negotiation or compromise: the Indians will be able to reclaim and rebury any bones and burial goods in the state collection.

Unfortunately, much of this archaeological treasure—371 skeletal remains and more than 100,000 artifacts, including jewelry, tools and musical instruments—has barely been studied, especially not with the latest analytical tools for dating, identifying and interpreting ancient fragments. It is hard not to wonder what secrets remain in this rich legacy left by America's first settlers. Curator Riddell hardly seems to be exaggerating when he warns: "In reburying this collection, we are unwittingly assisting the Indians in destroying their past." —By Frederick Golden. Reported by Alessandra Stanley/ Patrick's Point

---

*Captain Jack led a small group of Modoc Indians in Northern California who held off the U.S. Army for six months in 1873. After he shot a general, he was hanged and his head was shipped East for scientific analysis but never put on display. The Smithsonian has now agreed to return it to the Indians.

DETERMINING THE MAIN IDEAS OF PARAGRAPHS IN A NEWS MAGAZINE ARTICLE

Bloodsuckers from France

"If there's anything in the world I hate, it's leeches—filthy little devils!" Humphrey Bogart growled in *The African Queen*. He had just climbed out of a river, covered with the little suckers. Doctors tend to be less squeamish. But even for them leeches have long been associated with archaic medical practices, like bloodletting to cure everything from gout to mental illness. Lately, however, the unlovable little creatures have been having a minor revival. At New York's Montefiore Hospital and Medical Center doctors are using them effectively to help save reattached fingers.

Critical to the success of any replant surgery on a severed part is the restoration of blood flow through the injured tissue by reconnecting arteries and veins. Rejoining arteries is surgically difficult. Repairing much narrower and thinner-walled veins is often impossible. After surgery, fresh blood flows into the reattached part, but deoxygenated blood may not be able to flow away through the veins. Result: swelling, pain and sometimes loss of the part. Says Microsurgeon Berish Strauch: "You may spend many hours salvaging a part only to have it die three, four or five days later."

One rough and ready way to get rid of excess blood is to stick the skin with pins to make it bleed, but that has to be done repeatedly and causes damage to the tissue. Enter the leech. Surgeons at Montefiore got the idea from visiting French colleagues who have been pressing the tiny bloodletters into medical service for years. Placed on the reattached digit, a leech happily punctures the skin and drains off accumulated blood. A 1-in.-long leech can take in 6cc to 10cc of blood during a single 20-min. repast, so there are few punctures in the patient's skin. When the leech is full, it simply drops off. Blood continues to ooze from the skin for a few hours more because of a potent anticloting chemical that leeches produce. Relieving blood congestion gives the damaged blood vessels time to grow and establish a new circuit.

So far, the New York doctors have employed leeches imported from France, at $3 a leech, on eight patients with good results. Says Strauch: "It's as if the leeches were designed for the use to which we've put them." As for patient reaction, Strauch says: "People are a little concerned when we first propose leeches, but when we explain they usually go along. And once they see the reattached part becoming pink and healthy looking, they think it's a pretty good idea.

DETERMINING THE MAIN IDEAS OF PARAGRAPHS IN A NEWS MAGAZINE ARTICLE

Bloodsuckers from France

"If there's anything in the world I hate, it's leeches—filthy little devils!" Humphrey Bogart growled in *The African Queen*. He had just climbed out of a river, covered with the little suckers. Doctors tend to be less squeamish. But even for them leeches have long been associated with archaic medical practices, like bloodletting to cure everything from gout to mental illness. Lately, however, the unlovable little creatures have been having a minor revival. At New York's Montefiore Hospital and Medical Center doctors are using them effectively to help save reattached fingers.

Critical to the success of any replant surgery on a severed part is the restoration of blood flow through the injured tissue by reconnecting arteries and veins. Rejoining arteries is surgically difficult. Repairing much narrower and thinner-walled veins is often impossible. After surgery, fresh blood flows into the reattached part, but deoxygenated blood may not be able to flow away through the veins. Result: swelling, pain and sometimes loss of the part. Says Microsurgeon Berish Strauch: "You may spend many hours salvaging a part only to have it die three, four or five days later."

1.

Introductory Remarks

These introductory sentences indicate that the article is going to be about bloodsuckers. They also arouse the reader's interest and set a somewhat humorous tone for the article.

Main Idea Statement

Doctors at a New York hospital are using bloodsuckers to save reattached fingers.

2.

Main Idea Statement

Blood flow must be restored if a reattached finger is to be replanted successfully.

Supporting Ideas

1. *Rejoining arteries is difficult.*
2. *Rejoining veins is almost impossible because they are narrower and thinner-walled.*
3. *After surgery blood may flow to the finger through the arteries but may not be able to flow away through the veins. The results may be pain and the loss of the part.*

One rough and ready way to get rid of excess blood is to stick the skin with pins to make it bleed, but that has to be done repeatedly and causes damage to the tissue. Enter the leech. Surgeons at Montefiore got the idea from visiting French colleagues who have been pressing the tiny blood-letters into medical service for years. [Placed on the reattached digit, a leech happily punctures the skin and drains off accumulated blood.] A 1-in.-long leech can take in 6cc to 10cc of blood during a single 20-min. repast, so there are few punctures in the patient's skin. When the leech is full, it simply drops off. Blood continues to ooze from the skin for a few hours more because of a potent anti-clotting chemical that leeches produce. Relieving blood congestion gives the damaged blood vessels time to grow and establish a new circuit.

So far, the New York doctors have employed leeches imported from France, at $3 a leech, on eight patients with good results. Says Strauch: "It's as if the leeches were designed for the use to which we've put them." As for patient reaction, Strauch says: "People are a little concerned when we first propose leeches, but when we explain they usually go along. And once they see the reattached part becoming pink and healthy looking, they think it's a pretty good idea.

3.
Main Idea Statement (see bracketed text)

This sentence partially states the main idea of the paragraph. A complete statement of the main idea would be something to the effect that New York surgeons learned from French doctors that bloodsuckers could help save reattached fingers because they can effectively remove accumulated blood.

Supporting Ideas

1. *Leeches remove 6 cc to 10 cc of blood in 20 minutes.*
2. *After the leech drops off, blood oozes for several more hours.*
3. *Leeches are more effective than pricking the finger with pins because they remove more blood for a longer period of time with fewer punctures of the skin.*

4.
Main Idea Statement

1. *Leeches have been used effectively with eight patients.*
2. *Once patients see that leeches are effective they react positively to the idea.*

DETERMINING THE MAIN IDEAS OF PARAGRAPHS IN A PHYSICS TEXT

2.3 What Does Gravity Do?

Gravity cannot be seen or heard. So if you are to learn what it is, you must study what it *does*. That is, you must study the effect it has on objects you can see and measure. What effect of gravity can you observe? What effect of gravity have you been observing all along as you worked your way through this chapter?

Lay your pencil on the desk and flick it with your finger. What do you observe? If you had not pushed your pencil, would it have moved? Use your finger to pull your pencil toward you. Both the push and the pull of your finger set the pencil in motion. A push or a pull is called a *force*. Whenever a force is applied to an object, the object moves; unless, of course, there is some other force being applied to keep it from moving. Look at the situation the other way around. If something is set in motion, a force must have been applied to start it moving.

Hold your pencil an inch above the desk. Now release it. There was motion by the pencil; therefore a force must have been applied to it. At the beginning of the chapter you saw that the reason given for the motion of a falling object toward the earth was gravity. The effect of gravity on an object released above the earth's surface is motion. Therefore, an object under the influence of gravity experiences a force. This force is called the *force due to gravity* or the *gravitational force*. Force is usually represented by the letter *F*. To distinguish the force of gravity from other forces we represent it by an *F* or with a subscript *g*, or F_g.

The force of gravity is a pull between the earth and the falling object. Whenever an object is released above the earth's surface the object moves toward the earth. This has led to the generalization that gravity is an *attraction*. You have probably seen two magnets that attract. Magnets also can repel each other. But no one has ever seen gravity repel an object. So the gravitational force is considered to be a force of attraction only and will be so considered until somebody observes gravitational repulsion.

Now you can answer the question: What does gravity do? The answer is that gravity attracts with a force—the force due to gravity. So here is another observation about gravity that may be of some use to you in your continuing investigation of how objects fall.

From John W. Renner and Harry Packard: *Investigations in Physics,* p. 30. Copyright © 1974 by Houghton Mifflin Company. Used by permission.

DETERMINING THE MAIN IDEAS OF PARAGRAPHS IN A PHYSICS TEXT

2.3 What Does Gravity Do?

Gravity cannot be seen or heard. So if you are to learn what it is, you must study what it *does*. That is, you must study the effect it has on objects you can see and measure. What effect of gravity can you observe? What effect of gravity have you been observing all along as you worked your way through this chapter?

Main Idea Statement

The main idea is stated in these three sentences and could be paraphrased as follows: Since gravity cannot be seen or heard, only its effect can be studied.

Step-by-step listing of ideas leading to a conclusion which is the main idea.

Lay your pencil on the desk and flick it with your finger. What do you observe? If you had not pushed your pencil, would it have moved? Use your finger to pull your pencil toward you. Both the push and the pull of your finger set the pencil in motion. A push or a pull is called a *force*. Whenever a force is applied to an object, the object moves; unless, of course, there is some other force being applied to keep it from moving. Look at the situation the other way around. If something is set in motion, a force must have been applied to start it moving.

Main Idea Statement

Hold your pencil an inch above the desk. Now release it. There was motion by the pencil; therefore a force must have been applied to it. At the beginning of the chapter you saw that

Step-by-step listing of ideas leading to a conclusion which is the main idea.

From John W. Renner and Harry Packard: *Investigations in Physics,* p. 30. Copyright © 1974 by Houghton Mifflin Company. Used by permission.

Copyright © 1985 by Allyn and Bacon, Inc. Reproduction of this material is restricted to use with *A Guidebook for Teaching Reading,* by Pauline L. Witte.

the reason given for the motion of a falling object toward the earth was gravity. The effect of gravity on an object released above the earth's surface is motion. Therefore, an object under the influence of gravity experiences a force. This force is called the *force due to gravity* or the *gravitational force*. Force is usually represented by the letter *F*. To distinguish the force of gravity from other forces we represent it by an *F* or with a subscript *g*, or F_g.

Main Idea Statement

Ideas that lead up to the main idea.

The force of gravity is a pull between the earth and the falling object. Whenever an object is released above the earth's surface the object moves toward the earth. This has led to the generalization that gravity is an *attraction*. You have probably seen two magnets that attract. Magnets also can repel each other. But no one has ever seen gravity repel an object. So the gravitational force is considered to be a force of attraction only and will be so considered until somebody observes gravitational repulsion.

Main Idea Statement

Additional information about gravity as a force of attraction.

Now you can answer the question: What does gravity do? The answer is that gravity attracts with a force—the force due to gravity. So here is another observation about gravity that may be of some use to you in your continuing investigation of how objects fall.

Summary Statement

The question in the heading is repeated. The answer is the main idea of the entire selection.

DETERMINING THE MAIN IDEAS OF PARAGRAPHS IN A SOCIAL STUDIES TEXT

The German Democratic Republic

Although the German Democratic Republic (East Germany) is smaller in size and in population than the German Federal Republic (West Germany), it includes the chief area from which prewar Germany supplied itself with food. This was bound to create difficulties for West Germany after the division of Germany. About 17 million people live in East Germany.

The economy of East Germany is not as industrial, or as strong, as that of West Germany. The contrast is due chiefly to the Soviet policy of drawing from the satellites the things needed in the Soviet Union. From East Germany, the Soviets have taken machinery and equipment. They have demanded large quotas from the farms and factories. In addition, the area is not rich in minerals.

Berlin, once the chief center of government, culture, and commerce for all of Germany, has been a divided city since the end of World War II. Partially cut off from the area it used to serve, East Berlin offers fewer job opportunities than it did before the war.

For a time, East Germans crossed the line daily to jobs in West Germany. Many of them took the opportunity to stay in West Germany. They sought a new and freer life. To put a halt to this steady decrease in population, the East German government built a wall in Berlin separating the two Germanies. Since then, some Germans have gone to great lengths to reach the freedom of West Germany. Tunnels dug inch by inch, over long periods of time, have burrowed under buildings and across the border between the two parts of divided Germany. Through these, some people have fled to the West. One East German family even fled to the West in a balloon they had built.

The chief agricultural areas of East Germany are on the fertile loess lands between Magdeburg and Leipzig, and on the Baltic coastal area east of Lubeck (lu'bek). (See map, p. 329.) Before World War II, crop yields here, even on poor soils, were very high. The farmers used a large amount of fertilizer and could draw on the advice of skilled farm experts.

In the northern area, the chief crops are rye and potatoes. In the central area around Leipzig, the farms produce rye, oats, wheat, barley, and sugar beets. But the greater part of East Germany, like West Germany, is not suitable for farming. Either the soil is too sandy, the slopes too steep, or the summers too cool.

The contrast between the standards of living of the people in East Germany and West Germany is striking. Workers' riots in East Germany in 1953 were quickly put down by Soviet tanks and troops. When the economic condition of the country continued to be depressed, the Soviet Union tried to revive the economy. East Germany joined the trade agreement and the Warsaw Pact. In recent years, East Germany has tried to increase exports to the West and decrease its dependence on the Soviet Union. The economy grew at a much faster rate in the 1960's and throughout the 1970's.

DETERMINING THE MAIN IDEAS OF PARAGRAPHS IN A SOCIAL STUDIES TEXT

PARAGRAPH 1

Main Idea: *East Germany is smaller in size and population than West Germany but it supplied most of the food before World War II. This has caused problems for West Germany now that the country is divided.*

Detail: *17 million people live in East Germany.*

PARAGRAPH 2

Main Idea: *"The economy of East Germany is not as industrial, or as strong, as that of West Germany."*

Supporting Ideas: 1. *The main reason for the poor economy is that the Soviets have taken many things such as machinery and large farm quotas from East Germany.*
2. *Another reason is that East Germany has few mineral resources.*

PARAGRAPH 3

Main Idea: *Berlin is now a divided city.*

Supporting Ideas: 1. *Berlin was once the center of government, commerce, and culture for Germany.*
2. *Because it is now divided there are fewer job opportunities.*

PARAGRAPH 4

_____

_____

_____

_____

_____

_____

PARAGRAPH 5

_____

_____

_____

_____

_____

PARAGRAPH 6

_____

_____

_____

_____

_____

PARAGRAPH 7

_____

_____

_____

_____

_____

A WRITING APPROACH TO UNDERSTANDING THE CONCEPT OF MAIN IDEA

1. List five "first time" experiences you have had.

   1. _____

   2. _____

   3. _____

   4. _____

   5. _____

2. Circle the number of the experience that would be most interesting to write a paragraph about.

3. Write the topic sentence for the paragraph.

   _____

   _____

4. List the supporting ideas you will use.

   _____

   _____

   _____

   _____

   _____

5. Write the paragraph on a separate sheet of paper.

WRITING PARAPHRASES

Write a paraphrase for each of the following:

1. The increased number of thumbers on the highway was a real distraction to most drivers.

2. The word photosynthesis defines itself because "photo" refers to light while "synthesis" means the building of a complex substance from simpler substances.

3. To sell successfully and to feel happy while working, you must really know what you are selling.

4. The Phoenicians were imitators and improvers rather than creators.

5. Parity is the price relationship between prices received and prices paid out by farmers. This system of parity was established by Congress in the 1930s so that there would be a fair relationship between the prices which farmers paid out for labor, interest, supplies, and equipment and the price they received for products such as cotton, corn, or milk. Some products, such as cattle, hogs, chickens, and many fruits and vegetables, are not covered by price-support programs.

PARAPHRASE PRACTICE

Testing

EXAMS BARELY MAKE PASSING GRADE, SCIENCE PANEL SAYS

By Christopher Connell
The Associated Press

Washington—A National Academy of Sciences panel is urging undergraduate colleges to re-examine their mandatory use of admissions tests taken by nearly 2 million high school students each year.

A report released recently by the academy's Committee on Ability Testing concluded most colleges are not highly selective, so students who apply to them should not have to incur the "unneccessary expense and inconvenience" of taking the Scholastic Aptitude Test or the American College Test.

"There is also danger that students with poor or mediocre test scores may be discouraged from applying even to non-selective institutions in the mistaken belief that their chances of being admitted are small," the panel said.

The 19-member committee was established by the academy's national research council to review the field of testing in America, from schools to jobs.

In general, the 241-page report, which capped three years of study, provided a cautious vote of confidence in testing. But it warned against putting too much stock in test scores or using them as the sole means of selection for a job or college seat.

"Tests can only measure ability as it exists at the moment of testing," the report said, adding, "No important decision about an individual's educational future should be based on a single test score considered in isolation."

The report downplayed "intelligence" tests, saying the label can be misleading "insofar as it encourages misunderstandings . . . or false notions about intelligence—that it is a tangible and well-defined entity like a heart."

It said it is particularly important not to use a numerical cutoff score in making decisions about mental retardation or placement in special education programs.

On the question of minorities, the report said, "the evidence indicates that predictions made from test scores are as accurate for black applicants as for majority applicants . . ."

There is only scanty evidence available on how other minority groups test, the report said.

But it said that where "many applicants (are) capable of succeeding, admissions decisions should be based on social and educational values broader than a comparison of predicted grade averages."

Although tests came under criticism in the 1970s as elitist and unfair to minorities, they originally took hold in this country "as a liberating tool," the report said.

By identifying talent and intellectual ability wherever it may exist in society, tests would, it was felt, act as a democratizing force," the report said.

The committee, composed of professors and testing experts, was chaired by Yale psychology professor Wendell R. Garner.

The study was financed by the Carnegie Corp., the National Institute of Education, the Office of Personnel Management, the National Institute of Mental Health and the Ittleson Foundation.

The *Capital Times*, February 16, 1982. Used by Permission of the Associated Press.

PARAPHRASE PRACTICE

PARAGRAPH 1
1. What word could be used instead of "mandatory"?

PARAGRAPH 2
2. What word or words could be used instead of "are not highly selective?"

PARAGRAPH 3
3. Rewrite this paragraph using two sentences.

PARAGRAPH 6
4. Rewrite this paragraph using one sentence.

PARAGRAPH 7
5. Paraphrase this entire paragraph.

PARAGRAPHS 9, 10, 11, and 12
6. These paragraphs could be combined to convey one main idea. Write this idea in the space below.

STUDY SKILLS PROJECT

1. *Courses for the current marking period*   *Grades you received*

_____   _____

_____   _____

_____   _____

_____   _____

_____   _____

_____   _____

2. Star the course you have selected for this study skills project.

3. What grade would you like to receive in this course for the next marking period? _____

4. Reading course requirements for this project:
   a. A completed log for _____ from _____ to
      (name of course)   (date project begins)

   _____
   (date due)

   b. Your notes, outlines, maps, and other materials that demonstrate how you applied specific study strategies and skills.

Name _____

Date _____

APPLYING STUDY SKILLS

Date _____

Study Technique _____

Text or Source of
Material _____

Chapter or Article
Title _____

Issue Date/Page No. _____

SAMPLE LOG — AMERICAN HISTORY

Date: 8/10/80

Class Activity: Teacher talked about the exploration of North America.

Comment: I understand what the teacher was saying but my notes are still disorganized.

Assignment: Read pp. 56–87 for tomorrow

Date: 8/11/80

Class Activity: Teacher discussed the French explorers in North America.

Comment: I didn't answer any of the questions because I forgot to read the assignment.

Assignment: Same as yesterday

Comment: I read it but I didn't get much out of it.

COURSE ANALYSIS FORM

Subject _____

Analyzing the Course	Yes	No
1. Do you like this subject?		
2. Do you have a good background in this subject?		
3. Did you take this course because you really wanted to learn more about this subject?		
4. If you have taken a similar course before, did you receive an acceptable grade?		
5. Does the teacher present the material in a way that is understandable to you?		
6. Do you think that you will be able to receive an acceptable grade in this course?		

Total number of yeses

_____

TEXTBOOK ANALYSIS FORM

Select a section that is at least several paragraphs long from the beginning of the text. Read this section carefully and then answer the following questions:

1. How many words and/or terms are there in this section that you don't know or are uncertain about? _____

2. Reread the first paragraph in the section. Does it have a clearly expressed main idea? _____ If so, what is it? _____

   _____

   _____

3. Write the main (most important) idea expressed in the entire section

   _____

   _____

4. Did this section have headings and subheadings? _____
   Were you able to use these headings and subheadings to help you determine the main ideas? _____

5. Were the above questions difficult for you to answer? _____

6. Are you able to learn easily from this book? _____

PREVIEWING A CHAPTER

After previewing a chapter from a content area text, write responses to the following:

1. What is the main topic of the chapter?

2. List two subtopics discussed in the chapter.

    A.

    B.

3. Write five facts you know or thoughts you have about the main topic of the chapter. (These should be your own ideas, not just a listing of topics you remember from previewing the chapter.)

    A.

    B.

    C.

    D.

    E.

4. List two study aids included in this chapter and explain how you would use each of them.

    A.

    B.

TYPES OF TESTS

Teacher-made Tests   *Tests that are written by the teacher*
These tests usually test material presented in lectures and class discussions, as well as reading assignments. When studying for teacher-made tests, students ought to focus on ideas the teacher stressed.

Textbook Tests   *Tests developed by textbook authors*
These tests reflect the organization of ideas presented in the text. Often they have a multiple choice or fill in the blank format. Questions may reflect factual recall or interpretive thinking.

Fill in the Blank   *Student answers a question or completes a sentence with a one- or two-word response.*
These test questions usually require the recall of facts or details.

Multiple Choice   *Students select best answer from a number of choices*
Multiple choice questions may test details:

Example: The season in which this story takes place is
a. winter
b. summer
c. spring

Or multiple choice questions may require main idea recall or interpretive thinking:

Example: The best title for this story would be
a. *America Makes Friends*
b. *Touring the World*
c. *People are Funny*

True or False   *Student indicates whether a statement is true or false, correct or incorrect*
These questions may require recall of facts and details but often interpretive thinking also is involved in answering them.

Short Answers   *Students write a complete sentence to answer a question*
Sentence completion questions can test literal recall as well as interpretive thinking. Even when testing recall, these questions require the students to kow the information well enough to put it in their own words.

Essay   *Student writes a paragraph or more to answer a question*
Essay tests require the student to demonstrate an understanding of both the general concepts presented and the ideas that support these concepts. The ability to summarize ideas and show how ideas are related is important when writing responses for essay tests.

Course	*Type of Test Usually Given*
_____	_____
_____	_____
_____	_____
_____	_____
_____	_____
_____	_____
_____	_____

PREVIEWING ARTICLES WITHOUT HEADINGS

1. Read and ponder the title. Sometimes the author sets the mood or tone of the article with the title. Is the title straightforward? Does it represent an attempt to be humorous or sarcastic? Does it raise a question in the reader's mind? After thinking about the title, study any available graphic aids.

2. Read the first two paragraphs, searching for an explanation of the subject, the author's purposes, or any clues to how the ideas are organized. Sometimes the initial paragraph is written just to interest the reader; if so, read it quickly and look for a clear statement of purpose in the second paragraph.

3. Skim through the article. Are there any words, dates, or figures that seem to "jump out?" If there are, stop and read them.

4. When skimming, note any organizational or structural clue words such as *first, second, in addition,* or *finally.* Note terms the author uses more than once.

5. Read the final paragraph, searching for a summary of the author's thoughts. The author may, in one paragraph, restate the main ideas and draw a final conclusion based on these ideas. A paragraph such as this can provide a focus for organizing and remembering the ideas in the article.

APPLYING PREVIEWING SKILLS

Another Sort of Smoke

MARIJUANA: "JUSTIFIES SERIOUS NATIONAL CONCERN"

More than 25 million Americans spent some $24 billion in 1980 for the illegal privilege of regularly smoking marijuana. Another 25 million have tried the drug at least once, making it the most widely used illegal substance in the country. A major reason: the tenacious belief among marijuana smokers that the occasional joint does little, if any, harm. Last week the Institute of Medicine of the National Academy of Sciences issued a long-awaited, 188-page report on the effects of marijuana. Its main finding: widespread use of the drug "justifies serious national concern." But after 15 months of study, the academy concluded that there is, as yet, insufficient research to decide whether or not marijuana causes irreversible long-term health damage. The 22-member study committee, chaired by Arnold Relman, editor of the *New England Journal of Medicine*, analyzed 1,000 scientific studies of the health effects associated with marijuana and called for further research. Among its conclusions:

Behavioral Effects. The principal active element in marijuana, delta-9-tetrahydrocannabinol (THC), like alcohol, impairs motor coordination, the ability to follow a moving object and to detect a flash of light. Since these functions are necessary for safe driving, the report notes, their impairment "may suggest a substantial risk." The effects may last four to eight hours after the time the user feels a "high," unlike alcohol, which is more quickly metabolized. Marijuana hampers short-term memory, slows learning and produces distortions of judgment, including reactions of panic and confusion. Consequently, there is special concern since much of the heavy use of marijuana "takes place within the school setting." Says Charles O'Brien, a professor of psychiatry at the University of Pennsylvania School of Medicine and a member of the committee: "There's no way a student's brain can function normally when he uses marijuana daily. It's a definite risk, but there's no way to evaluate that risk in a quantitative way." Mild withdrawal symptoms that sometimes occur among heavy users indicate the drug can lead to physical dependence, but the committee stressed that so far there is no evidence that marijuana actually causes addiction.

Heart and Lung Damage. Like heavy cigarette smoking, chronic heavy marijuana use may lead to cancer of the respiratory tract and seriously impair the lungs. It can raise the heart rate and blood pressure, as does stress. Such effects are serious for people who suffer from hypertension, cerebrovascular disease and coronary atherosclerosis (fatty deposits in the blood vessels of the heart.)

Impairment of Reproductive and Immune Systems. Regular marijuana use cuts down on the number and activity of sperm, but there is no proof of resulting loss of fertility. Studies on animals have shown a decrease in ovulation and female reproductive hormone levels. Marijuana is known to pass through the placenta, but the committee found "no evidence yet" of birth defects in human fetuses. Nor is there conclusive evidence that marijuana causes any chromosome damage or suppresses the body's ability to protect itself against infection.

The report emphasized the need for more detailed long-term study because marijuana is widely used, and its components remain in the body for long periods, accumulating at levels that may be far higher than the levels after a single dose. The study urged further research into ways THC and other marijuana derivatives can be of greater use in treating glaucoma, asthma and the nausea and vomiting associated with chemotherapy in cancer patients. The aim: to find ways of increasing the medically beneficial uses of marijuana while diminishing its potentially harmful effects.

Medical science's uncertainty about the serious risks of marijuana has apparently been noted by at least one segment of the population. Also released last week was a University of Michigan study that revealed regular marijuana use among 17,000 high school seniors across the country has dropped from a high of 11% in 1978 to 7% last year. The most frequently cited reason: the teen-agers' concern about possible adverse effects of marijuana smoking on physical and psychological health.

APPLYING PREVIEWING SKILLS

Suggestion 1: Read and ponder the title. Study any graphic aids that appear.

The title and the one subtitle of the article on Reproduction Page 66 indicate that marijuana smoking is a serious national problem. A glance at the subheadings shows the specific problem areas discussed in the article.

Suggestion 2: Search for an explanation of the topic in the first one or two paragraphs.

The first paragraph clearly states the problem: Marijuana is widely used in the United States today and does cause health damage, although the research does not clearly show if this damage is irreversible and long-term.

Suggestion 3: Skim.

The following phrases seem to stand out:

"$24 billion spent"
"principal active element—(THC)"
"effects may last four to eight hours"
"Mild withdrawal symptoms"
"may lead to cancer of the respiratory tract."
"no evidence yet of birth defects."
"marijuana usage among high school seniors has dropped."

Suggestion 4: Look for organizational or structural clues.

The last sentence of paragraph 1 ("Among its conclusions:") indicates that the rest of the article will describe the findings of a study committee chaired by the editor of the *New England Journal of Medicine.*

Suggestion 5: Read final paragraph or paragraphs for a summary.

The first sentence in the final paragraph does provide a summary because it states that medical science is uncertain about the effects of marijuana. The rest of the paragraph, though, introduces new information about the decline in the use of marijuana among teenagers.

MEMORY AND THOUGHT

Understanding how the mind works—how human beings think, remember, solve problems, and create ideas—is one of the most fascinating and challenging goals of psychology. For simplicity's sake, psychologists treat all cognitive or mental activities—from memorizing lists of numbers to writing poems and inventing new technologies—as *information processing*. This involves three steps: input, central processing, and output. *Input* refers to the information people receive from their senses. *Central processing* refers to the storing (in memory) and sorting (by thought) of this information in the brain. *Output* refers to the actions that result from processing.

Psychologists know a great deal about how the senses take in information. . . . They also know a great deal about how people behave. However, exactly what happens between sensory input and behavior output remains something of a mystery. In this chapter we will focus on this mystery, describing what psychologists have learned so far about information processing.

Taking Information In

Input comes through the senses in many forms—voices, musical sounds, sweet tastes, pungent odors, colorful images, rough textures, painful stings. At any given moment a confusing array of sights, sounds, smells, and other sensations compete for your attention. If you accepted *all* these inputs, you would be completely overwhelmed. Two processes help people to narrow sensory inputs down to a manageable number: selective attention and feature extraction.

SELECTIVE ATTENTION

The ability to pick and choose among the various available inputs is called *selective attention*. For example, if you are at a large party where the music is turned up and everyone is talking, you can focus on friend's voice and ignore all other sounds. In a way, selective attention is like tuning in a specific television channel.

Unlike a television dial, however, selective attention does not completely block out the other programs or stimuli. You may be listening attentively to what a friend is saying, but at the same time you are unconsciously monitoring information that is coming in over other channels. If your name is mentioned in a conversation going on three feet away, you will notice it and tune into that input. If someone strolls by dressed in a bathing suit, snorkel, and fins, you will notice him. The "cocktail-party phenomenon," as selective attention is sometimes called, allows you to concentrate on one thing without tuning out everything else that is happening.

From *Understanding Psychology,* Second edition. Copyright © 1974, 1977 by Random House, Inc. Reprinted by permission of CRM Books, a Division of Random House, Inc.

Laboratory experiments have shown how selective attention works (Hernández-Peón).[1] For example, if people are asked to pay attention to an auditory stimulus, the brain waves that record their response to sound will get larger. While this is happening, the brain waves that record their response to what they see will get smaller because they are not paying close attention to visual stimuli. If the same people are asked to pay attention to visual stimuli, the reverse occurs. Visual brain waves increase while auditory brain waves decrease. A similar experiment showed that a certain kind of brain wave diminished but did not disappear when people were given a problem to solve or were drawn into conversation. Such experiments seem to indicate that the brain somehow evaluates the importance of the information that comes in over different channels. Top-priority information is allowed to reach the highest brain centers, whereas unimportant information is suppressed.

What makes one input more important than another? Information leading to the satisfaction of such needs as hunger and thirst has top priority. (A person who is very hungry, for example, will pay more attention to his dinner than to the dinner table chitchat.) We also give priority to inputs that are strange and novel, such as an individual who comes to a party dressed for snorkeling. A third director of attention is interest: The more interested you are in something, the more likely you are to notice it. For example, most people "tune in" when they hear their name mentioned: we're all interested in what other people have to say about us. Likewise, if you become interested in chess, you will suddenly begin to notice newspaper articles about chess, chess sets in store windows, and references to chess moves in everyday speech (for example, "stalemate"). These inputs are not new. They were there last year and the year before, but you simply weren't interested enough to notice them.

FEATURE EXTRACTION

Selective attention is only the first step in narrowing down input. The second step is to decide which aspects of the selected channel you will focus on. This process, called *feature extraction*, involves locating the outstanding characteristics of incoming information. For example, if you want to identify the make of a car, you look for distinctive features—the shape of the fenders, the proportion of height to length, and so on. For the most part, you ignore such features as color, upholstery, and tires, which tell you little about the make of the car. Similarly, when you read, you focus on the important words, skimming over such words as "the," "and," or "for example."

Being able to extract the significant features of an input helps a person to identify it and compare it to other inputs. For example, you are able to distinguish faces from one another, and at the same time see resemblances. You may notice that all the members of a family have similar noses, yet you are able to recognize each person on the basis of other features.

---

1. R. Hernández-Peón, "Reticular Mechanisms of Sensory Control," in *Sensory Communication,* ed. W. A. Rosenblith (New York: Wiley, 1961), pp. 497–520.

Obviously, feature extraction depends to some extent on experience—on knowing what to look for. This is especially true where fine distinctions must be made. It takes considerable expertise to distinguish an original Rembrandt from a skillful forgery. Most of us cannot say what vineyard produced the wine we are drinking in what year, but a gourmet who knows what to look for can.

Like selective attention, feature extraction is an evaluative process. If you are reading a novel for pleasure, you may look for the "juicy" parts; if you're reading an historical biography to prepare for an exam, you concentrate on the facts.

Storing Information

In order to be used, the inputs that reach the brain must be registered, held onto, perhaps "filed" for future reference. We call the storage of inputs *memory*. Psychologists distinguish among three kinds of memory, each of which has a different purpose and time span. *Sensory storage* holds information for only an instant; *short-term memory* keeps it in mind for about twenty seconds; *long term memory* stores it indefinitely.

SENSORY STORAGE

The senses seem to be able to hold an input for a fraction of a second before it disappears. For example, when you watch a movie you do not notice the gaps between frames—the actions seem smooth because each frame is held in sensory storage until the next frame arrives.

Psychologists have measured the length of sensory storage by testing subjects with inputs such as that shown in Figure 3.4. [Three lines of digits and numbers appear in a square frame in this figure.] This image is flashed on a screen for one-fiftieth of a second, and immediately afterward the subject is signaled to recite one of the lines he or she has seen. The subject is usually able to report all four items on the required line if the signal is sounded within a quarter of a second after the exposure. (However, they cannot do this if the signal is delayed for a second or more.) It is therefore thought that the subject retains a brief image of the whole picture so that he or she can still read off the items in the correct row after the picture has left the screen (Sperling).[2]

The information held momentarily by the senses has not yet been narrowed down or analyzed. It is like a short-lived but highly detailed photograph or tape recording. However, by the time information gets to the next stage—short-term memory—it has been analyzed, identified, and exemplified so that it can be conveniently stored and handled for a long time.

---

2. G. Sperling, "The Information Available in Brief Visual Presentations," *Psychological Monographs*, 74 (1960), no. 11.

SHORT-TERM MEMORY

The things you have in your conscious mind at any one moment are being held in short-term memory. Short-term memory does not necessarily involve paying close attention. You have probably had the experience of listening to someone only partially and then having that person accuse you of not paying attention. You deny it, in order to prove your innocence, and you repeat to him, word for word, the last words he said. You can do this because you are holding the words in short-term memory. However, in all probability, the sense of what he was saying does not register on you until you repeat the words out loud. Repeating the words makes you pay attention to them. This is what psychologists mean by rehearsal.

Rehearsal. To keep information in short-term memory for more than a few seconds, you have to repeat it to yourself, in your mind or out loud. When you look up a telephone number, for example, you can remember the seven digits long enough to dial them if you repeat them several times. If you are distracted or make a mistake in dialing, the chances are you will have to look the number up again. It has been lost from short-term memory.

Psychologists have measured short-term memory by seeing how long a subject can retain a piece of information without rehearsals. The experimenter shows the subject or card with three letters on it, such as CPQ. However, at the same time the experimenter makes the subject think about something else in order to prevent her from rehearsing the letters. For example, she might ask the subject to start counting backward by threes from 798 as soon as she flashes the card. If the subject performs this task for only a short time, she will usually remember the letters. But if she is kept from rehearsing for more than eighteen seconds, the information is gone forever. Thus short-term memory seems to last for less than twenty seconds without rehearsal.

Chunking. Short-term memory is limited not only in its duration, but in its capacity as well. It can hold only about seven unrelated items. If, for example, someone quickly reels off a series of digits to you, you will be able to keep only about seven or eight of them in your immediate memory. Beyond that, confusion among them will set in. The same would be true if the unrelated items were a random set of words. We may not notice this limit to our capacity because we usually do not have to store so many unrelated items in our immediate memory. Either the items are related (as when we listen to someone speak) or they are rehearsed and placed in long-term memory.

The most interesting aspect of this limit, discovered by George Miller,[3] is that it involves seven items of any kind. Each item may consist of a collection of many other items, but if they are all packaged into one "chunk" then there is still only one item. Thus we can remember about seven unrelated sets of initials, such as . . . DDT or SST . . . even though we could not remember all the letters separately. This occurs because we have connected or "chunked" them together previously, so that DDT is one item, not three.

---

3. George Miller, Eugene Galanter, and Karl Pribram, *Plans and the Structure of Behavior* (New York: Holt, 1960).

One of the tricks of memorizing much information quickly is to chunk together the items as fast as they come in, by making up connections with them, so that, in effect, they become fewer.

Even with chunking, short-term memory is only a temporary device. It contains information labeled "of possible interest." If the information is worth holding onto, it must be transferred to long-term memory.

LONG-TERM MEMORY

Long-term memory involves all the processes we have been describing. Suppose a person goes to see a play. As the actors say their lines, the sounds flow through sensory storage. Selective attention screens out other sounds, and feature extraction turns sounds into words. These words accumulate in short-term memory and form meaningful phrases and sentences.

The viewer attends to the action and changing scenery in much the same way. Together, they form chunks in her memory. An hour or two later, she will have forgotten all but the most striking lines, but she has stored the meaning of the lines and actions in long-term memory. The next day, she may be able to give a scene-by-scene description of the play. Throughout this process, the least important information is dropped and only the essentials are retained. A month or two later, the woman may only remember a brief outline of the plot and perhaps a few vivid images of particularly impressive moments. In time she may not remember anything about the play. Other, more recently stored items block access to earlier memories, or may even replace them. But if she sees the play again, she will probably recognize the lines of the play and anticipate the actions. Although it has become less accessible, it is still stored in long-term memory.

THEORIES OF MEMORY

What happens in the brain when something is stored in long-term memory? This question is highly controversial. Although psychologists agree that some physiological changes must occur in the brain, they do not always know what these changes are.

One theory is that memory is due to changes in the form of protein molecules in the brain. In one experiment, a number of mice were trained to run through a maze, avoiding alleys where they would receive an electric shock. Then the mice were injected with a chemical known to disrupt protein production in the brain. Afterward the mice could no longer remember the safe way out of the maze (Flexner).[4] Recently researchers (Flood, Bennett, and Orme)[5] have been able to control the amount of "amnesia" in mice by injecting varying amounts of the chemical for certain time periods

---

4.   L. Flexner, "Dissection of Memory in Mice with Antibiotics," *Proceedings of the American Philosophical Society*, 111 (1967), pp. 343–346.
5.   J. Flood, E. Bennett, and A. Orme, "Relation of Memory Formation for Controlled Amounts of Brain Protein Synthesis," *Physiology and Behavior* 15 (1975), pp. 97–102.

after the training task. The more of the protein-blocking chemical the mice receive, the more forgetful they become. It may be that senility is related to the cessation of protein production in the brain.

Another theory focuses on chemical-electrical changes in the brain. It may be that memory develops when the characteristics of the synapses change chemically. When information is learned, some pathways in the brain are facilitated, others inhibited. To date, it is impossible to say which of these theories is closer to the truth.

To complicate matters further, memories seem to be distributed over wide areas of the brain, rather than located in particular areas. No one cell, or group of cells, can be removed to destroy a memory. Indeed, Karl Lashley[6] found that he had to destroy most of the upper part of a rat's brain to erase memory of a problem it had learned to solve. As a result, many psychologists believe that memories may be stored in the brain in multiples, so that destroying one area of the brain simply removes one copy.

All these ideas remain highly speculative. Many psychologists believe, however, that a better understanding of the processes underlying memory will be reached in the near future.

---

6. K. Lashley, *Brain Mechanisms and Intelligence* (Chicago: University of Chicago Press, 1929).

A HERITAGE OF CHANGE

Someone once said that "American History is the story of change." Perhaps more than any other people on earth, we are accustomed to constant change in our lives, in our ways of doing things. We move often. In fact, in any five year period, half of us move from one home to another. As we look around us, there is always evidence of change. Farms become homes and shopping centers. Houses are torn down to make way for apartment buildings. Old offices and stores are replaced by new skyscrapers.

Change is not new to America. While the Revolutionary War was still going on, settlers were pushing westward into Tennessee, Kentucky, and Ohio, opening up new lands, pushing back the frontier.

From wilderness to farms and cities. As the frontier pushed forward, forests were cleared for farms. Later, farms were paved over to make cities. Today herds of cattle graze where buffalo roamed. Wheat and corn grow where prairie grass waved in the wind. Indian trails have become highways, and small trading posts have grown into great cities with factories, homes, schools, and offices. Not every change has been for the better, of course. Many a stream where the Indians could catch their fill of fish is now too polluted for even the hardiest breeds of fish. And many forms of wildlife have completely disappeared from our country.

Different people and different ways. Some of the biggest changes in the history of the United States have come from the people themselves. At the time our nation won its independence, most Americans were from a few countries in northern Europe or from Africa. In the years that followed, millions of others came from southern and eastern Europe, from Asia, from Canada and Latin America. Each group made its own contributions to our culture. Today our nation is a great blend of many cultures.

Our society has changed, too. The greatest change of all was the ending of slavery. No longer can one man own another; no longer can one of us live by the sweat of another.

The status of many other groups has changed too. Women today have the right to vote. Workers have the right to organize unions. These rights seem very natural to us now. But it was not always that way. Such rights are the result of change.

From muscle power to machines. Many of the changes in our history are the result of industrialization. With it came more and more motor power and less and less animal or human power. Farming was once very slow, hard work. Hour after hour, the farmer walked behind a plow pulled by a team of horses. He could plow only about two acres a day. Now, a man riding on a tractor, with his radio for company, can easily plow 80 or more acres in a day.

From *Exploring World Regions: Western Hemisphere* by Herbert H. Gross et al. Copyright © 1975 by Follett Publishing Company. Reprinted by permission of Allyn and Bacon, Inc.

Corn pickers, combines, cotton pickers, potato-diggers, and hundreds of other machines help farmers do their work easily and quickly. Long ago a farmer could feed only one or two people besides himself. Now one American farmer, with all his machines, can feed an average of more than 45 people! Without such changes in farming, we could never feed our growing population.

From letter writing to television. When the Declaration of Independence was approved by the Continental Congress, horseback riders carried the news to distant towns. Some people did not learn about the Declaration until many days later. Today we hear news almost as soon as it happens, on television or radio. We can often watch events halfway around the globe while they are actually happening. And the voice of a distant friend is only as far away as the telephone.

These modern systems of communication have also helped to bring our nation together. Now we can share the same information, whether we live in the center of New York City, or on a lonely ranch in Wyoming. What a change from the days of the frontier!

From handmade to machine-made. One of the biggest changes has come in the way we make things. Cloth was once woven by hand, and suits and dresses sewed by hand. Workers cut trees with an ax and sawed boards by hand. Nails, paper, shoes, books, dishes, shovels, furniture, rugs, knives, clocks, wagons, and pots and pans were all handmade. Today all these items and almost everything else we use is made by machine. And because machine-made goods are usually cheaper, many families today can afford things that only the very rich could have had in the past.

Of course, changing the way things are made has changed the kind of jobs we have, too. With machines to do much of the heavy work, there is less dirty and back-breaking labor to be done. More people today produce services instead of goods. But we must not forget that the changes may not have been good for everyone. It is harder for an unskilled worker to find a job today than it was at times in the past. And many factory jobs have become boring because of the work done by machines. Just think of the difference between being a worker on an automobile assembly line, putting on one part as each car comes down the line, and being a wagonmaster who built the whole wagon from start to finish.

From hardship to comfort. The early settlers faced many hardships. They were often hungry and many starved. They had few doctors, if any, and no schools. Even young children had to work in the fields to help their families survive. And imagine what the life of a slave was like.

While many Americans still do not have easy lives, most of us are far better off than our forefathers. We have better food, better clothing, and better housing. We have more schools and more time to enjoy music, art, reading, and sports. By almost any standard, we are far more comfortable than the early citizens of our nation.

From horsepower to atomic power. When we talk about the great changes in transportation and production, we are often talking about a change in power. Long ago human and animal muscle supplied most of the power that was used. Horses pulled plows and carriages. Spinning wheels and looms were driven by human feet and hands. Water pumps were cranked by hand.

Today almost everything is powered in some way by electricity or by gasoline, diesel, or steam engines. This use of nonanimal power has helped us to produce the abundance we now have. But supplies of fuel are not unlimited. The whole world is using more oil than ever before. The use of coal is going up, too. Even atomic energy, which many think is the answer, has the problem of what to do with radioactive wastes. If we are to keep the advantages of our new machines, we must use fuel wisely. We once thought we could keep on using more and more fuel for anything we wanted. But that, too, has changed.

SELECTIVE ATTENTION

1) The ability to pick and choose among the various available inputs is called selective attention. 2) For example, if you are at a large party where the music is turned up and everyone is talking, you can focus on a friend's voice and ignore all other sounds. 3) In a way, selective attention is like tuning in a specific television channel.

4) Unlike a television dial, however, selective attention does not completely block out the other programs or stimuli. 5) You may be listening attentively to what a friend is saying, but at the same time you are unconsciously monitoring information that is coming in over other channels. 6) If your name is mentioned in a conversation going on three feet away, you will notice it and tune into that input. 7) If someone strolls by dressed in a bathing suit, snorkel, and fins, you will notice him. 8) The "cocktail-party phenomenon," as selective attention is sometimes called, allows you to concentrate on one thing without tuning out everything else that is happening.

From *Understanding Psychology*, Second edition. Copyright © 1974, 1977 by Random House, Inc. Reprinted by permission of CRM Books, a Division of Random House, Inc.

A HERITAGE OF CHANGE

1) Someone once said that "American History is the story of change." 2) Perhaps more than any other people on earth, we are accustomed to constant change in our lives, in our ways of doing things. 3) We move often. 4) In fact, in any five-year period, half of us move from one home to another. 5) As we look around us, there is always evidence of change. 6) Farms become homes and shopping centers. 7) Houses are torn down to make way for apartment buildings. 8) Old offices and stores are replaced by new skyscrapers.

9) Change is not new to America. 10) While the Revolutionary War was still going on, settlers were pushing westward into Tennessee, Kentucky, and Ohio, opening up new lands, pushing back the frontier.

11) **From wilderness to farms and cities.** 12) As the frontier pushed forward, forests were cleared for farms. 13) Later, farms were paved over to make cities. 14) Today herds of cattle graze where buffalo roamed. 15) Wheat and corn grow where prairie grass waved in the wind. 16) Indian trails have become highways, and small trading posts have grown into great cities with factories, homes, schools, and offices. 17) Not every change has been for the better, of course. 18) Many a stream where the Indians could catch their fill of fish is now too polluted for even the hardiest breeds of fish. 19) And many forms of wildlife have completely disappeared from our country.

From *Exploring World Regions: Western Hemisphere* by Herbert H. Gross et al. Copyright © 1975 by Follett Publishing Company. Reprinted by permission of Allyn and Bacon, Inc.

WRITING MARGINAL NOTES

1. Underline key ideas that you want to remember and then rewrite these ideas in margins, using your own words. Or underline main ideas and then in the margin write "Main Idea" or the abbreviation "M.I."

2. Number supporting details in the text. Write "Supporting Details" (S.D.) in the margins.

3. Write "ex." in the margin next to portions of text where the author gives examples that explain the main idea.

4. Write a note in the margin to point out any organizational guides the author uses such as introductory statements, transitional words and phrases, or summaries.

5. Underline unknown words in the text. Write definitions in the margins.

6. Write any insights, thoughts, or questions you have about the topic in the margins. Time spent writing down your own ideas is well worth the effort. Relating the text to your own experience and to information you already have helps you to remember.

7. Write notes emphasizing ideas in the text that your teacher stressed in a class lecture or discussion. Your teacher may use these ideas to form the basis for test questions.

8. Underline ideas or portions of text which you have difficulty understanding. Write a note in the margin as a reminder to find a resource that will help you to understand the material.

A NEWSMAGAZINE ARTICLE WITH MARGINAL NOTES

Birds May Do It, Bees May Do It

A GROUP OF SCIENTISTS CONSIDER WHETHER ANIMALS REALLY THINK

Loath—unwilling

Main problem—How to measure intelligence?

Anthropomorphism = giving human characteristics to nonhuman beings.

Though humans are understandably loath to relinquish their monopoly on intelligence, observers have long believed that a good case can be made for the animal mind. At a weekend symposium at the National Zoo in Washington, D.C., a group of scientists put their brains together to decide whether or not animals think. Their conclusion: an unequivocal maybe.

The central problem in arriving at an answer is how to measure intelligence. Homo sapiens has a hard time devising IQ tests for its own species, much less trying to assess the brains of others. One trap: interpreting animal behavior in human terms. Notes Theodore Reed, former director of the National Zoo: "The public perception of animal intelligence abounds with anthropomorphic fantasies."

One of the most widely held misconceptions, for example, is that dolphins have an authentic language. The mammals do exchange clicks and whistles in isolated laboratory tanks. But Sheri Lynn Gish, a Smithsonian research associate, points out that although the calls made by dolphins in captivity show definite patterns, it is not known if the patterns constitute a language. Moreover, says Gish, dolphins have not been studied in the open sea, where they may really communicate by nudges and scrapes.

First paragraph summarizes the article—*Maybe* animals think.

Unequivocal = there is no doubt

Misconception about the language of dolphins

Benjamin Beck—animal expert

Two indexes of intelligence:

1) ability to use tools

2) language behavior

Animal Behaviorist Benjamin Beck of the University of Illinois at Chicago calls attention to still another human delusion, the species bias. Says he jokingly: "On tests for giraffes, where intelligence might be equated with neck length, humans test out below horses and ostriches."

Despite the difficulties, scientists have been trying to devise ways of evaluating animal intelligence. So far, none of them works perfectly. One theory holds that the bigger the brain size in proportion to the body and the more creased the cerebrum portion, the brighter the animal. But, notes Beck, "the human cerebral cortex occupies no greater a proportion in the human brain than in any other primate."

Current research has focused on the use of tools by animals as a signal of intelligence. Chimpanzees, for example, get at termites by jabbing their nests with twigs. The assassin bug of South America, also a termite fancier, approaches its prey by gluing nest material on its back to serve as camouflage. But, says Beck, the bug's behavior is probably "innate or genetically prewired." Another scientific index is the ability of animals to transmit information through so-called language behavior. Bees, foraging for pollen, return to the hive and perform an intricate figure-eight dance to map the route for other bees. Biologist James Gould of Princeton University says, however, that the dance is in the bees' genes, not their minds.

What is species bias?

Brain size in proportion to body size is not an indication of intelligence.

Animal use of tools— innate or learned?

Nevertheless, there are examples of behavior suggesting that animals can process information and make judgments. Gould points out that honey bees, fed sugar water that is gradually moved away from the hive, anticipate where the food will be placed. Seagulls break open shellfish by dropping them on hard surfaces, flying low when their target is small. At the Yerkes Regional Primate Research Center in Atlanta, chimpanzees have been conditioned to communicate through symbols and are able to distinguish between signs that mean food and those that refer to nonedible items. Says Duane Rumbaugh: "Apes have the capacity to use symbols that represent things not present in time and space—the essence of semantics, in human parlance." The chimps have also demonstrated self-awareness. One, while watching itself on a television monitor, directed a flashlight beam into its mouth, apparently curious about what its throat looked like.

Still, no animal species is likely to prove more intelligent than Homo sapiens. However, as Psychologist Colin Beer of Rutgers University puts it, "Human intelligence has made us dominant, but has also brought us great suffering. The balance sheet of the costs and benefits of intelligence has yet to be tallied."

Summary—human intelligence has made us dominant—but has it really made us happy?

Examples which show that animals can think:

1) Bees anticipate where they will be fed

2) Seagulls break open shellfish by dropping them on hard surfaces

3) Chimps can be taught to communicate through symbols and demonstrate self-awareness

MEMORY AND THOUGHT

According to psychologists all mental activities are a form of information processing

Understanding how the mind works—how human beings think, remember, solve problems, and create ideas—is one of the most fascinating and challenging goals of psychology. For simplicity's sake, psychologists treat all cognitive or mental activities—from memorizing lists of numbers to writing poems and inventing new technologies—as *information processing*. This involves three steps: input, central processing, and output. *Input* refers to the information people receive from their senses. *Central processing* refers to the storing (in memory) and sorting (by thought) of this information in the brain. *Output* refers to the actions that result from processing.

Introduction
Provides an overview

Psychologists know a great deal about how the senses take in information. They also know a great deal about how people behave. However, exactly what happens between sensory input and behavior output remains something of a mystery. In this chapter we will focus on this mystery, describing what psychologists have learned so far about information processing.

Purpose of this chapter

Taking Information In

Input comes through the senses in many forms—voices, musical sounds,

From *Understanding Psychology*, Second edition. Copyright © 1974, 1977 by Random House, Inc. Reprinted by permission of CRM Books, a Division of Random House, Inc.

The world around us contains too much information to take in at one time.

Selective Attention and *Feature Extraction* help us to cope with all this information.

sweet tastes, pungent odors, colorful images, rough textures, painful stings. At any given moment a confusing array of sights, sounds, smells, and other sensations compete for your attention. If you accepted *all* these inputs, you would be completely overwhelmed. Two processes help people to narrow sensory inputs down to a manageable number: selective attention and feature extraction.

SELECTIVE ATTENTION

Partial definition of *Selective Attention*

The ability to pick and choose among the various available inputs is called *selective attention.* For example, if you are at a large party where the music is turned up and everyone is talking, you can focus on a friend's voice and ignore all other sounds. In a way, selective attention is like tuning in a specific television channel.

Unlike a television dial, however, selective attention does not completely block out the other programs or stimuli. You may be listening attentively to what a friend is saying, but at the same time you are unconsciously monitoring information that is coming in over other channels. If your name is mentioned in a conversation going on three feet away, you will notice it and tune into that input. If someone strolls by dressed in a bathing suit, snorkel, and fins, you will notice him. The "cocktail-party phenomenon," as selective attention is sometimes called, allows you to concentrate on one thing without tuning out everything else that is happening.

Complete definition of *Selective Attention*

How *Selective Attention* works.

Laboratory experiments have shown how selective attention works (Hernández-Peón).* For example, if people are asked to pay attention to an auditory stimulus, the brain waves that record their response to sound will get larger. While this is happening, the brain waves that record their response to what they see will get smaller because they are not paying close attention to visual stimuli. If the same people are asked to pay attention to visual stimuli, the reverse occurs. Visual brain waves increase while auditory brain waves decrease. A similar experiment showed that a certain kind of brain wave diminished but did not disappear when people were given a problem to solve or were drawn into conversation. Such experiments seem to indicate that the brain somehow evaluates the importance of the information that comes in over different channels. Top-priority information is allowed to reach the highest brain centers, whereas unimportant information is suppressed.

Brain waves show how people focus their attention.

We pay attention to what is important. But how do we decide what is important?

What makes one input more important than another? Information leading to the satisfaction of such needs as hunger and thirst has top priority. (A person who is very hungry, for example, will pay more attention to his dinner than to the dinner table chitchat.) We also give priority to inputs that are strange and novel, such as an individual who comes to a party

Good question! Can be used to organize the rest of the information given in this paragraph.

---

*R. Hernández-Peón, "Reticular Mechanisms of Sensory Control" in *Sensory Communication,* ed. W. A. Rosenblith (New York: Wiley, 1961), pp. 497–520.

dressed for snorkeling. A third director of attention is interest: The more interested you are in something, the more likely you are to notice it. For example, most people "tune in" when they hear their name mentioned: we're all interested in what other people have to say about us. Likewise, if you become interested in chess, you will suddenly begin to notice newspaper articles about chess, chess sets in store windows, and references to chess moves in everyday speech (for example, "stalemate"). These inputs are not new. They were there last year and the year before, but you simply weren't interested enough to notice them.

FEATURE EXTRACTION

Definition of *Feature Extraction*

Selective attention is only the first step in narrowing down input. The second step is to decide which aspects of the selected channel you will focus on. This process, called *feature extraction,* involves locating the outstanding characteristics of incoming information. For example, if you want to identify the make of a car, you look for distinctive features—the shape of the fenders, the proportion of height to length, and so on. For the most part, you ignore such features as color, upholstery, and tires, which tell you little about the make of the car. Similarly, when you read, you focus on the important words, skimming over such words as "the," "and," or "for example."

What is the difference between *Selective Attention* and *Feature Extraction?*

Being able to extract the significant features of an input helps a person to identify it and compare it to other inputs. For example, you are able to distinguish faces from one another, and at the same time see resemblances. You may notice that all the members of a family have similar noses, yet you are able to recognize each person on the basis of other features.

Why is Feature Extraction important?

Obviously, feature extraction depends to some extent on experience— on knowing what to look for. This is especially true where fine distinctions must be made. It takes considerable expertise to distinguish an original Rembrandt from a skillful forgery. Most of us cannot say what vineyard produced the wine we are drinking in what year, but a gourmet who knows what to look for can.

Success at Feature Extraction depends on experience. We have to learn what to look for.

S.A. and F.E. are evaluative processes.

Like selective attention, feature extraction is an evaluative process. If you are reading a novel for pleasure, you may look for the "juicy" parts; if you're reading an historical biography to prepare for an exam, you concentrate on the facts.

A HERITAGE OF CHANGE

The main heading introduces the idea that Americans have always been involved in change. Each of the subheadings indicates the type of change that is described in the section that follows.

Someone once said that "American History is the story of change." Perhaps more than any other people on earth, we are accustomed to constant change in our lives, in our ways of doing things. We move often. In fact, in any five year period, half of us move from one home to another. As we look around us, there is always evidence of change. Farms become homes and shopping centers. Houses are torn down to make way for apartment buildings. Old offices and stores are replaced by new skyscrapers.

Interesting fact

Change is not new to America. While the Revolutionary War was still going on, settlers were pushing westward into Tennessee, Kentucky, and Ohio, opening up new lands, pushing back the frontier.

From wilderness to farms and cities. As the frontier pushed forward, forests were cleared for farms. Later, farms were paved over to make cities. Today herds of cattle graze where buffalo roamed. Wheat and corn grow where prairie grass waved in the wind. Indian trails have become highways, and small trading posts have grown into great cities with factories, homes, schools, and offices. Not every change has been for the better, of course. Many a stream where the Indians could catch their fill of fish is now too

Not all change has been good. We have damaged our environment.

From *Exploring World Regions: Western Hemisphere* by Herbert H. Gross et al. Copyright © 1975 by Follett Publishing Company. Reprinted by permission of Allyn and Bacon, Inc.

polluted for even the hardiest breeds of fish. And many forms of wildlife have completely disappeared from our country.

Different people and different ways. Some of the biggest changes in the history of the United States have come from the people themselves. At the time our nation won its independence, most Americans were from a few countries in northern Europe or from Africa. In the years that followed, millions of others came from southern and eastern Europe, from Asia, from Canada and Latin America. Each group made its own contributions to our culture. Today our nation is a great blend of many cultures.

Our society has changed, too. The greatest change of all was the ending of slavery. No longer can one man own another; no longer can one of us live by the sweat of another.

All people have rights no matter who they are, what they do, or whey they come from.

The status of many other groups has changed too. Women today have the right to vote. Workers have the right to organize unions. These rights seem very natural to us now. But it was not always that way. Such rights are the result of change.

Main Idea
Machines have
changed farming

From muscle power to machines. Many of the changes in our history are the result of industrialization. With it came more and more motor power and less and less animal or human power. Farming was once very slow, hard work. Hour after hour, the farmer walked behind a plow pulled by a team of horses. He could plow only about two acres a day. Now, a man riding on a tractor, with his radio for company, can easily plow 80 or more acres in a day.

Important term

Corn pickers, combines, cotton pickers, potato-diggers, and hundreds of other machines help farmers do their work easily and quickly. Long ago a farmer could feed only one or two people besides himself. Now one American farmer, with all his machines, can feed an average of more than 45 people! Without such changes in farming, we could never feed our growing population.

From letter writing to television. When the Declaration of Independence was approved by the Continental Congress, horseback riders carried the news to distant towns. Some people did not learn about the Declaration until many days later. Today we hear news almost as soon as it happens, on television or radio. We can often watch events halfway around the globe while they are actually happening. And the voice of a distant friend is only as far away as the telephone.

Main Idea
Communication is much faster now and we can communicate over greater distances.

These modern systems of communication have also helped to bring our nation together. Now we can share the same information, whether we live in the center of New York City, or on a lonely ranch in Wyoming. What a change from the days of the frontier!

From handmade to machine-made. One of the biggest changes has come in the way we make things. Cloth was once woven by hand, and suits and dresses sewed by hand. Workers cut trees with an ax and sawed boards by hand. Nails, paper, shoes, books, dishes, shovels, furniture, rugs, knives, clocks, wagons, and pots and pans were all handmade. Today all these

Main Idea
The effects of the change from handmade to machine-made goods.

Positive Effects

items and almost everything else we use is made by machine. And because machine-made goods are usually cheaper, many families today can afford things that only the very rich could have had in the past.

Of course, changing the way things are made has changed the kind of jobs we have, too. With machines to do much of the heavy work, there is less dirty and backbreaking labor to be done. More people today produce services instead of goods. But we must not forget that the changes may not have been good for every one. It is harder for an unskilled worker to find a job today than it was at times in the past. And many factory jobs have become boring because of the work done by machines. Just think of the difference between being a worker on an automobile assembly line, putting on one part as each car comes down the line, and being a wagonmaster who built the whole wagon from start to finish.

Negative Effects

Main Idea
Supporting Details
1.
2.
3.
4.

From hardship to comfort. The early settlers faced many hardships. They were often hungry and many starved. They had few doctors, if any, and no schools. Even young children had to work in the fields to help their families survive. And imagine what the life of a slave was like.

While many Americans still do not have easy lives, most of us are far better off than our forefathers. We have better food, better clothing, and better housing. We have more schools and more time to enjoy music, art, reading, and sports. By almost

Main Idea
Supporting Details
1.
2.

any standard, we are far more comfortable than the early citizens of our nation.

From horsepower to atomic power. When we talk about the great changes in transportation and production, we are often talking about a change in power. Long ago human and animal muscle supplied most of the power that was used. Horses pulled plows and carriages. Spinning wheels and looms were driven by human feet and hands. Water pumps were cranked by hand.

This statement is really the main idea for both of the following paragraphs.

How power was supplied in the past.

Today almost everything is powered in some way by electricity or by gasoline, diesel, or steam engines. This use of nonanimal power has helped us to produce the abundance we now have. But supplies of fuel are not unlimited. The whole world is using more oil than ever before. The use of coal is going up, too. Even atomic energy, which many think is the answer, has the problem of what to do with radioactive wastes. If we are to keep the advantages of our new machines, we must use fuel wisely. We once thought we could keep on using more and more fuel for anything we wanted. But that, too, has changed. The change in the way power is supplied has caused us to rely on fuels. Now we have shortages of these fuels.

How power is supplied today.

APPLYING NOTETAKING SKILLS

The Unresolvable Question

When does a human being begin to exist? That question is at the very heart of the abortion debate, yet it is far from susceptible to a sure answer. This much is beyond serious dispute: biological life begins at fertilization, when the female's egg is united with the male's sperm. But does a collection of cells constitute a human being? Some biologists believe that fertilization does mark the beginning of humanity, since the fertilized egg is a distinct and unique genetic entity. This belief shores up the anti-abortion argument of Catholic bishops as well as those of secular pro-life groups. John T. Noonan, a professor of law at the University of California at Berkeley, explains the church's theological position this way: "Once conceived, the being was recognized as man because he had man's potential. The criterion for humanity, thus, was simple and all-embracing: if you are conceived by human parents, you are human."

Others argue that human life does not start until a week or so after conception, when the fertilized egg has traveled through the Fallopian tube and implanted itself in the wall of the uterus. "We are able to discern [the embryo's] presence and activity beginning with implantation," wrote Dr. Bernard Nathanson, former chief of obstetrical services at New York City's St. Luke's Hospital, in his 1979 book *Aborting America*. "If this is not 'life,' what is?"

Others pinpoint the beginning of human life when the heart of the embryo begins beating, around the fourth week of pregnancy, or when the central nervous system has developed to the stage where simple reflexes are evident, around the sixth week. By the eighth week, the embryo is undergoing the transition to a fetus and is definitely recognizable as a human being—a stage that some defend as the beginning of human life. Says Dr. Maurice J. Mahoney of the Yale University School of Medicine: "For me, humanness requires that some process of development has taken place which gives the embryo a human form, so that it has a nervous system, a heart and circulatory apparatus, and indications of human shape."

Protestant Theologian Paul Ramsey, a professor of religion at Princeton, declines to identify the precise moment when life begins. But he argues that science now offers evidence of human characteristics in the fetus far earlier than once believed. "I do not say human life begins with conception," says Ramsey, "but science has given us ample factual grounds for believing that the unborn child is an independent human being within the time span [that is, six months] in which the law now says this unborn child can be killed."

Some pro-choice biologists counter that human life does not begin until the fetus becomes viable, by which they mean sufficiently developed to survive outside the uterus. In 1973, when the Supreme Court gave women the legal right to have abortions up to the moment of viability, that age was placed between 24 to 28 weeks. Since then the age at which a fetus is considered viable by medical experts has slowly dropped; doctors are now able to keep alive fetuses as young as 20 weeks and weighing 500 gm (1.1 lbs.). Indeed, Dr. Norman Fost of the Medical School of the University of Wisconsin-Madison believes that the day will eventually arrive when all fetuses can be kept alive—in the laboratory if not in a nursery.

But is any of this relevant? Some experts argue that it is futile to rely on biological data at all in trying to determine when life begins. "Most biological data can never be decisive," says Lisa Cahill, a Catholic and assistant professor of theology at Boston College. "Any particular biological line that might be drawn, such as implantation or viability, is relative to the individual fetus, and each fetus reaches each stage at a slightly different time." Yet even if every fetus developed at precisely the same rate, a consensus would never be reached on when human life begins. "The question is unresolvable," says Fost. "It's not a question that doctors or religious authorities can be helpful on because it's not certifiable. It is just a matter of individual opinion."

APPLYING STUDY SKILLS

Date _July 9, 1981_

Study Technique _____ _Notetaking_ _____

Text or Source of
Material _____ _Time Magazine_ _____

Chapter or Article
Title _"The Unresolvable Question"_

Issue Date/Page No. _____ _April 6, 1981, p. 23_ _____

> <u>Main Topic:</u> _One of the important issues surrounding the abortion debate centers around the question "When does human life begin to exist?"_

When does life begin?—different points of view

1. The Catholic church and other pro-life groups believe that life begins when the sperm and egg unite.

2. Some say human life begins when the fertilized egg is implanted in the wall of the uterus, about a week after conception.

3. Others maintain that human life begins at the fourth week when the heart begins to beat. Some say it begins at the sixth week when the nervous systems develops. Still others argue that the embryo must have some type of human form to be considered human life. This form develops around the eigth week.

4. Protestant Theologian Paul Ramsey won't say when he thinks life begins. But he does say the human life is in existence during the first six months when it is legal to abort the fetus.

5. Pro-choice biologists say human life does not begin until the fetus is able to survive outside the uterus.

6. The conclusion reached in the article is that the question of when human life begins is really irrelevant. There can be so many different answers to the question that it is up to each individual to decide.

APPLYING STUDY SKILLS

Date   *July 9, 1981*

Study Technique   *Summarizing*

Text or Source of
Material   *Time Magazine*

Chapter or Article
Title   *"The Unresolvable Question"*

Issue Date/Page No.   *April 6, 1981, p. 23*

    "When does human life begin?" a question prompted by the abortion debate is the topic of this article. Many people have many different answers. Catholic and pro-life groups maintain that human life begins at the moment of conception. Pro-choice groups say that it does not begin until the fetus is able to survive outside the uterus. Others believe human life begins at various points during the pregnancy such as when the fertilized egg becomes implanted in the wall of the uterus during the first week or at the fourth week when the heart begins to beat. The conclusion reached in the article is that the question "When does human life begin?" is irrelevant. There is no one definite answer. The point at which human life begins is a matter of individual belief.

USING THE QUESTIONING STUDY TECHNIQUE

Fast Shuffle for Card Counters?

A NEW JERSEY COURT SAYS THEY HAVE BEEN GETTING A BAD DEAL

The stranger draws a pair of fours and decides to split them. The dealer frowns, the crowd mutters. Splitting fours is not supposed to be a percentage move in blackjack, but maybe he knows what he is doing anyway. He is ahead for the night and attracting attention. Is he a pro, or just a tourist on a streak? With his fours now split, he draws two weak hands—15 and 16—and stands on both. The dealer hits his own two with a queen, then a jack—bust. The stranger wins again! But what's this? Suddenly the table is surrounded by sternfaced casino employees in immaculate business suits. They indicate a sign near by: "We reserve the right to exclude professional card counters from play . . ." The man protests. The casino insists. A steely hand clamps around his arm, and a thumb gestures toward the exit. "Out."

Such scenes have been enacted thousands of times wherever gambling is legal in the U.S. In Atlantic City's seven casinos, there have been about 1,500 evictions of suspected card counters in the past three years. Many of the ousted patrons have protested to the New Jersey Casino Control Commission, to no avail. One was a New Jersey state legislator. Another, Atlantic City Businesswoman Ruth Altman, objected that "I couldn't count cards if my life depended on it."

Some, however, have actually been "counters": serious or even professional players who have mastered a complex system of mathematical charts and memorization. By varied estimates, such systems give the player a competitive edge of from 1.5% to 4.38% over the house. Counters say, correctly, that they are doing nothing illegal, only making blackjack a game more of skill than of chance. Too much so, say the casinos, who maintain that counters threaten their hefty profits (Atlantic City casinos are currently winning more than $18 million a month at their blackjack tables). Now, in a case involving Kenneth Uston, the self-styled "king of the card counters," a New Jersey appeals court has made a ruling that may lead to a resolution of the question.

The flamboyant Uston . . . was banned from playing blackjack at Resorts International Hotel Casino in Atlantic City in 1979. He went to the New Jersey Casino Control Commission, charging that he had been discriminated against and citing state legislation that called for "maximum public participation" in gaming. The commission held that the casino had a common-law right to exclude a player for any reason it chose. Uston appealed in the courts. In last week's decision, a three-judge panel of the appellate division of New Jersey Superior Court unanimously rejected the commission's theory, saying it applied only to outright undesirables. Under New Jersey's Casino Control Act, said the panel, only the commission, if anyone, has the authority to decide if counters should be excluded.

So, Uston and his fellow counters are going to rush straight to the tables and clean up, right? Don't bet on it. The commission and the hotel quickly won a stay of the action, pending appeal to the State Supreme Court; until then, counters remain *personae non gratae.*

There are several systems of counting, all tricky in execution but relatively simple in concept. In one common method the general idea is to assign a value to each card—plus one for low cards (three through seven), zero for twos, eights and nines, minus one for the rest (ten through ace). The player keeps a running count of the cards that have been played. By matching the count against memorized strategy charts that anticipate virtually every conceivable situation, he determines his odds and bets accordingly. When he figures the deck is "ripe," he may bump his bet to the limit.

To become even a novice at counting, says Uston, requires at least 50 hours of memorization. Beyond that, he says, very few players—maybe 18 in all the world—have the "steady nerves, discipline and adequate financing" to become top professionals. Other estimates put the number of true counters at up to 150, or even more. Attorney Joel Sterns, who represented Resorts International in the New Jersey case, claims that half the casino's 1979 "win" in blackjack was lost to "an influx of professional card counters."

A sure way to frustrate the system is to change the rules. One ploy is to use more frequent shuffles of the deck. But casinos dislike frequent shuffling because it slows down the game (hence their take) and irritates even noncounters. Charges Uston's attorney, Morris Goldings: "Casino owners not only want suckers but also suckers who lose at the most rapid pace possible." Nevertheless, should the New Jersey Supreme Court uphold last week's ruling, the Atlantic City casinos are expected to seek some such change in rules from the commission.

In Las Vegas, where the state allows casinos wide latitude for setting their own policies, most already use more frequent shuffling, among other variations. Some allow acknowledged counters to play but restrict them to small bets.

Other Las Vegas establishments actively discourage or even prohibit counters—notably including Uston. Twice Uston has gone to the federal courts to try to regain admission to casinos on the ground that he has a constitutional right to play in a public facility. And if he is finally vindicated in New Jersey, he vows a relentless effort to apply the precedent to bolster his case out West. All of which only seems to reaffirm Damon Runyon's dictum: "There is no such thing as a 'friendly' game of cards in which money is involved."   —*By Jeff Melvoin. Reported by Raji Samghabadi/New York*

APPLYING STUDY SKILLS

Date   *August 2, 1981*

Study Technique   *Questioning*

Text or Source of
Material   *Time Magazine*

Chapter or Article
Title   *"Fast Shuffle for Card Counters?"*

Issue Date/Page   *May 25, 1981, p. 80*

Questions from title and subtitle

1.   *What is a card counter?*
     (A person who has mastered a complex system of mathematical charts that gives that person an advantage when playing blackjack at gambling casinos.)

2.   *Have card counters been getting a bad deal, as the New Jersey court says?*
     (Casinos in Las Vegas and New Jersey have prohibited card counters from playing. Counters say that this is not fair; they have a right to play in a public facility. A New Jersey appeals court seems to agree with the card counters.)

Questions from the introduction and first paragraph of the text

1.   *Why do casinos exclude professional card counters?*
     (In order to make the kind of profits they feel they need to make, casino owners must consistently win more than they lose. Professional card counters seem to have an edge over the casino. Therefore casinos exclude them.

2. *How does card counting work?*
   (The general idea behind card counting is that a numerical value is assigned to each card. The player keeps track of the cards that have been played. This enables him to have a fairly accurate idea of which cards are left in the deck. Based on memorized strategy charts the player can then decide what his odds of winning are before he places his bet.)

3. *Is card counting really effective?*
   (For someone who has mastered the system, card counting does seem to result in more wins than losses.)

Questions from the last paragraph

1. *Who is Kenneth Uston?*
   (A person who has mastered the system of card counting and as a result has been evicted from many casinos. He is the person who has taken the casinos in Atlantic City to court.)

Additional questions based on a reading of the entire article?

1. *Will the New Jersey court decision enable card counters to play?*
   (No, the casinos appealed the New Jersey appeals court decision and won a stay of action.)

2. *Do casinos have any way of preventing card counters from winning?*
   (Yes, they can shuffle the deck more often and they can change some of the rules.)

APPLYING STUDY SKILLS

Date   _January 21, 1982_

Study Technique   _Questioning_

Text or Source of
Material   _Understanding Psychology_

Chapter or Article
Title   _"Memory and Thought"_

Issue Date/Page   _pp. 51–56_

1. *What do I already know about how people think and remember? Or, how do I think and remember?*
    (Individual answers)

2. *What are the three steps involved in information processing?*
    (A.   Taking information in)
    (B.   Central processing or storing of information)
    (C.   Actions that result from the stored information)

3. *What do scientists know about how people remember and think?*
    (Psychologists know a great deal about how our senses take in information and they know much about how people actually behave. But what happens in the brain between the time when people take in information and when they act on this information is still a mystery.)

4. *What two processes help people to deal with all the information they take in?*
    (Selective attention and feature extractions help people to narrow information down so that they can deal with it.)

5. *How is selective attention different from feature extraction?*
    (Selective attention helps you to choose among various inputs. You selectively attend, for example, if you choose to listen to just one person's voice when several people are talking.)
    (Feature extraction means that you locate the most important parts of the input you have selected and you focus on those parts. Instead of carefully paying attention to each word a person is saying to you, you focus on the ideas or the meaning of what is being said.)

6. *What are the most important ideas to remember about storing information?*
   (A.   The storing of information is called memory
   (B.   There are three types of memory:
       a.   Sensory storage—lasts an instant
       b.   Short-term memory—lasts about 20 seconds
       c.   Long-term memory—lasts indefinitely)

7. *What is sensory storage?*
   (Brief not thought-about impressions that our senses take in form the basis of sensory storage.)

8. *What is short-term memory?*
   (Short-term memory consists of impressions or inputs you have in your conscious mind at any one moment.)

9. *How do rehearsal and chunking help to keep information in short-term memory?*
   (When information is repeated or rehearsed, it is more likely to remain in memory. Chunking is a process of organizing information so that it can be remembered in meaningful groups. Scientists have found that the mind is able to remember only about 7 unrelated items.)

10. *What kind of information is stored in long-term memory?*
    (Long-term memory contains representations of experience and sensations that people have had throughout their lives. It also contains records of details such as words, names, and dates as well as ideas and concepts that people have learned.)

11. *What theories do scientists have about what happens in the brain when information is stored in long-term memory?*
    (One theory states that memory is due to changes in the form of protein molecules in the brain. Another suggests that memory occurs because of chemical-electrical change in the brain.)

12. *Are specific memories stored in specific places in the brain?*
    (No, scientists have found that no one cell or group of cells can be removed to destroy a memory.)

SUGGESTIONS FOR OUTLINING

Outlining Passage with Headings

1. Skim the passage to find main divisions. Carefully read the headings, subheadings and first and last paragraphs as you skim.

2. Read the entire passage carefully.

3. Decide if the headings and subheadings do in fact reflect the organization of the article.

4. If the headings and subheadings seem suitable, rewrite them in the form of complete sentences to form the major subdivisions of the outline. If the headings and subheadings do not reflect the organizational structure of the passage, make necessary revisions.

5. Complete the outline by writing in the facts and details you want to remember in relationship to the main ideas of the selection.

Outlining Passage Without Headings and Subheadings

1. Read and think about the title.

2. Read the first paragraph of the passage to determine if it provides a key to the organization. If not, then read the second paragraph.

3. Read the final paragraph. Does it include a summary of the main points presented in the passage?

4. Read the entire passage and write the main subdivisions of the outline.

5. Reread the passage and complete the outline with the important facts and details.

OUTLINING A NEWSMAGAZINE ARTICLE

Going Gentle into That Good Night

A DOCTOR STUDIES PATIENTS' RECOLLECTIONS OF DYING

Owen Thomas appeared dead on arrival at the New York Infirmary last December. His heart, liver, intestines and a lung had been slashed in a knife fight. The 20-year-old fish-market laborer had no pulse, no blood pressure and no breath left in a body that was already "very cold to touch," according to Dr. Daryl Isaacs, who was in charge of the emergency room. Yet five minutes later, Thomas' hearbeat was restored, a recovery that Isaacs described as "the most wondrous thing we've ever experienced."

After awakening from eight hours of surgery, Thomas told a story about his "death" that was no less wondrous. The normally down-to-earth Brooklyn youth remembered floating into a dark void. "I was going some place, and then I saw my brother," says Thomas, meaning his brother Christopher, who had died in a 1979 car accident. "He put his two big hands on my shoulders and pushed me back, saying, 'You can't come here; there's no room.'"

Owen Thomas had lived through what is sometimes called a near death experience (NDE), a vivid, memorable sense of sights, sounds and events that occur while an individual is clinically dead or very close to the point of no return. Discussion of this phenomenon and other aspects of dying achieved an almost faddish popularity in the early and mid-1970s, following the publication of two bestsellers: *On Death and Dying*, a study of terminally ill patients, by Psychiatrist Elisabeth Kübler-Ross, and *Life After Life*, by Psychiatrist Raymond Moody.

Neither author took a particularly scientific approach to NDEs. Moody's style was anecdotal. Kübler-Ross did not actually write about NDEs, but lectured on the subject. Now comes a new book, *Recollections of Death: A Medical Investigation* (Harper & Row; $13.50). The author is Dr. Michael Sabom, 37, a cardiologist at Atlanta VA Medical Center and assistant professor of medicine at Emory Univeristy. Like most doctors, he was initially skeptical about "'far-out' descriptions of afterlife spirits and such." When asked to help lead a church-group discussion of Moody's book, he decided to do a little research with his own critically ill patients. "Five years and 116 interviews later," he says, "I am convinced that my original suspicions were wrong."

In approaching his far-out subject, Sabom was determined to be "objective and systematic. Patients were asked standardized questions and did not at first know the purpose of his study. Rather than limiting it to people claiming to have had an NDE, as Moody did, Sabom questioned a random sample of patients who had suffered near fatal medical crises, defined as any unconscious bodily state that "would be expected to result in irreversible biological death in the majority of instances." Three-quarters had been in cardiac arrest. A few had already been given up for dead. One soldier, for instance, was discovered to be alive only when a mortician saw blood flowing from a vein in which he was about to inject embalming fluid.

Sabom found that 40% of his random sample had vivid memories of their brush with death. A third had what he calls purely "autoscopic" experiences, in which they remember floating at ceiling height above the operating table (or battlefield) and looking down on their own lifeless bodies. About half had "transcendental" experiences, in which they recall traveling through a dark tunnel toward a bright light. Some, like Owen Thomas, encountered other figures or entered unearthly landscapes like those painted by Hieronymus Bosch. Several patients reported both autoscopic and transcendental elements.

What astonished Sabom was the uniformity of the patients' accounts. All recalled a sense of timelessness, an awareness of their own deaths, and a strong sense of reality. (It was "realer than here," said one man.) Patients remembered an absence of physical pain, a feeling of tranquility and even delight ("That was the most beautiful instant in the whole world when I came out of that body!")

Sabom could discern no religious or other differences between patients who had NDEs and those who did not. The two groups contained roughly equal numbers of atheists and frequent churchgoers, college grads and high school dropouts. Even prior awareness of the existence of near death experiences did not predispose patients to have them. Nor did race, occupation or sex, though, curiously, women who had NDEs were more likely to recall seeing their loved ones.

What was a serious scientist to make of such findings? Could the recollections be nothing more than dreams or hallucinations induced, perhaps, by drugs, lack of oxygen or brain seizures? Could they have been triggered by betaendorphin, the body's naturally occuring opiate, which, Biologist-Author Lewis Thomas has suggested, may be released at the moment of death to "ensure that dying is a painless and conceivably pleasant experience"?

Sabom does not think so. As evidence, he cites patients who had extremely sharp autoscopic memories. They were often able to describe the minutiae of their own cardiopulmonary resuscitation: readings on a monitor, the color of an oxygen mask, the number of electric shocks administered, the exact position of doctors around the table and what they talked about (in one case, golf). These memories, Sabom found, conformed precisely with doctors' accounts. Was it possible that some chronic cardiac patients were simply familiar enough with CPR procedures (from experience and television) to fantasize accurately about what took place? Sabom put this to the test by asking longtime heart patients who had not had NDEs to describe such procedures. Twenty out of 23 made major errors in their accounts.

Kübler-Ross jeopardized her standing in the medical profession by asserting she knew "beyond a shadow of a doubt" that there was life after death. Sabom is more cautious. "Personally, I believe in life after death," he says. "But I do not believe the work I have done proves life after death." What it does suggest, he thinks, is that dying brings about a "splitting apart of the nonphysical part of our being from the physical part." How this split occurs and the nature of the nonphysical part are, of course, elusive matters. Many of the patients in the study, notes Sabom, have died since he spoke to them. "It's an eerie feeling to know that now they may know, while I'm still here wondering about what they said."   —By Claudia Wallis

OUTLINE OF "GOING GENTLE INTO THAT GOOD NIGHT"

I. Introduction
   A. Owen Thomas appeared dead on arrival at a New York infirmary last December.
   B. He recovered.
   C. He told a story about his own death.
      1. He was floating in a dark void.
      2. He saw his brother who said there was no room for him.
II. Background of the Near Death Experience (NDE)
   A. Vivid memories of events that occur while an individual is clinically dead.
   B. NDEs were faddish in the mid 1970s.
   C. Two popular books about the subject were written by:
      1. Kübler-Ross.
      2. Moody.
III. Sabom, a cardiologist, has written a new book.
   A. Initially Sabom was skeptical of NDEs.
   B. Then he did some research with his own patients.
   C. After 5 years began to believe in NDEs.
IV. Sabom tried to be objective and systematic.
   A. He asked all patients the same questions.
   B. He questioned a random sample.
   C. 40% had vivid memories of NDEs.
      1. A third had "autoscopic" or out-of-the-body experiences.
      2. About half had "transcendental" experiences. They experienced the feeling of traveling down a dark tunnel toward a bright light.
V. Sabom was surprised by the uniformity of patients' accounts in spite of the fact that there were no real differences among patients.
   A. They all recalled
      1. A sense of timelessness.
      2. A strong sense of reality.
      3. Absence of pain.
   B. There were no real differences among patients in terms of:
      1. Religious beliefs.
      2. Education.
      3. Race.
      4. Occupation.
      5. Sex.
VI. Sabom's conclusions:
   A. He does not believe that NDEs are induced by drugs, lack of oxygen, or brain seizures.
   B. He believes in life after death but does not believe that his own work proves it.

OUTLINE OF "A HERITAGE OF CHANGE"

I. The history of America shows that the country has been essentially changing.
   A. Americans move often.
   B. Americans have changed their environment.
   C. The American people have been involved with change ever since the country began.

II. There are many examples of change that have occurred in America.
   A. People changed the land from wilderness to farm to cities.
   B. The people who changed the United States came from many different places. Some of the changes these people made included:
      1. Freeing slaves.
      2. Giving women the right to vote.
      3. Giving workers the right to organize.
   C. Many changes occurred in America when machine power replaced human or animal power for farming and for transportation.
   D. Through television and other forms of modern communication people today quickly know about events that occur in other parts of the country.
   E. Most goods today are made by machine rather than by hand as they were years ago.
      1. In one way this is a good change because people have less back-breaking work to do.
      2. In another way this is a negative change because:
         a. There are fewer jobs for those who are unskilled.
         b. Many factory jobs which consist of running machines are boring.
   F. Most Americans have more comfortable lives now than Americans did in the early years of our country.
      1. People are healthier and do not have to work as hard.
      2. There is better food, clothing, and shelter.
      3. There are more schools and leisure activities.
   G. Changes in transportation and production have been changes from animal power to machine power.
      1. This power is provided by oil or atomic fuel.
      2. The problem is that the supplies of oil and atomic energy are limited and atomic energy has dangers associated with it.

SAMPLE OF A GRAPHIC OVERVIEW

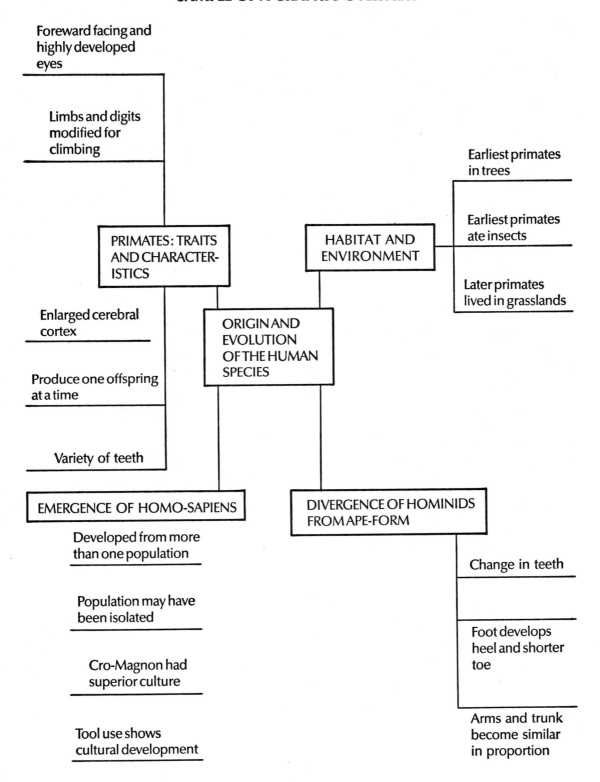

GRAPHIC OVERVIEW OF "MEMORY AND THOUGHT"

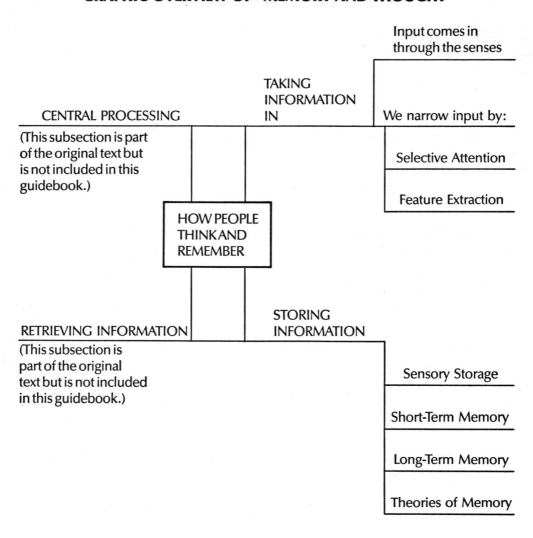

GRAPHIC OVERVIEW OF "STORING INFORMATION"

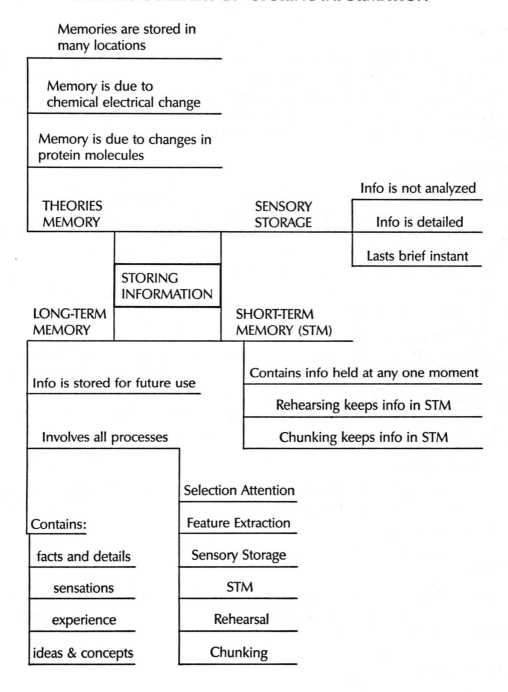

SOME SUGGESTIONS FOR USING PARTICULAR STUDY APPROACHES

Underlining

Underlining can be done quickly and it is an appropriate study strategy to use when students can write in their texts. This strategy appears to be useful for material that contains detailed information that is not difficult for the reader to understand. Using this approach would probably help students organize information prior to taking multiple choice, fill-in-the-blank, or true-or-false tests.

Writing Marginal Notes

Like underlining, this approach can be used when students are permitted to mark in their texts. Students may use the approach to draw attention to main ideas and supporting details and facts as well as to write notes in the margins that will help them to understand and recall difficult concepts. Marginal notetaking seems to be a study procedure that would help students prepare for most types of tests.

Notetaking and Summarizing

Writing notes and summaries are time-consuming procedures. For this reason they are not good study choices if the material to be studied contains many ideas that are fairly easy to understand. Using these procedures, though, helps students to think about and organize complex concepts. If students expected their teachers to give a short essay or an essay exam, one or both of these procedures would probably be a good study selection.

Student Questioning

Writing questions and answering them takes time. Similar to notetaking and summarizing, this procedure is a good choice when studying complex material in preparation for an essay exam.

Outlining

The process of outlining seems to help students learn complex information and organize facts and supporting details. To use it effectively requires both time and effort, but writing an outline helps prepare students to take most types of tests.

Graphic Overview

Preparing a graphic overview based on headings and subheadings or larger divisions in text helps students quickly organize information for review. A graphic overview based on ideas within a subsection of text requires more time, but assists students as they attempt to understand complex ideas and retain supporting facts and details. A series of graphic overviews can help students study for most types of tests.

SELECTING STUDY STRATEGIES

Part One: Sample

Type of Material: Biology text
Chapter on skeletal structure
Many details and facts

Purpose for Reading: Teacher assigned it
Will be tested on it

Difficulty Level: I understand the idea. But there are many facts to remember.

Type of Test: Multiple Choice

Study Approach: Outlining

Part Two: Exercise

Select a reading assignment from one of your content area courses and write responses for each item below.

Type of Material:

Purpose for Reading:

Difficulty Level:

Study Approach:

STUDY SKILLS PROJECT

Name   _____

Date   _____

Course   _____

Study Strategies Used   _____

                            _____

                            _____

                            _____

                            _____

                            _____

                            _____

Previous Grade   _____

Expected Grade   _____

Write a paragraph below that explains which study strategy worked most effectively for you. Give specific reasons for or examples of its effectiveness.

SPEED READERS DON'T READ; THEY SKIM

"I took a speed-reading course, learning to read straight down the middle of the page and I was able to go through War and Peace *in 20 minutes. It's about Russia."*—Woody Allen

The advertisements that describe speed-reading courses try to sound like scientific reports on a major advance in human education, but they are closer to science fiction. They claim that an average person can triple his reading speed with no loss in comprehension; the advertisements support this claim with one piece of irrefutable data—a money-back guarantee.

1. What is the main idea of this paragraph? Restate it in your own words.

Speed reading has become big business. Evelyn Wood Reading Dynamics, the most popular speed-reading method, claims to have graduated more than 500,000 students, who presumably have paid more than $85,000,000 to increase their reading speed. Very few of these students have asked for their money back; they apparently felt that they had gained a valuable skill. But what exactly have they learned? Can we increase our reading speeds without adversely affecting comprehension? The evidence suggests that we cannot. In the past few years I have studied the research on reading, conducted experiments on speed reading, and attended an Evelyn Wood Reading Dynamic course. I now feel that speed reading is about five percent sense and 95 percent nonsense. *Speed-reading courses cannot do what they say they do. They do not increase your reading speed, they teach you to skim and scan material, and to sample the ideas in an article or book.* We should not use the term reading to describe this piecemeal process, nor should we expect this process to produce the level of comprehension we expect from reading. Skimming may be a valuable skill, but let the buyer beware. Woody Allen's anecdote leaves much unsaid, the least of which is about *War and Peace.*

This is the main idea of this paragraph.

Most advocates of speed reading insist that they teach reading, not skimming or scanning. They claim that their methods produce a difference in quantity, not quality. It makes good business sense to call their product reading—after all,

Reprinted from *Psychology Today* Magazine. Copyright © 1972. American Psychological Association.

few persons would pay $175 to learn to skim faster. But do the claims and methods make scientific sense? Let's look at some of the evidence.

A third factor, purpose, or reason for reading also determines how fast the reader decides to read.

Buggy

The rate at which a person reads depends on *two factors—his ability and the difficulty of the material.* S. E. Taylor found that the average reading rate of students increased from about 80 words per minute in the first grade to about 280 words per minute in college. (Each student read material geared to his own grade level.) Other researchers have shown that most adults seem to read between 150 and 300 words per minute. The Evelyn Wood organization refers to such rates as typical of the horse-and-buggy era of reading; its graduates supposedly can read more than 1,000 words per minute. Other instructors have claimed that their students can read 1,000,000 words per minute. Research does not support these claims, however.

2. How fast can adults really read?

Most researchers contend that there is a limit to our reading speeds. In a sense, these limits help define reading. As these limits are approached, most researchers will contend that there is a change in the quality of the information processed as well as the quantity.

Steps: To assimilate the contents of this article, a normal reader will:
1. look at the words in sequence, moving the eyes from left to right across the page
2. let the eyes fix on each word long enough to store the meaning of the symbols in short-term memory, and then move on to the next word.
3. stop, regress to a previous point, and begin again whenever the complete thoughts contained in the symbols elude understanding; and
4. read especially difficult passages subvocally—that is, moving the lips—if it is necessary.

This section explains what happens during normal reading.

When we read normally, our eye movements are under immediate control of the material being read. *Our eyes do not move faster than our information-processing ability function.* We usually read at a rate that makes complete sense of written

3. What does information-processing mean?

material. Several researchers have shown that an intelligent individual reading very easy material cannot comprehend most of the material at rates above 500 or 600 words per minute. There is evidence that suggests that persons who read normally at 200 or 300 words per minute cannot function at faster rates because of the distracting influence of conscious eye movement. If we become conscious of the individual parts that make up the act of reading, we are no longer reading. Most reading researchers agree that reading rates above 800 to 1,000 words per minute are physiologically impossible. What do speed readers do at that rate if they are not reading?

Fragments. In an Evelyn Wood Reading Dynamics course, most persons learn to:
1. Look at the small group of words in the middle of each line long enough to store the bit of information it carries, independent of the words that are on either side. Move the eyes straight down the middle of the page.
2. Try to get as much information as possible without attempting to understand or store the complete line of thought the writer intended to communicate. Continue to skip until the material is covered.
3. Make inferences unhesitatingly about what the author intended to communicate, on the basis of the fragments of information gathered.

Obviously, Evelyn Wood Reading Dynamics teaches its students to skip over material. Most people call this skimming, not reading. It is hard for an observer to tell the difference between skimming and true reading. An intelligent person with the proper background needs only a few clues to infer a great deal about a piece of material. But we should give credit where credit is due. A person might skim a new introductory text in psychology at 2,000 words per minute, then show a tremendous amount of knowledge about the book. However, this feat is not impressive if the skimmer happens to be a professor who has taught introductory psychology for 10 years.

4. Why can the psychology professor "read" the psychology text at 2,000 words per minute?

J.F.K. One speed-reading course claims, in a brochure, that President Kennedy could read newspapers at 1,200 words per minute. President Kennedy was a well-informed person who could make sense of almost any newspaper article just from the information in the headline and lead paragraph. By skimming newspapers, Kennedy could decide whether an article was worth reading at a normal rate. One of the most important uses of skimming is to make sure that the ideas that deserve to be read are read and that the ideas that deserve to be skimmed are skimmed.

5. Why could J.F.K. read newspapers so fast?

This sentence states an important idea.

Skimming occurs at rates higher than 1,000 words per minute, but it is a limited skill. The chances are good that the speed reader will miss a vital point and fail to make sense of the whole. One advocate of speed reading, Henry McLaughlin, has acknowledged this aspect of speed reading; he admits that the recall of speed readers is sometimes mere fabrication. When speed-reading courses claim to have students who can read at 1,000,000 words per minute, we should react as we would to a magician's trick. There is more to a book than meets the eye at that rate.

Eye. Persons who conduct speed-reading courses usually claim to correct four basic "faults" of the normal reading process. They say that a person can increase his reading speed with no loss in comprehension by learning to 1) read without regressing; 2) read vertically instead of horizontally; 3) read visually instead of orally; and 4) read concepts and thought-units instead of single words. The course operators may say that their approach to improved reading is based on scientific research, but scientific research does not indicate that these supposedly faulty practices are in fact detrimental to reading.

6. What are the four faults the Evelyn Wood course claims to correct? Are these really faults?

For example, Guy Buswell showed as early as 1922 that poor readers do regress more than good readers. But there is no evidence that regression causes poor reading. Most researchers, such as E. C. Poulton, view regressive eye movement as a symptom of poor reading, not a cause. (In a sense, this reflects one of the major problems encountered by psychologists who study reading. The primary effects of reading are covert. It is very difficult to investigate a complex internal thought process by analyzing overt behavior.)

Lip. Most persons occasionally look back at material they have just read; nearly everyone will stop to reread a difficult passage. We regress to give the material and ourselves a second chance. To suggest that we can pass over difficult passages without losing comprehension is nonsense. In contrast, efficient skimming requires that we pass over large amounts of material as quickly as possible. To that extent, it makes sense for the speed reader to learn to stop regressing.

Speed-reading courses also misinterpret the data on subvocalization, or silent speech. A. W. Edfelt has done extensive research with persons who move their speech muscles (e.g., lips and tongue) when they read. He found that more silent speech occurs in a poor reader than in a good reader and that as the content of the text becomes more difficult, silent speech increases in all readers. He concluded that we cannot view silent speech as a habit detrimental to reading. Apparently, speed-reading courses have again confused correlation with causation. In fact, David Wark has conducted research which he interpreted as suggesting that individuals should talk to themselves to improve their reading comprehension. The visual approach to increasing reading speed appears to be nonsense.

Movie. Speed-reading courses usually teach students to read vertically, moving their eyes straight down the middle of the page. They are supposed to learn to see an entire line at one time. This technique probably evolved from research done with a tachistoscope. This device flashes words and phrases on a screen for varying lengths of time. It was found that some subjects could remember five words flashed on a screen for only 1/10 of a second, giving a pseudo reading rate of 3,000 words per minute. Unfortunately, the tachistoscope experiments do not resemble the reading process. The difference is similar to the differences between a movie and a slide projected on a screen. In normal reading there is no halt in the action that allows the reader to read what he has just perceived from the after-image remaining on the retina of the eye. When new words continually erase old words on the retina as happens with a movie, two or three words are the most that the eye can see in one fixation. The research by Luther Gilbert indicates that a person cannot possibly perceive an entire line at one instant in either normal reading or in skimming.

S. E. Taylor compared the eye movements of a group of Evelyn Wood graduates to those of a group of regular readers. Photographs revealed that there was no difference between the groups. The speed readers did not move their eyes in a vertical line: their eyes moved unsystematically often horizontally, in a skipping manner similar to the eye movements of un-trained readers who were skimming the material.

Chunk. Speed-reading courses teach students to look for thought-units rather than individual words. This practice probably is grounded in tachistoscope research and in the work of an eminent psychologist, George A. Miller, at Rockefeller University, who advocates that persons chunk bits of information into thought patterns, concepts and ideas. Pursuing this idea, I presented to students reading material that had been pre-chunked. I arranged phrases of two to five words in vertical column on a page. (I tried different arrangements of words in other experiments but the results were the same.) Prechunking the information increased neither reading speed nor comprehension. I might note that in the Evelyn Wood Reading Dynamic course that I took, it was recommended that the students learn to read in thought-units, but there was no instruction as to how to accomplish it. For good reasons—there is no research evidence that people can be taught to read this way.

Aspirin. If speed reading does work, it does not work for the reasons that are put forth by its supporters. Perhaps we should just accept it as a benign mystery like aspirin and let it go at that: you pay $175 for an eight-week course and something happens to you that lets you triple your reading speed with no loss in comprehension. But does it really work?

It remains for us to examine the evidence used by speed-reading advocates to support their claims. In an article describing her method, Evelyn Wood cites an experiment by William Liddle: "At the University of Delaware, a careful study of the Evelyn Wood Reading Dynamics technique was made by William Liddle, a Ph.D. candidate, using a control and an experimental group. In reading nonfiction he found no significant differences in comprehension between the two groups, despite the fact that the experimental group read at 1,300 wpm—better than three times the speed of the control group." Interestingly, the article fails to mention the second part of Liddle's experiment, in which he tested the comprehension of the same two groups on fiction material. Liddle did find a statistically significant drop in comprehension for the speed readers when they were reading fiction. It seems reasonable to conclude that if

This section describes the evidence Evelyn Wood uses to support her cause.

7. *What were the two findings from Liddle's experiments?*

an individual is taught to triple the rate at which he reads fiction, he will experience a significant loss in comprehension.

But what about finding no difference between the speed readers and normal readers for nonfiction material? Does this mean that individuals can learn to triple the rate at which they read nonfiction material with no significant loss in comprehension? Let's look closer at the evidence. The speed readers did score lower than the normal readers on the nonfiction test (68 percent versus 72 percent), but the difference was not large enough to be statistically significant. Statistical significance testing is an art, the results of which depend directly upon the number of subjects used in the experiment and the sensitivity of the measuring instrument. I suspected that the reason Liddle found no statistically significant difference for nonfiction might have been because the test was not sensitive to major losses in comprehension. In order to test this hypothesis, I gave Liddle's comprehension questions on the nonfiction material to a comparable group of subjects without letting them read the material first.

Carefully note what is said in this sentence.

Comprehension scores for this control group are good. They averaged 57 percent on material they had never seen before. The speed readers who supposedly read the nonfiction material comprehended only 11 percent more than this non-reading control group. Thus, my hypothesis was supported. The nonfiction test was insensitive to major losses in comprehension since a group which had zero comprehension received an average score of 57 percent.

8. What is being said about Liddle's comprehension questions?

Norm. It is impossible to know exactly what degree of comprehension the speed readers achieved on Liddle's nonfiction material. But, the scores of the speed readers were so close to the nonreaders that it would be unreasonable to conclude from this evidence that an individual can learn to triple his reading rate on nonfiction with no loss in comprehension. Liddle's research provides the only scientifically collected data directly relevant to the claims made by speed-reading courses. And, his data can reasonably be interpreted as providing no support for the claim that individuals can be taught to triple their rate with no loss in comprehension.

It may seem strange that Liddle did not develop his test to measure how much of the material was actually comprehended. That is, Liddle did not develop his tests so as to prevent bright individuals from: a) extracting enough information from some of the questions to give away the answers to other questions, or b) using general background knowledge to figure out the answers to many of the questions. However, Liddle did develop his tests using traditional test-construction procedures that measure how an individual performs in relation to a norm. Several research studies have shown that college students can average around 40 to 70 percent on these norm-referenced reading tests without ever reading the passages. Someday, college courses on testing will start teaching students that the traditional test-building procedures are not appropriate for measuring change, or gain, or improvement, but that they are appropriate only for measuring individual differences. Until this change occurs, we can expect frequently to see ridiculous results, even when trained persons use standardized tests.

To circumvent the problem of standardized tests, I asked a group of individuals to rate subjectively their understanding of paragraphs that they had read. During the experiment, the reading rate of students was increased from 75 to 450 words per minute for a set of college-level paragraphs. Three different experimental groups said that the faster they read, the less they understood. At 75 words per minute they thought that they understood about 80 percent of the material; at 450 words per minute they said they understood only about 40 percent of the material.

Customer. If speed-reading courses really cannot do what they claim to do, why do so many persons continue to pay the high tuition prices? It seems natural that an unsatisfied customer would ask for his money back, when he realized that the course did not live up to its advertising. I suspect that one of the major reasons that persons do not ask for their money back is the nature of the tests the Evelyn Wood course uses to measure comprehension. Customers seem to be easily impressed by test scores—they will believe something that is not true if it can be given an appearance of scientific evidence.

9. *Why don't people ask for their money back?*

The instructor in the speed-reading course I took gave three tests. Reading Dynamics developed two of the tests for use in the course. I have already discussed how some of the most carefully developed tests are not sensitive to major losses in comprehension. It seems reasonable to question the validity of these two homemade tests. The third test was the Nelson-Denny

Reading Test, a commercially available standardized reading test. The published manual for the Nelson-Denny claims that it is a valid test with which to predict academic success, diagnose reading problems, and screen out superior readers, all aspects of measuring individual differences. The manual does not claim that the test is valid as a measure of: a) the improvement a person makes in reading rate or comprehension as a result of taking a training course, or b) the percent of material that he actually comprehended while he was reading.

Farce. It is readily acknowledged by psychological test experts that is is grossly invalid to multiply scores on tests that have been developed solely to measure individual differences. Yet, a careful reading of the fine print indicates that Reading Dynamics has actually guaranteed that the customer's Reading Efficiency Index will triple during the course; they have calculated this index by multiplying a person's reading-rate score by his comprehension score. In order to multiply test scores validly, the test must have been developed so that a score of zero means the total absence of the attribute being measured. The Reading Efficiency Index is a farce because it is relatively easy to get a person to skim over material and drive his rates to fantastically high levels. However, the tests used will erroneously show only small losses in the comprehension score; the Reading Efficiency Index will no doubt triple for almost every student. This invalid statistical index provides another piece of irrefutable data which undoubtedly satisfies the scientific tastes of many customers.

10. *What is Carver trying to say in this last paragraph?*

If you were a speed reader, you would have finished this article 10 minutes ago—and to judge from the evidence, you would not be a great deal wiser or better-informed.

WORKSHEET FOR "SPEED READERS DON'T READ; THEY SKIM"

These questions correspond to those on Reproduction Page 93. Write answers to each of these questions, referring back to Carver's article when necessary.

1.   What is the main idea of this paragraph? Restate it in your own words.

2.   How fast can adults really read?

3.   What does information-processing mean?

4.   Why can the psychology professor "read" the psychology text at 2,000 words per minute?

5.   Why could J.F.K. read newspapers so fast?

6.   What are the four faults the Evelyn Wood course claims to correct? Are these really faults?

FAULT 1
Is this a real fault?   Why not?

FAULT 2
Is this a real fault?   Why not?

FAULT 3
Is this a real fault?   Why not?

FAULT 4
Is this a real fault?   Why not?

7.   What were the two findings from Liddle's experiments?

8.   What is being said about Liddle's comprehension questions?

9.   Why don't people ask for their money back?

10.   What is Carver trying to say in this last paragraph?

SKIMMING PRACTICE

Due to Barrier Island Property

HURRICANES MORE DANGEROUS TODAY

By Philip J. Hilts
Washington Post News Service

Washington—The East and Gulf Coasts are due for a major natural disaster, according to Neil Frank, the nation's chief hurricane forecaster.

Developers, home buyers and local governments have all but ignored the possibility of killer storms. The development of some dangerous barrier islands means that "we are more vulnerable to the hurricane than we have ever been in our history," said Frank, director of the National Hurricane Center.

"Poor building codes, out-of-date evacuation plans and overdevelopment are setting the stage for a major disaster," Frank told the Senate subcommittee on environmental pollution recently.

People have a feeling of security because the country has not suffered a killer hurricane in a populated area in about 30 years, Frank said. He said he believes that federal disaster aid should not be offered to those who build knowing that their apartments or houses are in danger of being wiped away.

Some examples of the danger he cited:

- The worst single disaster in American history was a hurricane that hit Galveston Island off the Texas coast and killed 6,000 people in one swipe across the island at the turn of the century.

  Now, where those 6,000 were, tens of thousands of people live during the hurricane season. At the spot where the 6,000 were killed, a 17-foot seawall was built to protect the town of Galveston. The seawall has protected the city, but recently a developer put up a condominium on a sandbar in front of the seawall, and more are scheduled to be built, Frank said.

- In 1938 a hurricane hit West Hampton Beach on Long Island. "There were 179 homes on the barrier island before the storm," Frank said. "Only 26 remained after the storm. I visited Hampton Beach in 1979 and counted 900 homes in that same area."

- In 1954, there were 357 homes on a barrier island on the North Carolina coast, near Wilmington, called Long Beach Island. After Hurricane Hazel only five remained. Now, there are 2,000 homes on the same spot, Frank said.

- Other better known and dangerous areas are Hilton Head, Seabrook and Kiawah Islands off the South Carolina coast. Those islands were hit by the center of a storm in 1893 and wiped clean. About 2,000 died.

- Frank said there are few city evacuation plans and in every case where the problem has been studied it was found that people could not be evacuated in time. The National Hurricane Center can give about 12 hours of warning of a severe hurricane.

"There are 70,000 people in the Florida Keys today and their escape route is a narrow two-lane road with 50 bridges. It would take 20 hours to evacuate," Frank said. That estimate does not take into account what would happen if there was an accident blocking the one escape route.

"Recent comprehensive evacuation studies for (the) area around Ft. Myers, Fla., show it will take between 20 and 30 hours to evacuate . . . for Tampa Bay and Galveston Bay (there would be) evacuation times in excess of 20 hours."

The danger in a hurricane, contrary to the popular idea, is not so much from wind and rain, but from "storm surge." Nine of 10 people who die in a hurricane drown in the storm surge, Frank said.

The winds of the hurricane push up a great dome of water before it, perhaps 50 miles long. The rising water does not slam in like a tidal wave, but instead rises like a quick tide to flood coastal areas, sometimes reaching 20 to 25 feet above sea level. On top of this are powerful five-foot waves.

Since barrier islands are most often only about five feet or so above sea level, a major hurricane's storm surge can put an island under 10 to 20 feet of rushing water plus the five-foot waves. Few structures can survive it, Frank said, and no building code is written to take it into account.

Frank said that between 1900 and 1974 a total of 126 hurricanes struck land on the Atlantic and Gulf coasts. Of those, 52 were "major storms" with winds above 110 mph and a storm surge often over 10 feet.

In the 20 to 30 years since any of these hurricanes hit a heavily populated island, the barrier islands' populations have "skyrocketed," he said, making the next one to strike a populated island likely to be the nation's single worst disaster.

PROCEDURES FOR SKIMMING

How to Skim

1. Read titles, headings, subheadings, and any other typographical indicators of important ideas (such as words in italics or in darker print).

2. Does the first paragraph include a preview or an organizational structure for the information that is to follow? If it does, read it!

3. Read the first sentences of paragraphs.

4. Look at illustrations and read captions under pictures.

5. Note numbers, dates, and words that seem to stand out.

6. Does the last paragraph include a summary? If it does, read this paragraph.

WHEN TO SKIM

Skimming is an effective reading approach when you want to:

- Preview a chapter or selection to help recall information you already know about the topic.

- Decide whether a selection interests you or contains information you want to know.

- Review material you have already read.

- Search for specific facts.

- Stay up-to-date on a topic that you already know a great deal about.

DETERMINING READING RATE FOR ALL TYPES OF MATERIALS

Before the Reading

1. Count the number of lines on an average page.

2. Count the total number of words in ten lines. Then divide that total by ten to get the average number of words per line.

3. Multiply the results obtained in items 1 and 2 above to learn the average number of words per page.

After the Timed Reading

4. Count the total number of pages read during the timing.

5. Multiply that number by the average number of words per page.

6. Divide that number by the number of minutes read.

Example

1. 40 lines per page

2. 120 words in 10 lines = an average of 12 words per line

3. 40 × 12 = 480 words per page

4. 6 pages read during timing

5. 6 pages × 480 words per page = 2880 total words

6. 2880 total words divided by 10 minutes = 288 words per minute

APPENDIX C

Feedback Form

Your comments about this book will be very helpful to us in planning other books in the Guidebook for Teaching Series and in making revisions in *A Guidebook for Teaching Reading*. Please tear out the form that appears on the following page and use it to let us know your reactions to *A Guidebook for Teaching Reading*. The author promises a personal reply. Mail the form to:

Dr. Pauline L. Witte
c/o Longwood Division
Allyn and Bacon, Inc.
7 Wells Avenue
Newton, Massachusetts 02159

Your school: _____

Address: _____

City and State: _____

Date: _____

Dr. Pauline L. Witte
c/o Longwood Division
Allyn and Bacon, Inc.
7 Wells Avenue
Newton, Massachusetts 02159

Dear Pauline:

My name is _____ and I want to tell you what I think of your book *A Guidebook for Teaching Reading*. I like certain things about the book, including:

I do, however, feel that the book could be improved in the following ways:

There are some other things I wish the book had included, such as:

Here is something that happened in my class when I used an idea from your book:

Sincerely yours,

_____